Intentional Disruption

Expanding Access to Philosophy

Edited by

Stephen Kekoa Miller

Oakwood Friends School; Marist College

Series in Philosophy
VERNON PRESS

In the Americas:	*In the rest of the world:*
Vernon Press	Vernon Press
1000 N West Street, Suite 1200,	C/Sancti Espiritu 17,
Wilmington, Delaware 19801	Malaga, 29006
United States	Spain

Series in Philosophy

Library of Congress Control Number: 2021938620

ISBN: 978-1-64889-385-8

Also available: 978-1-64889-191-5 [Hardback]; 978-1-64889-296-7 [PDF, E-Book]

Cover design by Vernon Press using elements designed by Timothy Dykes, unsplash.com.

Table of contents

Foreword

Wendy C. Turgeon

St. Joseph's College

Started in the late 1960s-70s, the movement known as "Philosophy for/with children" began in the United States through the pioneering efforts of philosophers Gareth Matthews and Matthew Lipman. Lipman, along with his associate, Ann Margaret Sharp, started a program at the then-called Montclair College in New Jersey, which trained philosophers and teachers to bring philosophical enquiry into pre-college classrooms. To that end, they wrote carefully crafted "philosophical novels" geared to grade ranges and accompanying teachers guides to assist the teachers in exploring a wide range of philosophical questions and issues that were planted within each novel. Since that time, philosophy for young people has spread across the globe, and many different models and methodologies have grown up over the past fifty years. There are international and national organizations that champion philosophical inquiry in schools from Australia to Asia to Europe to South America. During this same period, we have witnessed a sustained and even growing reluctance to bring philosophy to pre-college classrooms as the emphasis in education shifts to quantifiable assessment, testing, and career preparation. The liberal arts, in general, are under attack at all levels of education, at least in the United States of America. Other countries may still be more hospitable to such disciplinary studies, but "P4/wC" (as it is often labeled) as a practice with children is still relatively rare in the US.

Despite that gloomy outlook, we have witnessed new generations of advocates for philosophy in the schools and beyond here in the US. The Philosophy Learning and Teaching Organization (PLATO) has grown up over the past 10+ years to be a rich source of materials, ideas, and opportunities for practitioners and theorists to gather and share ideas. This organization actively champions new programs through grants and publicity. The American Philosophical Association has also joined in opening its doors to those in pre-college philosophy. One of the most important recent developments is an explosive expansion of philosophy beyond the classroom model to inclusively embrace alternate spaces and peoples, constructing new avenues for engagement in philosophical dialogue. Philosophy in prisons, with retirees, in local community centers, and even the very young (babies and preschool ages) have found advocates who have developed rich models of diverse engagement. The authors included in this volume exemplify this kind of creative thinking, and while grounded in sound theory, they each offer practical ways (with careful guidance) on how to promote philosophical inquiry to a wide audience.

Stephen Kekoa Miller's opening essay, "What to Consider when Considering a Pre-college Philosophy Program", sets the tone by outlining concrete goals and methods for getting philosophy into a pre-college educational setting. Focusing on the twin familiar aims of critical thinking and ethical reasoning, Miller details why these values can be taught through philosophy in ways that are meaningful but not authoritatively imposed. He also tackles common concerns (can children handle philosophy? Won't it take time away from more "important" subjects?) with sound advice and good reasoning on how to respond to such skepticism. He honestly recognizes that philosophy will not cure the world or generate saints, but he persuasively builds a case for its value in terms of inviting young people to think clearly and compassionately about the world around them.

The following three essays take the reader to different geographic and cultural areas of the US, where philosophy has been introduced to diverse populations in dramatically different ways. Each essay presents, through the lens of personal experiences, the ways that philosophy can transform communities. In "The Iowa Lyceum: Graduate Students and Pre-College Philosophy", Colburn, Finley, and Glover detail a long-standing summer camp for philosophy sponsored by the University of Iowa. This camp is run by graduate students who value deeply the opportunity to work on their own pedagogy and explore new ways to introduce traditional materials to a non-college audience. The authors highlight that the learning goes in both directions: from the graduate students and profs to the campers but also from these young participants back to the facilitators. One of the essential aspects for valuing pre-college philosophy is this bi-directional exchange of personal and intellectual growth. All are invited into the "community of inquiry" as they collectively and cooperatively explore questions that matter. These experiences encapsulate what academic administrators clamor for in "high impact learning" activities. But as the authors conclude, the real goal is to help participants "develop a new approach to life."

While the Iowa Lyceum serves high school-aged young people looking for enrichment during their summers. Eric Kenyon's essay ("P4C and Community - Engaged Pedagogy") introduces how philosophy can impact the thinking of very young children, children in preschool. Kenyon tells his story of developing a service-learning/community engagement project for undergraduates at his college, Rollins College in Florida. A classicist by training, he crafted an exciting class that introduced the college students to Greek philosophers and thereby invited them to rethink their own educational histories and then go out to local elementary school classes to engage them in a self-same reflection. When the schools could no longer accommodate them, Kenyon looked to the campus laboratory preschool and, along with his colleagues at Rollins, found new ways to get very young children thinking about language, actions, and meaning through games and activities. His program offered internships to undergraduates to work with these preschoolers. Kenyon steps back from outlining his evolving program to offer cogent ways to realize the notion of the "pragmatic liberal arts" and innovative ways to think about teaching at all levels.

Marisa Diaz-Waian opens her inspiring personal story ("Philosophy in & By the Community") with an account of the trauma of losing her father. Living in Montana, Diaz-Waian offers a magnificent account of starting and expanding her philosophy program, "Merlin." Perhaps named for the wizard in the King Arthur legends, Merlin creates its own magical experiences for the people in her community. One of the most powerful sections in her essay is her extended metaphor of doing philosophy as gardening. I have never read such an entrancing and spot-on account of why philosophy is both difficult and exhilarating. In many ways, the central part of Diaz-Waian's essay captures what every contributor to this volume knows: that philosophy as an activity—rather than a study—creates opportunities for people to come together and form communities, not necessarily of homogenous thinking, but rather of shared diverse viewpoints and excitement in the project of living a life. Implementing a spice metaphor, she traces how her Community Philosophy programming addresses the four areas of space, action, people and philosophy itself. Beyond this imaginative and riveting account of what philosophical inquiry can offer a community, she then proceeds to provide some concrete examples from among her programs: doing philosophy with children, philosophy walks/hikes, and an array of seasonal activities from hayrides to other celebratory events. Finally, she shares some benefits but also real challenges that she has faced and stresses how important "place" is in designing any program. The community in which you live, both the community of persons and the natural/urban world around you, shapes how and why you will want to invite philosophy into the lives of people. This offers a theme echoed in many of the essays in this volume: adapt models to work for your situation and do not be afraid to try new things.

The next three essays invite us to consider the rewards and challenges of doing philosophy with young people. We are again traveling around the country from a small city in the south to rural Indiana, back to the East Coast city of Philadelphia. Kronsted and Wurtz in "Philosophical Horizons: P4/WC and Anti-Racism in Memphis, TN" offer a frank and refreshing account of recognizing institutional racism everywhere and overtly in Memphis. They detail the process by which they recrafted their approach to introducing philosophy to young people so as to consciously disrupt the ingrained but often unnoticed threads of dominance and power among the participants. They uncover ways in which the traditional models of doing pre-college philosophy may still include such implicit racism, even if it is clearly not intended. The three key Lipmanian ideals of reasonableness, impartiality, and feelings of social solidarity may not work in positive ways within a community of persons of color that is acutely aware of its treatment at the hands of white people. Kronsted and Wurtz detail ways in which they had to rethink their approach to allow the young people from this minority community to experience and grow their own sense of agency. Interestingly enough, one key move was to get philosophy out of the schools and into a more neutral and liberating territory, in their case, a rock climbing gym. This essay reveals the depth of self-reflection necessary to truly engage others in philosophy and how we need to become aware of our own hidden prejudices, assumptions, and biases. The sincerity of their reflections here offers a guide for all of us, regardless of how or where we want to do philosophy.

Continuing in the theme of caveats to doing philosophy, Sarah Vitale ("Overcoming Barriers: Pre-college Philosophy Programs in Neoliberalism") provides a cogent account of the contemporary pressures in education: the degrading of the humanities to the status as useless material, the "corporationalization" of education (education as a business), and how funding shifts (from the overall government to property taxes) disadvantage the economically less wealthy. This creates tensions for philosophy in the school programs as so often, these programs are diametrically opposed to the neoliberal values of quantifying success. As a relatively new faculty member in Indiana, she ambitiously began her "Philosophy Outreach Program", which encouraged schools to begin philosophy clubs, and from her college class, "Philosophy for High School", she prepared undergraduates to go out to work with teens in the schools. The college students learn valuable skills from developing materials and managing social media accounts and get the opportunity to inspire and support high school students in their own learning. They also worked on setting up and running a philosophy conference. This model offers insights into developing service-learning classes and encouraging undergraduates to share their own love of philosophical inquiry with younger individuals.

The third essay in this trio, "Bringing Philosophy into Philadelphia Classrooms," is written by Dustin Webster, Stephen Esser, and Karen Detlefsen. They detail the history and structure of the "Penn Project for Philosophy for the Young" [P4Y]. Beginning in 2014 as a philosophy club sponsored by the University of Pennsylvania and run by Professor Detlefsen and a graduate student, Robert Willison, to help high school kids to be college-ready, P4Y has subsequently grown to include many different programs and activities for pre-college students at all levels. They offer an exciting array of different programming ideas to inspire readers to consider new ways to bring philosophy to young people: writing projects, science and philosophy, ethics bowls, and what has been termed broadly as "public philosophy"—using philosophical reflection to inform and guide our thinking about real-life issues and events through writing for the public sector. Additionally, they have been working with area teachers on ways to introduce philosophy into the traditional pre-college subjects. All of this activity has impacted the university itself, which now offers a Graduate Certificate in Public Philosophy, a potentially powerful credential for philosophy graduate degree candidates looking for careers both within the academy and without. They are also engaged in research on the efficacy of their programs, information critically useful for anyone who wants to introduce a philosophy program into an educational institution or apply for funding. Towards the end of their account of the Penn programs, they offer some practical advice on how to make these ideas a reality.

The final essay in this insightful volume is by Joseph Aloysius Murphy, "Once a philosopher in Hiding: Teaching Philosophy in Spanish in the USA." Like the other authors in this text, Murphy shares his personal story. These stories contextualize the journeys experienced by each contributor and serve to situate their practice both in their personal lives and in the lives of their communities. This powerfully reminds us that philosophy is not a disembodied activity but very much one "in the flesh" located in a certain place. Murphy shares his struggles in getting his school to take philosophy seriously and how too often lip service is given to "critical thinking" and "ethics", but the need for sustained understanding and practices of these terms is not acknowledged. His own approach is to teach a philosophy course but completely in Spanish. This allows a LOTE class to include philosophy as both a practice in the language but also as ... well, philosophical inquiry. One of his sections that is particularly riveting is his account of why he tells his students that he is not interested in their opinions. While that might appear to be harsh, he quickly pivots to demonstrate how important careful thinking, reason-giving, and sound argumentation is in supporting an opinion. Given recent rhetoric about "alternative facts" and "truth" as what one wants to believe, this section is timely and offers some concrete suggestions for implementing in any classroom...or one's personal exchanges with family and friends. In the end, he details his work on the American Philosophy Open, a competition for high school students to write a philosophical essay; the winners in the US can attend the international competition. Murphy's story is inspiring as a teacher who persevered and ended up developing a robust program in philosophy in his own school.

These essays are invaluably important in a number of ways:

1. They all offer a personal narrative which humanizes the theory into the struggle of the practice. In each case, they persevere and succeed.
2. They offer diverse models for introducing philosophy to people outside of the college environment but in ways that are highly successful and

genuinely philosophical. Every one of these contributors has solid training in philosophy itself, and this shows in both their astute reflections on the nature of philosophical inquiry and clearly impact the success of their endeavors.

3. There is not one "right" way to do philosophical inquiry, and the creative alternatives captured in each essay serve to free us from some artificial standard or any unilateral model.

4. They demonstrate the power of philosophy in a wide range of places around the US but, by extension, clearly applicable to other regions of the world. The ways in which their programs are designed to fit their communities is critically important. A sense of place permeates each author's account and reflects what their community cares about.

5. They provide honest appraisals of the challenges faced by those wishing to introduce such programs: from securing funding (an ongoing battle for most of them), finding spaces that work well for their goals and their participants, being accepted by administrative authorities (both at the college and pre-college level), and finally going against the tide of the neoliberal landscape which measures learning in terms of economic production (Vitale's term but present in each contributor's experiences.)

6. Finally, they capture the joy, the fun, the exhilaration of doing philosophy with others. They show us that, whether we live in a rural area, an inner city, a small town, or anywhere, there is a thirst for opportunities to think about the things that really matter.

In conclusion, readers will find this volume to be an invaluable resource as snapshots of what creative people can offer the world, how philosophy can speak to deep human concerns and needs, and a primer on how to make it happen in your community. The twelfth-century theologian and philosopher Bernard of Clairvaux claimed that we are "standing on the shoulders of giants" as we use the insights of the past great thinkers to look ahead. While our authors are all inspired by the work of Lipman, Matthews, Sharp and the many other more recent "giants" in the field of philosophy with children, they can serve as our own giants as we look forward to see what we can do to build on their insights and discoveries.

Wendy C. Turgeon
5/21/2021

Chapter 1

What to Consider when Considering a Pre-college Philosophy Program: Frequently Asked Questions from Those considering Starting a Pre-College Program or Improving an Existing One

Stephen Kekoa Miller

Oakwood Friends School; Marist College

Abstract

This chapter comes out of a number of years consulting with elementary, middle school and high school teacher and administrators interested in beginning philosophy programs. Here, I share some of these, give some perspectives on them and finally share resources for those who might now be considering philosophy programs in their institutions. This chapter also serves to give context the following eight chapters which describe some of the creative and exciting things being done in pre-college philosophy across the country.

Keywords: pre-college philosophy, ethics curricula, P4C, critical thinking, philosophy of education, Oakwood Friends School

***

Are these good times or bad times for philosophy in schools? The early 21st century has given us the Crisis in the Humanities, budgetary cutbacks for college philosophy and adjacent departments and an ever-broadening testing regime that moves us further away from the ideal of a philosophical education. Despite this, there are also growing numbers of institutions, individuals and programs bringing philosophy outside of traditional academic locations. Public philosophy has brought it into prisons, farmers markets, museums and parks. More and more secondary schools are also exploring the introduction of philosophy into their curricula. However, the counter-cultural nature of the field which prioritizes questioning over accepting answers can make it difficult to articulate a rationale and to convince school boards and administrations.

Over the past five years or so, through my involvement with the Philosophy For Children (often abbreviated P4C or P4/wC) movement and especially as a board member of the Education Committee of the Philosophy Learning and Teaching Organization (PLATO), I have been asked to consult with a wide range of schools and programs looking to start philosophy programs. These have ranged from a middle school in Poland to high schools in Lebanon to a small hybrid start-up in China to public and private schools in the United States to programs that exist outside of school walls altogether. While the schools and programs are very different from each other, they have often had some of the same questions for me. In this chapter, I'd like to share some of these, give my perspective on them and finally to share resources for those who might now be considering philosophy programs in their institutions.

Famously, philosophers themselves have long loved to debate what philosophy itself is and ought to be. When considering it as a course subject or program, this just adds a layer of complexity and uncertainty. However, having a clear sense of what goals one has can help a lot to figure out what the program should look like. Here are some questions I have fielded about pre-college philosophy. Some of these may initially seem to be less interesting, but bear with me. In practice, philosophy in schools advances a number of goals that educators value but often does so in ways that are nearly the opposite of how many educators would go about them. After introducing some of these questions and offering thumbnail sketches of answers, I'll try to sort this out.

What Should a Pre-College Philosophy Program Aim For?

There are two distinct questions here that I'll look at separately, as schools often have very different goals for pre-college philosophy and for pre-college ethics programs. By far, the most common goal for general pre-college philosophy is the development of critical thinking skills. Much research has shown that pre-college philosophy is quite good at this. From SAT to GRE, philosophy studies correlate strongly with higher scores. But what else could/should it look to do?

One of the often-overlooked benefits of studying philosophy involves its place in intellectual history. Students in the United States all study history, but many fewer of them study art history, science history, music history or general cultural history. Some amount of the history of philosophy can serve to greatly enhance a student's understanding of the relationships between these fields, the rationale behind some cultural movements and especially, the development of science, another underdeveloped part of our curriculum. Science textbooks tend to present consensus beliefs of the time, but usually fail to show earlier conclusions that have been abandoned but were reasonable at the time, introducing a flawed view of the nature of scientific inquiry.

While the term has become culturally contested, philosophy at its heart aims to discover what is true. Historically, it has investigated this in nearly every important area of human endeavor. While a philosophy class is not necessarily going to deliver a student to truth, it does a lovely job of showing students the range of possible answers and criteria for sorting them out. This aspect of philosophy looks far ever vital in regards to world trends which suggest that any belief held fervently enough can be held to be true.

Finally, and possibly most importantly, philosophy should offer a chance to train students to be much more conceptually precise. This is really key when looking at how many of our social debates play out; in many cases, they end up foundering not on substantial disagreements but on semantics. Having a class come to a conceptual definitional agreement can be really useful here. Defining fairness, justice, race, gender, God, etc.... goes a long way towards gaining understanding and an ability to communicate even if no one agrees on the conclusions.

There are of course many, many other possible ends to strive for in philosophy programs, most obviously being the actual content of specific classes.

What Methods Are Available to Do Philosophy with Pre-College Students?

The classic method of actually doing philosophy with a group of pre-college students is referred to as a Community of Inquiry. There is extensive material available concerning the methodology for this, but broadly speaking, it is a moderated discussion focused on a specific question or topic. Depending on the levels of the students, conversation can be prompted by picture books, artworks, philosophical texts, case studies or simply a question. Many practitioners also suggest that students are best served by having them choose the topics themselves. The main idea here though is that even if there is no final resolution arrived at on the question in dispute, the session need not have failed. There can still be significant progress in the students' understanding of the topic at hand, ability to articulate reasons for their opinions and ability to understand how reasonable people can disagree. There are also different views in the field about who is an appropriate moderator, how much training is needed and how much guidance the moderator should give to the group. Some programs successfully employ high schoolers in moderation, some with undergraduate or graduate students, and some rely exclusively on trained, credentialed professionals. In general, however, the moderator aims to keep the participants on task by getting them to respond specifically to the previous speaker, aiming to avoid a series of non-sequiturs and assuring that everyone follows agreed-upon discussion norms.

Another infamous way to approach this is referred to as the Socratic Method, although confusingly, no one seems to agree on exactly what this means. The Socratic Method is much more centered around the teacher, but the teacher uses questions rather than statements to help get the students to an understanding. Optimally, this method would not involve beginning with a particular answer or destination in mind, but in exploring a topic through questions and follow-up questions. This is very different from how law schools employ the method, where they do aim towards a set answer. Socrates himself seemed to think one of its biggest virtues lies in disabusing us of false belief. Plato's dialogues also show this method to illustrate that learning is dialogic and not solitary. Thus, the key aspect here is the fact that like the Community of Inquiry, it shows that learning is social...we do best when we do it together.

Should a Pre-College Philosophy Program Focus on Critical Thinking Skills?

One of the most common goals of pre-college philosophy is often aiming to improve critical thinking skills. On a fairly regular basis, studies come out showing that philosophy can help with LSAT, GRE, MCAT, Common Core, SAT and more. Whatever one thinks about testing regimes, at this time, they do affect the lives of children. Many schools and programs have looked to philosophy to assist here. Especially at a time when most students' only exposure to any kind of logic or formal reasoning skills is in Geometry class, this can be helpful.

Learning to avoid fallacies and to structure sound, valid arguments is indeed an important skill. It assists in essay writing, communicating effectively and perhaps most essentially, it helps us to avoid being suckers. The ability to spot fallacious arguments that other people who would deceive us or harm us is a skill philosophy has long excelled at.

Of course, this is not enough. Simply avoiding fallacies and arguing consistently can still lead us to immoral or harmful conclusions. Michael Pritchard emphasizes the need to have "reasonableness" accompany any training in rationality. He describes it as "Having social features...the reasonable person respects others and is prepared to take into account their views and their feelings."[1] A pre-college philosophy program, thus, would seem to want to train students to be both critical and reasonable thinkers. This would mean practicing the kind of epistemic humility that's referred to as Fallibilism. This position begins with the premise that anything I now believe may turn out to be wrong. As

---

[1] Pritchard, 3.

Kronsted and Wurtz show in Chapter 5 in this book, however, "reasonableness" itself can be a problematic standard as well, since how we define it can lead to silencing some voices and views.

What Should a Pre-College Ethics Program Aim For?

The Hastings Center brought together a committee to answer this question for higher education. The report it generated in 1980 is a useful starting point. This report suggests that Ethics programs in higher education ought to aim for five things: "Stimulating the moral imagination, recognizing ethical issues, developing analytical skills, eliciting a sense of moral obligation and personal responsibility and tolerating and resisting disagreement and ambiguity."[2] Most of these are handled separately in this introduction, but the second and third are worth thinking about.

While it may seem obvious to those in the field, simply being able to recognize the difference between moral claims and empirical claims is actually a relatively rare skill among students. Whether through a whole ethics program or a single stand-alone lesson, the ability to differentiate between these types of claims is really important. Understanding what type of claim is involved also prompts the students about what evidence and counter-evidence would look like. As an example here, I often find that with both college and pre-college Bioethics students, empirical facts are often offered as disproof of moral claims. Being able to recognize among kinds of claims will not eliminate moral disagreements but do stand a good chance of helping to make them more fruitful.

While the report uses the language of "developing analytical skills," it is most helpful to think of this as being able to use analytical skills correctly. Again, many of my college and pre-college students are strong math and science students, evincing a good grasp of basic analysis. However, even when they can tell apart moral and non-moral claims, they struggle to find a vocabulary for how to articulate moral problems. Some of this can be overcome by philosophy training in basic logic. However, the students tend to be particularly ill-trained in the use of values language. In this case, one of the most useful analytical skills that they can develop in an ethics class would be conceptual clarity. A discussion of fairness will always be better if the class agrees on what the term means and then applies it to situations. Using values language with precision and accuracy would go a long way towards improving moral discourse.

---

[2] "The Teaching of Ethics in American Higher Education," 30.

Shouldn't Schools That Are Not Religiously Affiliated Be Concerned about the Fact That Many People Understand Ethics as a Religious Perspective?

This is an interesting question that initially caught me by surprise due to the ubiquitous calls for schools to teach students morality. Of course, those who come from a religious background worry about whose understanding would be taught. As an interesting perspective here, many public school systems in European countries that have historically been religiously homogeneous allow families a choice: while studying ethics is mandatory, families choose secular/philosophical ethics or religious doctrine courses. While many conversations I've had with practitioners in this system suggest it allows the classes to function without a lot of controversy, it also lets some students avoid the important task of questioning their own beliefs.

Briefly, like with many rich humanities classes, a good ethics course would expose students to a wide range of views, teach them arguments around each and explore the significance these carry. They are able to do this without concluding with relativist conclusions. It is a popular move to have students read Plato's *Euthyphro* and to conclude that religion and ethics should be seen as separate fields with different strategies of justification. Ethics can be well taught in a fully secular manner, but this question still needs to be taken seriously in how to present the curriculum to parents in such a way that makes it clear that philosophy and ethics in particular are not contrary to a religious perspective. In fact, living in a pluralistic society, this is essential.

Will Pre-College Ethics Classes Make Students Morally Better?

This is a tricky one. The most commonly described aim of pre-college ethics I have come across looks to have the program bring about improved moral behavior in students. I myself suggested that a robust ethics curriculum could do just this when pitching my idea to the Board of Managers at Oakwood Friends School, the small Quaker school I work. The Board accepted my argument; however, shortly after getting the program underway, I came across some evidence that it might not be true. My favorite example of this is the survey by Schwitzgebel and Rust showing that college ethics professors were much more likely to judge eating animals to be morally wrong but no more likely than the average person to have that judgement make them eat animals less.[3] So what's going on here?

There's a lot of evidence that pre-college ethics can teach students to analyze, understand and process moral terms more effectively. However, a lot of highly-reported and trendy scholarship in moral psychology has indicated that

---

[3] "The Moral Behavior of Ethics Professors," 293.

emotions, priming, context, habits and moral imagination all seem to influence our behavior more than we previously had thought. Some have then suggested that a curriculum that teaches students moral reasoning is ill-suited to training them to behave better. It's become clear that the above list of cognitive and environmental factors matter a lot to how we act. However, some data also seems to suggest that even normative ethics survey courses might help students act better even if that's not the case with their teachers, that younger students may be affected more than the meat-eating university teachers by doing ethics.

No definitive study on all of this has been done yet; however, the same authors of the study on professors' views on meat did a version for students. The results here were quite different. In the article, they describe their results this way:

> We obtained 13,642 food purchase receipts from campus restaurants for 495 of the students, before and after the intervention. Purchase of meat products declined in the experimental group (52% of purchases of at least $4.99 contained meat before the intervention, compared to 45% after) but remained the same in the control group (52% both before and after). Ethical opinion also differed, with 43% of students in the experimental group agreeing that eating the meat of factory farmed animals is unethical compared to 29% in the control group.

Ultimately, the studies that have been conducted (see bibliography) seem to show (preliminarily) that the earlier a student can be exposed to moral reasoning, the more likely it is to affect how they act. Work is now being done with students as young as pre-K which points to just this (see *Ethics for the Very Young*).

How Can a School Teach Ethics in a Pluralistic Society?

In a globalized world with most societies now highly diverse, what should an ethics curriculum look like? Or, put another way, whose ethics should be taught? Important moral questions continue to be the areas of greatest social unrest and disagreement. Many people take this fact to be enough to convince them to oppose any ethics education in pre-college settings. When one adds to this the constitutional mandate to separate government from religion, many schools choose to just ban discussion of the most controversial, and by extension, important topics.

Firstly, Bernard Williams' distinction between "thick" and "thin" moral disagreements can be useful here. Simply put, Williams suggests that some disagreements are more fundamental than offers ("thick") while others that appear to be deep moral disagreements when looked at more closely turn out to only appear so. In practice, then, we can usually find meaningful agreement on basic moral principles ("thin" ones such as most disagreements about politeness...societies value politeness but disagree about the content of impoliteness).[4] In line with the discussions above, one key task of an ethics curriculum is to help students become better at recognizing moral claims and at disentangling "thick" and "thin" ones. This part should be relatively uncontroversial.

However, human societies do have real moral differences both internally and between each other, and it shouldn't be the schools' job to give students final answers to these. While students could benefit from looking at different perspectives on areas of deep moral disagreement like abortion, schools wouldn't say what the final answer is. Most schools, though, wouldn't permit even this. Importantly, however, schools can go further than a position of moral neutrality. This is because schools themselves have moral codes both explicit (mission statements, behavioral codes, etc...) and implicit (demands that students treat each other with respect are often not explicitly written out). David Annis describes some of these school moral values in a helpful way, reminding us that schools all believe cheating to be not only against the rules but morally *wrong*.[5] While schools vary enormously in how much explicit moral language is used, all schools enforce and operate with extensive implicit moral codes. These themselves serve as a great starting point for developing a curriculum. In a pluralistic society that often seems not to agree on anything, when we look closer, we find that most schools do in fact agree on a core set of academic and moral values. We can all agree with the value of freedom of expression while wanting to set ground rules which limit some forms of expression which undermine others' ability to express themselves.

If My Pre-College Ethics Program Does Want to Make Students Morally Better, What Should We Do?

Here's an area that there is much debate about, but there are some concrete strategies that have been shown to have potential. Some of the work in this area has constellated around three approaches: community service/ service learning, narrative fiction and social/ emotional learning curricula. While this is not the place to explore the nuances of this field, one issue that complicates these efforts is the fact that if done poorly, each of these has the potential to result in the opposite of its intended effect. Delivered badly, each can make students become more biased, selfish and confirmed in their previous understandings. As an

---

[4] *Ethics and the Limits of Philosophy*, 141.

[5] "Teaching Ethics In Higher Education: Goals, And The Implications Of The Empirical Research On Moral Development," 193.

example here, having students engage in service to a community they previously had no exposure to has the potential to expand their moral imagination. However, simply exposing students without proper preparation and processing can harden their pre-existing prejudices. It's not the job of philosophy or ethics programs to design community service, literature curricula or SEL programs, but it could well serve as an important part of these to do the conceptual work involved with questioning assumptions, implications and concepts. Philosophy, and in particular the Community of Inquiry model can be a great way to do some of the needed processing to help move some of these efforts to genuinely help students to question their own preconceptions.

David Annis spells out how he thinks we should foster moral development in this way:

* Engage the students in logical thinking and critical analysis about ethical issues. They must actively participate in this and it must be throughout the course.
* Expose them to moral conflicts and controversies where their views are challenged.
* Use Socratic questioning to draw out and challenge the students' views. There is evidence that the use of such Socratic questioning can have a significant impact on moral development.
* Expose students to moral reasoning that is at a higher stage than the level at which they are reasoning. E.g., if a student attempts to solve a moral problem by appealing to certain limited factors, show him or her what other factors need to be considered and how they are to be balanced. Some researchers have found that exposing subjects to moral reasoning one stage above their present level improved moral development.
* Explain the rationale or justification underlying a principle or rule. E.g., we can use Kantian notions of respect for persons, autonomy, utilitarianism to explain the duty of truth-telling or promise-keeping
* Encourage examining ethical problems from different perspectives. Taking the perspective of the other person increases student interest, understanding, and empathy. When students show greater interest in ethical discussions, it has a positive impact on their moral reasoning. Discussing ethical issues that the students raise or may face also increases student interest.
* Encourage empathy and explore the affective domain. Moral development in part involves a growing awareness of others. Empathy is an important part of this. It involves a cognitive element - discerning what another person is experiencing (what feelings, thoughts, emotions the person is having, what the person

is going through) and an affective element, viz., reacting with an emotional response that is similar, e.g., you are made happy by another's joy, sad by another's suffering.[6]

Ultimately, techniques which enhance students' empathy, moral reasoning, ability to see from others' perspectives, emotional intelligence and affect students' habits seem best suited to achieve this.

What Content Will Pre-College Philosophy Teach My Students?

One of the most common questions I get from people starting pre-college philosophy programs involves the basic idea of *what* exactly to teach...what should be in the curriculum? There is great value in a history of philosophy or a survey of normative ethics curriculum. In both cases, the class would teach critical thinking but also culture, history and intellectual history. However, this usually doesn't allow as much time for actually *doing* philosophy, which is messy, inefficient and counter-cultural.

Almost certainly, a pre-college philosophy curriculum would want to spend time helping students develop conceptual clarity. Even young middle school students benefit by learning about the categories of Necessary and Sufficient Conditions, and applying these to various topics. This skill is also one that easily transfers to other disciplines and students come to see the importance of having everyone in a classroom agree on the meaning of a concept before analyzing and evaluating it.

Pre-college philosophy is also uniquely situated to be a useful place to engage recent work dealing with gender identity, sexual orientation, race, ethnicity, disability, religious identity, environmental ethics and other really important social issues in the process of being rethought. In aiming for conceptual clarity, philosophy allows us a chance to at the very least come to some agreement about the terms we use. Even if we continue to disagree, this allows the conversation to occur. A classic example of this is that in order to have a discussion about God, all parties need to agree on how that term will be used; atheists, agnostics and theists should all be able to agree on the content of what they are disagreeing about.

Perhaps most counter-culturally, in the era of testing regimes, Socrates made clear what one of the main parts of philosophy should consist in: unlearning[7]. All of us believe things that are untrue. Many of these beliefs might harm us,

---

[6] "Teaching Ethics In Higher Education: Goals, And The Implications Of The Empirical Research On Moral Development," 200.

[7] See Miller, Stephen Kekoa. "Socratic Aporia in the Classroom and the Development of Resilience."

whether it be in terms of believing something false about what might make our bodies healthy or false political or social claims that lead to poor life choices. Ultimately, Socrates shows how believing something false might cause us to live diminished lives. This is important, but a hard sell.

Won't Pre-College Philosophy Courses/ Programs Cause Students to Suffer in Other Subjects by Having Them Give Up Time That Could Be Spent on Them?

It's important to start by admitting that philosophy in a classroom, if well done, is going to be inefficient. Philosophy is inefficient if the goal of education is information delivery. In a good philosophy class, some questions that may seem obvious or settled may be seriously opened for doubt. Other things which may seem obviously wrong might be considered. Philosophy classes will spend time thinking about how we know things, how we know we know them and why they matter. The actual knowledge claims will fade in importance compared to these. So, if a school's educational mission and method involve content mastery over a large set of specific facts, philosophy classes may well be seen as threatening to this view. Teachers who approach teaching this way may well be annoyed by students asking how they know what they claim or why it matters. However, teachers quickly find that spending time on these questions tends to inflame more interest in the content of these fields. Looking at the foundational questions of other disciplines is interesting, but also promotes more sophisticated grasp of these fields as well. In the end, though, it usually isn't so good at information delivery.

Are Children Really Able to Handle Philosophy?

Many people remember the one philosophy course they took in college, recall how challenging the reading was, and come to think that the idea of younger students engaging with philosophy seems ridiculous. Much of the work in this field starts with an important distinction between *doing* philosophy and *learning* philosophy. Children as young as pre-K and elementary school can *do* high-level philosophical work on important philosophical problems. I have had second-grade students come to the same conclusions as Aristotle about the nature of courage after being prompted by a picture book. There was no need at all to talk to them about Aristotle. These students were definitely doing philosophy though.

While much has been written about this, one really important point to consider here involves capacities. Gareth Matthews reminds us that children's ideas are not undeveloped so much as different in what they are best at.[8] Your average 5th grader is going to be significantly less able to read and understand abstract philosophical texts than a graduate student. However, it's also really clear that the 5th grader will likely be better at thinking subjunctively...about how things could be different. As we age and get better at grasping how things are, we get worse at thinking about how else the world could be. There is great virtue in having children and adults do philosophy together, the more mixed-age the better.[9] Older children may benefit from reading philosophical texts; critical reading skills develop quickly when exposed to the complexities and precision of the writing of professional philosophy. That said, picture books, artworks, poems, short stories and our own life stories are enough to get us doing philosophy well. Another interesting perspective here involves how commonly I have heard P4C practitioners describe how, after doing philosophy with younger people, came to rethink how they approached it with their college courses, even using picture books.

Was Socrates Right...Can Philosophy Teach Students How to Live?

No. This is one of the most important areas where philosophy can be useful however. In a globalized world where people are exposed to many different ways of living, philosophy can expose students to entirely different systems of final ends. While there is no way to logically prove or disprove the validity of any of them, exploring different ways of living expose us to options we may not have thought of. As an example, Aristotle, Buddhism and most modern American career counselors offer entirely different ways of conceiving of what it means to live a good life. Harry Frankfurt's work on the relationship between what we care about/ love and what matters also gives a unique perspective.[10] This aspect of philosophy, *eudaimonia* or the good life, is especially important in the globalized world because we no longer have consensus communal norms about virtues and proper ends. MacIntyre's influential book *After Virtue*[11], talks about how this lack can lead to a nihilism that collapses into substituting pursuit of money or career success for aims which tend to actually make human beings happy. A philosophy session on some of the empirical findings about subjective well-being[12] couldn't answer these questions but would be a

---

[8] Matthews, *The Philosophy of Childhood.*

[9] See Miller, "Restoring Wonder" in Wartenberg, Thomas E. *Philosophy in Classrooms and Beyond: New Approaches to Picture-Book Philosophy.* Rowman and Littlefield Publishers, 2019.

[10] See *The Reasons of Love.* Princeton University Press, 2019.

[11] McIntyre, 2014.

[12] See Stone, Arthur A., and C. J. Mackie. *Subjective Well-being: Measuring Happiness, Suffering, and Other Dimensions of Experience.* National Academies Press, 2013.

wonderful way to inspire these important conversations. Finally, Megan Laverty suggests how the Socratic Method itself might offer a pathway to engage this:

> Hence the question, "What is the good human life?" is translated by the Socratic Method into a question about "How should one ('I', 'we') live?" This is a potent translation because it shifts attention from determinations of "goodness" and "human life" to questions about how we live, as well as our reflections on how we live and what it is to live well. This questioning has three dimensions. First, we have to ask ourselves how we think we would like to live – what for us as human beings constitutes the ideal life? Second, who would we want to be? Third, what would we want to be like? In attempting to answer these questions we need to establish how truthful these answers are, and we do this by considering how they relate to what we already do and how we respond to what others do. To examine our activities in this way is to attempt to discover how we feel about the kinds of values, beliefs, and commitments that our activities give expression to: are we proud? ashamed? ambivalent? And so on. [13]

How Will My Program Be Able to Engage Students in Philosophy, a Notoriously Difficult Subject?

It turns out that to many peoples' surprise, it's really pretty easy to get students to engage with philosophy. It may be hard to get them to read abstract, technical texts, but playing with ideas comes easily to children. One point many authors, especially Matthews, stress is the ways that children may actually be superior to adults in their ability to use the subjunctive, the "what-if," while adults, the holders of experience with the world are often hindered by this grasp of "what-is." Ultimately, perhaps one of the most exciting things about pre-college philosophy is that it allows people of different age groups to think together. The more the emphasis is placed on actually "doing" philosophy rather than "learning" philosophy, the more students tend to respond. The chapters in this book show a host of creative methods people have used to do just this. Recent innovations involving Ethics Bowls, philosophy camps, philosophy in museums and parks demonstrate that philosophy needn't be the staid and arid activity it is sometimes thought to be. As a final note, though: philosophy's reputation as being a troublemaker is well-founded. However, if

---

[13] Laverty. "Philosophy of Education: Overcoming the Theory-Practice Divide," 41.

inquisitive, thoughtful and engaged students are what a school is seeking, pre-college philosophy may be just the right thing.[14]

Bibliography

Annis, David B. "Teaching Ethics In Higher Education: Goals, And The Implications Of The Empirical Research On Moral Development." *Metaphilosophy* 23, no. 1-2 (1992): 187-202. doi:10.1111/j.1467-9973.1992.tb00749.x.

Frankfurt, Harry G. *The Reasons of Love*. Princeton University Press, 2019.

Laverty, Megan. "Philosophy of Education: overcoming the theory-practice divide, *Paedeusis*, Volume 15 (2006): No.1 pp. 31-44.

MacIntyre, Alasdair C. *After Virtue: A Study in Moral Theory*. Bloomsbury, 2014.

Matthews, Gareth B. *The Philosophy of Childhood*. Harvard University Press, 1996.

Miller, Stephen Kekoa. "Restoring Wonder" in Wartenberg, Thomas E. *Philosophy in Classrooms and Beyond: New Approaches to Picture-Book Philosophy*. Rowman and Littlefield Publishers, 2019.

Miller, Stephen Kekoa. "Socratic Aporia in the Classroom and the Development of Resilience." Analytic Teaching and Philosophical Praxis. https://journal.viterbo.edu/index.php/atpp/article/view/1002.

Pritchard, Michael S. *Reasonable Children: Moral Education and Moral Learning*. University Press of Kansas, 1996.

Schwitzgebel, Eric, Bradford Cokelet., and Peter Singer. "Do Ethics Classes Influence Student Behavior? Case Study: Teaching the Ethics of Eating Meat." Cognition. July 25, 2020. https://www.sciencedirect.com/science/article/abs/pii/S001002772030216X?dgcid=coauthor.

Schwitzgebel, Eric., and Joshua Rust. "The Moral Behavior of Ethics Professors: Relationships among Self-reported Behavior, Expressed Normative Attitude, and Directly Observed Behavior." *Philosophical Psychology* 27, no. 3 (2013): 293-327. doi:10.1080/09515089.2012.727135.

Stone, Arthur A., and C. J. Mackie. *Subjective Well-being: Measuring Happiness, Suffering, and Other Dimensions of Experience*. National Academies Press, 2013.

"The Teaching of Ethics in American Higher Education: An Empirical Synopsis." *Ethics Teaching in Higher Education*, 1980, 153-69. doi:10.1007/978-1-4613-3138-4_6.

Williams, Bernard, A. W. Moore., and Jonathan Lear. *Ethics and the Limits of Philosophy*. Routledge, 2015.

Recommended Resources:

Annis, David B. "Teaching Ethics In Higher Education: Goals, And The Implications Of The Empirical Research On Moral Development." *Metaphilosophy* 23, no. 1-2 (1992): 187-202. doi:10.1111/j.1467-9973.1992.tb00749.x.

---

[14] Many thanks to Tom Wartenberg for showing me about the world of Philosophy for Children. Especially huge thanks go to Anna Bertucci for the unending support without which none of this would have been possible.

Aristotle., and William David Ross. *The Nicomachean Ethics of Aristotle*. Oxford University Press, 1971.

Bingham, Charles W. *Authority Is Relational: Rethinking Educational Empowerment*. State University of New York Press, 2008.

Brenifer, Oscar. "How to Avoid Children's Questions." *Thinking: The Journal of Philosophy for Children* 16, no. 4 (2003): 29-32. doi:10.5840/thinking200316413.

Burroughs, Michael D. "Ethics Across Early Childhood Education." *Ethics Across the Curriculum—Pedagogical Perspectives*, 2018, 245-60. doi:10.1007/978-3-319-78939-2_15.

Burroughs, Michael D., and Deborah Tollefsen. "Learning To Listen: Epistemic Injustice And The Child." *Episteme* 13, no. 3 (2016): 359-77. doi:10.1017/epi.2015.64.

Burroughs, Michael D., and Tugce B Arda Tuncdemir. "Philosophical Ethics in Early Childhood: A Pilot Study." *Journal of Philosophy in Schools* 4, no. 1 (2017). doi:10.21913/jps.v4i1.1420.

Cameron, J. M. "The Teaching of Philosophy. An International Enquiry of Unesco. Pp. 230. UNESCO. 9s. 6d." *Philosophy* 30, no. 114 (1955): 273-74. doi:10.1017/s0031819100034847.

Dewey, John. *Democracy and Education: An Introd. to the Philosophy of Education*. Free Press., 1968.

Dewey, John. *Experience and Education: By John Dewey*. Macmillan, 1975.

Dewey, John., and Charles Alexander McMurry. *The First Yearbook of the Herbart Society for the Scientific Study of Teaching*, Prepared for Discussion at the Denver Meeting of the National Education Association. Bloomington, IL: Pantagraph. 1895.

Easterlin, Richard A. "Does Economic Growth Improve the Human Lot? Some Empirical Evidence." *Nations and Households in Economic Growth*, 1974, 89-125. doi:10.1016/b978-0-12-205050-3.50008-7.

Flanagan, Owen J. *Moral Sprouts and Natural Teleologies: 21st Century Moral Psychology Meets Classical Chinese Philosophy*. Marquette Univ. Press, 2014.

Flanagan, Owen J. *Varieties of Moral Personality: Ethics and Psychological Realism*. Harvard University Press, 1993.

Frankfurt, Harry G. *The Importance of What We Care About: Philosophical Essays*. Cambridge University Press, 1998.

Frankfurt, Harry G. *The Reasons of Love*. Princeton University Press, 2019.

Gazzard, Ann. "Philosophy for Children and the Discipline of Philosophy." *Thinking: The Journal of Philosophy for Children* 12, no. 4 (1996): 9-16. doi:10.5840/thinking19961243.

Gosnell, Nelda., and Henry Frankel. "Can We Help Children Think?" *Thinking: The Journal of Philosophy for Children* 1, no. 3 (1979): 74-76. doi:10.5840/thinking19791318.

Goucha, Moufida. *Philosophy: A School of Freedom: Teaching Philosophy and Learning to Philosophize: Status and Prospects*. UNESCO Publishing, 2007.

Haidt, Jonathan. "The Emotional Dog and Its Rational Tail: A Social Intuitionist Approach to Moral Judgment." *Psychological Review* 108, no. 4 (2001): 814-34. doi:10.1037/0033-295x.108.4.814.

Howard, Jason J. *Conscience in Moral Life: Rethinking How Our Convictions Structure Self and Society*. Rowman and Littlefield Publishers, 2014.

Johnson, Mark. *Moral Imagination Implications of Cognitive Science for Ethics.* University of Chicago Press, 2014.

Karaba, Robert. "Reconceptualizing the Aims in Philosophy for Children." *Thinking: The Journal of Philosophy for Children* 20, no. 1 (2012): 50-54. doi:10.5840/thinking 2012201/27.

Kenyon, Erik. Diane Terorde-Doyle (Author), Sharon Carnahan (Author)., and Thomas Wartenberg (Series editor). *Ethics for the Very Young: A Philosophy Curriculum for Early Childhood Education.* Rowman and Littlefield, 2019.

Kozol, Jonathan. "Intelligent Subversion": an interview with author and activist Jonathan Kozol, *Reading Today*, 23(5), p10. (2006).

Kozol, Jonathan. *Letters to a Young Teacher.* Crown Publishers, 2007.

Kyle, Judy A. "Managing Philosophical Discussions." *Thinking: The Journal of Philosophy for Children* 5, no. 2 (1984): 19-22. doi:10.5840/thinking19845217.

Laverty, Megan. "Philosophy of Education: overcoming the theory-practice divide, *Paedeusis*, Volume 15 (2006): No.1 pp. 31-44.

Laverty, Megan. "The Role of Confession in Community of Inquiry." *Thinking: The Journal of Philosophy for Children* 16, no. 3 (2003): 30-35. doi:10.5840/ thinking20031636.

Lear, Jonathan. *A Case for Irony (The Tanner Lectures on Human Values).* Harvard University Press, 2011.

Lipman, Matthew, Ann Margaret Sharp., and Frederick S. Oscanyan. *Philosophy in the Classroom.* TPB, 2003.

Lipman, Matthew. *Natasha: Vygotskian Dialogues.* Teachers College Press, 1996.

Lipman, Matthew. *Philosophy Goes to School.* Temple University Press, 1988.

Lone, Jana Mohr., and Michael D. Burroughs. *Philosophy in Education: Questioning and Dialog in Schools.* Rowman and Littlefield, 2016.

Lone, Jana Mohr. *The Philosophical Child.* Rowman and Littlefield, 2015.

Matthews, Gareth B. *Dialogues with Children.* Harvard U.P., 1992.

Matthews, Gareth B. *Socratic Perplexity and the Nature of Philosophy.* Oxford Univ. Press, 2006.

Matthews, Gareth B. *The Philosophy of Childhood.* Harvard University Press, 1996.

McCall, Catherine C. *Transforming Thinking: Philosophical Inquiry in the Primary and Secondary Classroom.* Routledge, 2016.

Miller, Stephen Kekoa. "Contesting Harmful Representations." *Teaching Ethics* 17, no. 2 (2017): 213-26. doi:10.5840/tej201822655.

Miller, Stephen Kekoa. "Socratic Aporia in the Classroom and the Development of Resilience." Analytic Teaching and Philosophical Praxis. https://journal.viterbo. edu/index.php/atpp/article/view/1002.

Miller, Stephen Kekoa. "The Importance of Not Being Earnest." *Metodički Ogledi* 25, no. 2 (2019): 31-48. doi:10.21464/mo.25.2.2.

Millett, Stephan., and Alan Tapper. "Benefits of Collaborative Philosophical Inquiry in Schools." *Educational Philosophy and Theory* 44, no. 5 (2012): 546-67. doi:10. 1111/j.1469-5812.2010.00727.x.

Miller, Stephen. "Your Feelings Are Wrong." Analytic Teaching and Philosophical Praxis. https://journal.viterbo.edu/index.php/atpp/article/view/1147.

Morris, Ian. *Teaching Happiness and Well-being in Schools Learning to Ride Elephants.* Continuum, 2009.

Murris, Karin. "The Epistemic Challenge of Hearing Child's Voice." *Studies in Philosophy and Education* 32, no. 3 (2013): 245-59. doi:10.1007/s11217-012-9349-9.

Nussbaum, Martha Craven. *From Disgust to Humanity: Sexual Orientation and Constitutional Law.* Oxford University Press, 2010.

Nussbaum, Martha C. *Love's Knowledge: Essays on Philosophy and Literature.* Oxford University Press, 2009.

Nussbaum, Martha Craven. *Political Emotions: Why Love Matters for Justice.* Belknap Press of Harvard University Press, 2015.

Panaioti, A. "The Bodhisattva's Brain: Buddhism Naturalized, by Owen Flanagan." *Mind* 121, no. 482 (2012): 485-90. doi:10.1093/mind/fzs070.

Phillips, Christopher. *Socrates Café: A Fresh Taste of Philosophy.* Lutterworth Press, 2003.

Piaget, Jean. *The Moral Judgment of the Child Jean Piaget.* Routledge and Kegan, 1972.

Platon., and G. M. A. Grube. *Plato: The Republic.* Hackett Pub., 1974.

Pritchard, Michael S. *Reasonable Children: Moral Education and Moral Learning.* University Press of Kansas, 1996.

Rollins, Maughn. "Epistemological Considerations for the Community of Inquiry." *Thinking: The Journal of Philosophy for Children* 12, no. 2 (1995): 31-40. doi:10. 5840/thinking199512220.

Schwitzgebel, Eric, and Joshua Rust. "The Moral Behavior of Ethics Professors: Relationships among Self-reported Behavior, Expressed Normative Attitude, and Directly Observed Behavior." *Philosophical Psychology* 27, no. 3 (2013): 293-327. doi:10.1080/09515089.2012.727135.

Schwitzgebel, Eric, Bradford Cokelet., and Peter Singer. "Do Ethics Classes Influence Student Behavior? Case Study: Teaching the Ethics of Eating Meat." Cognition. July 25, 2020. https://www.sciencedirect.com/science/article/abs/pii/S001002772030216X?dgcid=coauthor.

Seligman, Adam B., Bennett Simon, Robert Paul Weller., and Michael J. Puett. *Ritual and Its Consequences: An Essay on the Limits of Sincerity.* Oxford University Press, 2008.

Stone, Arthur A., and C. J. Mackie. *Subjective Well-being: Measuring Happiness, Suffering, and Other Dimensions of Experience.* National Academies Press, 2013.

"The Teaching of Ethics in American Higher Education: An Empirical Synopsis." *Ethics Teaching in Higher Education*, 1980, 153-69. doi:10.1007/978-1-4613-3138-4_6.

Trickey, S., and K. J. Topping *. "'Philosophy for Children': A Systematic Review." *Research Papers in Education* 19, no. 3 (2004): 365-80. doi:10.1080/026715204200 0248016.

Turgeon, Wendy C. *Philosophical Adventures with Fairy Tales: New Ways to Explore Familiar Tales with Kids of All Ages.* Rowman and Littlefield, 2020.

Turgeon, Wendy., and Julia Jackson. "Wendy Turgeon." *Thinking: The Journal of Philosophy for Children* 19, no. 2 (2009): 30-31. doi:10.5840/thinking2009192/310.

"UNESCO Intersectoral Strategy on Philosophy." *Diogenes* 56, no. 4 (2009): 95-100. doi:10.1177/0392192109355525.

Walzer, Michael. *Thick and Thin: Moral Argument at Home and Abroad.* University of Notre Dame Press, 1994.

Wartenberg, Thomas E. *Big Ideas for Little Kids: Teaching Philosophy through Children's Literature.* Rowman and Littlefield Education, 2014.

Wartenberg, Thomas E. *Philosophy in Classrooms and Beyond: New Approaches to Picture-Book Philosophy.* Rowman and Littlefield Publishers, 2019.

Weinberg, Justin. "How Do Moral Philosophy Courses Affect Student Behavior?" Daily Nous. July 27, 2020. http://dailynous.com/2020/07/27/moral-philosophy-courses-affect-student-behavior/.

Williams, Bernard, A. W. Moore., and Jonathan Lear. *Ethics and the Limits of Philosophy.* Routledge, 2015.

Wolf, Susan R., and John Koethe. *Meaning in Life and Why It Matters.* Princeton University Press, 2012.

Chapter 2

The Iowa Lyceum: Graduate Students & Pre-College Philosophy

Danielle Colburn

University of Iowa

Cassie Finley

University of Iowa

Joe Glover

University of Iowa

Abstract

The Iowa Lyceum is a pre-college philosophy summer program hosted by the University of Iowa's philosophy department. The program is loosely affiliated with other Lyceum programs around the country but is unique in that it is entirely organized and run by philosophy graduate students. In this chapter, we lay out the history and structure of the Iowa Lyceum program, the values—practical, pedagogical, personal, and philosophical—pre-college instruction has not only for participants, but for the graduate students and faculty alike who help organize and execute the camp, and the pedagogical underpinnings which motivate the importance of exposing students to philosophy before college. Additionally, unique benefits of programs like the Iowa Lyceum are that they aid in the professional and personal development of graduate students while also serving the wider community by working towards developing intellectual virtues in high-school students. While the key insights offered in this chapter focus primarily on our experience as graduate student organizers, this chapter has broader appeal in the lessons learned from the Iowa Lyceum to others interested in establishing a successful pre-college philosophy program.

Keywords: pre-college philosophy, pedagogy, critical thinking, P4C, Philosophy for Children, graduate education, philosophy camp, Lyceum, dialogue, Community of Inquiry, teaching philosophy

***

The Iowa Lyceum, a week-long philosophy summer camp hosted at the University of Iowa, has been providing an environment for high-quality philosophical discussion to pre-college students ages thirteen to eighteen since 2013. The Lyceum was created by two graduate students, Gregory Stoutenberg and Kristopher Phillips, both of whom had pre-existing interests in public philosophy inspired by the Illinois Lyceum at the University of Illinois, Urbana-Champaign. Since the Iowa Lyceum's formation, it has carried on as one of the few pre-college philosophy programs run entirely by philosophy graduate students. The Lyceum as a concept traces its origins back to ancient Greece, where it marked a place for the public discussion of ideas. From this original Lyceum, Aristotle founded his school, out of which developed the connotations of a Lyceum as an institution devoted to public education. Like Aristotle's Lyceum, the Iowa Lyceum has the purpose of preparing its participants to critically engage with the world around them.

In what follows, we describe the Iowa Lyceum's approach to pre-college summer philosophy camp. This chapter is divided into three sections: (1) the origin and structure of the Iowa Lyceum, (2) the unique pedagogical values and challenges of pre-college philosophy, and (3) the general philosophical importance of pre-college philosophy programs.

The first section of the paper lays out the structure and motivations behind the organization of the Iowa Lyceum. We pay particular attention to the logistics and tasks required for running a pre-college philosophy program. Through our experience coordinating the Iowa Lyceum as philosophy graduate students, we are uniquely positioned to speak in favor of both pre-college philosophy programs generally as well as those which involve graduate student organizers. Thus, our experiences and advice will largely focus on the value of programs led by graduate students for organizers and participants alike. That being said, the information and ideas expressed within this chapter should still have relevance to a broader audience, including (but not limited to) graduate student supervisors, department chairs and administrators, and early career faculty. Finally, we discuss the philosophical underpinnings of the Iowa Lyceum and the transformative, intrinsic value of a pre-college philosophical education. Although pre-college philosophy programs certainly have instrumental value, we argue any skills or practical values that result from the experience are, and ought to be, secondary to the greater purpose of providing a holistic, transformative philosophical experience to participants.

The Iowa Lyceum: Origins and Structure

The Iowa Lyceum owes its inception to the antecedent interests of a few philosophy graduate students inspired by the Illinois Lyceum, coupled with the support of the philosophy faculty at the University of Iowa. The founding aim was to expose high school students to academic philosophy as a means for developing philosophical and logical skills prior to entering college, just as high school athletes develop physical skills pertaining to their sport through sustained practice. However, it became apparent soon after the program's implementation that the unique space created by the Lyceum was not, and should not be, limited to prioritizing skill-based outcomes. Rather, the participants' engagement and open-minded curiosity, combined with the enthusiasm of coordinators, create a transformative educational opportunity invaluable to all involved. The structure and pedagogical approaches, then, are grounded in efforts to facilitate this experience.

The structure of the Lyceum is similar to that of a philosophy conference, but with greater emphasis on participant engagement. In the past, we have focused each year's camp on a theme, such as "Justice", "Identity", or "Female Philosophers", which helps to encourage diverse presentation topics year to year. The theme is chosen with an eye towards the interests and competencies of the graduate student organizers, as it benefits both organizers and participants alike to have a topic in which organizers feel confident. Graduate students often TA for similar classes, so they usually have a common foundation of philosophical topics with which they feel comfortable exploring. These foundations are great sources for deciding on a year's theme, particularly if the coordinators have different philosophical backgrounds and interests.

As for the daily structure of the Lyceum, each day is broken into three or four sessions, consisting of introductory lectures given by graduate students and more focused presentations led by professors. At the beginning of the camp, graduate students offer introductory discussion sessions to help facilitate a comfortable discussion environment, prepare participants for professor discussions, and to introduce them to philosophy more generally. Professors then offer age-appropriate talks, with a focus on engaging participants in the discussion, as opposed to straightforward lecturing. Our goal is to give professors as much freedom as possible regarding the structure and content of their presentations. We encourage professors to relate their research to the general theme of the year, but as they are volunteering their time, we accept any topic on which they want to present. Given the wide range of faculty research interests, how they choose to tie their presentation to the year's theme creates an even wider range of topics to present to the participants. For instance, if a professor works on social and political philosophy, then their presentation for the year's theme of personal identity may engage the topic of how culture shapes an individual's identity. Meanwhile, another professor who works on philosophy of mind will discuss how the mind-body problem can cast doubt on identifying an individual with their body. We keep these sessions to about an hour in length, though we have also found success when professors combine their forces and lead two connected sessions back-to-back. Participants have always been given time to ask professors questions at the end of each presentation, but many of them are looking to continue these discussions amongst themselves. In previous years, the main opportunity for informal conversation amongst themselves was limited to the lunch break and the small breaks in between sessions. Moving forward, participants have expressed interest in having time after presentations specifically dedicated to open-ended discussion of the topic.

We finish the Lyceum with student presentations. Participants have the opportunity to present at the end of the week on a topic of their choosing—usually aligned with the week's theme—but are welcome to incorporate their own interests in selecting their topic. The participant presentations vary year to year, generally taking the form of either individual presentations or group debates, decided upon by each student based on their preferences. We also do not just leave them to fend for themselves in constructing their presentation or debate. Towards the end of the week, usually from Wednesday onwards, the graduate student organizers work with the participants in order to help them develop their presentation and provide feedback on the ideas they have. It can be a challenge to get participants to focus on a topic and to be confident in their own philosophical intuitions, but we make a point to reiterate that our expectation is not for them to produce a perfect presentation; rather, the presentations are an opportunity to present difficult, interesting questions within a supportive community of inquiry. Participants who choose a presentation, as opposed to the debate format, engage the group in a guided philosophical discussion which may draw from the material they have all learned over the course of the week. These elements emphasize the importance of *doing* philosophy—that is, having students *apply* their newly developed skills and reflections to real-world, as well as theoretical, questions and problems.

An important aspect of our program is that it is entirely free for participants, removing the potential financial limitations which can prevent the expansion of philosophy into different parts of the public sphere. In order to make this possible, we have received funding from various internal and external sources, including the University of Iowa's College of Liberal Arts and Sciences, the Philosophy Department, the American Philosophy Association (APA), and the Philosophical Learning and Teaching Organization (PLATO). Many colleges have funds available to support programs like the Lyceum, so seeking funding both through one's institution and through external sources ensures an equally accessible program to all prospective participants.

For a baseline, the cost of hosting the Lyceum with about 20 participants is $2,000—the majority of which is spent feeding participants a small breakfast and a hearty lunch, providing books to be used before and during the camp, and providing a Lyceum t-shirt, which serves the additional function of advertising the camp whenever past participants wear their shirt. Funding enables us to provide Lyceum participants with philosophical texts, encouraging further reading beyond the camp. These texts include a combination of physical and digital copies of books and articles. Offering participants cost-free philosophical texts affords students the opportunity to begin to build a philosophical library in their home well before attending college. These funds also cover the background checks required for working with minors and the membership fees for PLATO, the APA, etc., which provide the Lyceum organizers access to more funding opportunities.

It is worth noting that due to COVID-19, the 2020 Lyceum was held online. The online format (run via Zoom) was quite successful and meant we were able to allocate the food budget to provide books to participants; this allowed us to keep the budget below $1,000. While there is an important feature of community lost by not hosting the camp in a shared physical space, an online format could be a good starting point for a pre-college philosophy program with a smaller budget and fewer logistical concerns associated with hosting minors on campus.

Because the Lyceum is committed to making philosophy accessible to high school students, ages thirteen to eighteen, the students' application process is relatively simple. The application requires a short essay stating why they would like to participate in the Lyceum, as well as a brief note about how they heard about the program. The function motivating the application's format is two-fold: (i) the short essay demonstrates that the student is interested in philosophy and willing to put in the work, without burdening (and potentially excluding) students with hefty application requirements, and (ii) students' reports of how they came to hear about the Lyceum informs which community-outreach techniques are more effective in recruiting participants. By and large, the applications reflect word-of-mouth as the most effective means to bringing students into pre-college philosophy programs.

Therefore, one task for program organizers is to reach out to the community to raise awareness of the program and facilitate pre-college student interest. Since participants are from the area surrounding the university, community outreach—working with high schools and teachers—is of the utmost importance to establishing and maintaining a thriving pre-college philosophy program. In order to facilitate this communication, we keep a file of contacts from the local school districts, to whom we send flyers with information about the Lyceum a few months before the camp begins. They are then able to disseminate resources amongst colleagues, students, and parents and encourage participation in the program. Another option for community outreach is to post informational flyers on parent-access sites, though this often requires membership fees for posting and increases the costs without a guarantee of increased enrollment.

For programs involving contact with minors, it is essential for steps to be taken to protect participants. The University of Iowa has developed program requirements for working with children under the age of eighteen, which has been incredibly helpful in guiding organizers who may not have worked with children prior to the Lyceum. One important guideline involves communication with minors, both in person and electronically. Universities often have pre-established procedures for interacting with minors on campus, but one further way of ensuring that participants are aware of policies and protocol regarding their safety is through a centralized website. The Lyceum website provides a convenient location for finding official program documents, keeping a record of the progress that our program has made over the years, and commemorating important program contributors. A separate email address—independent of personal organizer email addresses and accessible to all program organizers—allows for better organization and smooth transitions of leadership from year to year. All email exchanges can be monitored by multiple people, aiding in the prevention of private correspondence between program organizers and minors. The separate email address also allows for a centralized list of contacts.

Additionally, a program manual provides important information about safety measures, relevant University contacts, and the appropriate protocols for when problems arise. The University of Iowa also requires complete background checks for anyone coming into contact with minors (including online interactions), as well as a brief training which covers the University policies for working with minors. It is worth noting that the manual reflects important safety protocols specific to the program, so separate manuals are required for delivering pre-college programs in different formats, i.e., on-campus versus online. Thus, an essential element to all pre-college philosophy programs is adherence to strict safety guidelines, including a presentation at the beginning of the camp to participants informing them of all necessary safety requirements. When working with minors, we as program organizers are responsible for the participants while they are in our care. In order to protect both participants and the program, it is important that agreement forms and waivers are kept on file for multiple years, even as the program changes hands from year to year.

The Graduate Student Experience at the Lyceum

The Iowa Lyceum is uniquely situated as one of the few pre-college philosophy camps organized and executed entirely by philosophy graduate students. By having graduate students run the camp, both participants and graduate students benefit; the knowledge that organizers and presenters gain from tailoring philosophical material to a pre-college audience is valuable as a means to improving teaching skills.

The involvement of graduate students in pre-college philosophy programs enables graduate students to develop their pedagogy in a unique setting. The Lyceum is structured so that pre-college students participate in discussions facilitated by graduate students. The graduate coordinators also offer a few lectures which cover general introductions to philosophy, logic and formal reasoning, and an introduction to the week's theme. The experience of teaching and organizing the Lyceum is the perfect opportunity for graduate students to explore different ways of presenting philosophical material to audiences who have no prior familiarity with philosophy. Common to many specialists, and perhaps particularly applicable to philosophers, is the lack of ability to communicate with those unfamiliar with the technicalities and methods within their field. As one becomes more specialized in philosophy, it is easy to get lost in technical language and discipline-specific vernacular. The experience of teaching high school students, then, requires reflection upon how one speaks and introduces concepts in order to make them accessible not just to pre-college audiences, but to the public at large.

Beyond the value of the Lyceum on graduate students' approach to teaching, learning how to present complex philosophical ideas is invaluable to one's scholarly development. An underappreciated aspect of graduate student teaching is the impact that teaching itself has on the philosophical thought of the teacher. In the words of Aristotle, "To teach will be the same as to learn", meaning when one teaches they are exercising their capacity to learn.[1] In clearly and carefully identifying and explaining arguments, concepts, and inferences made in academic philosophy, graduate students may learn to articulate their own thinking on seemingly disconnected issues. Given the dense interconnections between *prima facie* disparate areas of philosophy, clarifying concepts in, for example, the philosophy of science for a pre-college audience may help an instructor understand moves made in the realism debate in ethics.

Those new to philosophy also benefit from working with graduate students in particular, as graduate students are positioned to provide a bridge between participants' philosophical interests and the potentially intimidating language of academia. The ideal result is an accessible discussion exploring participants' philosophical questions within the structures of academic philosophy. Having graduate student mentors with whom participants can feel comfortable is more conducive to open communication than if participants were expected to

---

[1] *Physics* 202b8.

only engage directly with professors. Further, we have found that pre-college students are more likely to share their ideas if we specifically stop and ask each student to share a thought. It is less important at the pre-college level for organizers to edit the thoughts that participants share; rather, in order to develop confidence in younger students' ideas, it is most beneficial to directly encourage them to speak up.

Outside of the experience of running the program, graduate students are often still exploring their interests in philosophy and are preparing for careers either within or beyond academia, though most graduate students aim for the former. Having the opportunity to engage with pre-college philosophy can influence the rest of one's philosophical career, yet few graduate students are afforded the opportunity to explore pre-college philosophy, or public philosophy more generally. Just as one may discover a passion for philosophy of language, Aristotle, or philosophy of mind, graduate students may discover a passion for engaging with pre-college students through experience running the Lyceum—an opportunity not otherwise accessible to graduate philosophy students.

The relative scarcity of opportunities to pursue public philosophy in graduate education does not, however, entail that such programs are unimportant; rather, given the shrinking academic job market, opportunities outside of the academy are more essential than ever. Working with high school students exposes graduate students to possibilities for careers in K-12 education, administration, and the potential for further public philosophical engagement. Of course, having a program run entirely by graduate students poses distinct challenges for which organizers must accommodate—namely, the transition of leadership from year to year. The potential for disconnects during these transitions necessitates significant organization and communication among coordinators, which are applicable skills to any profession, but particularly essential to any career working with minors. The need for clear communication of safety protocols is crucial for any professional interactions with minors, which is central to K-12 instructors' training but often non-existent in higher education. A safely run pre-college program requires hypervigilance on the part of coordinators in adhering to these protocols and protecting participants' well-being. The logistics of establishing, organizing, and implementing a pre-college philosophy program involve maneuvering administrative systems, networking and communication to advertise the program, and event planning—all of which are skills invaluable to nearly any profession. This experience and resulting know-how can set a graduate student apart from their peers as a competitive candidate who has a demonstrated interest in community engagement and service.

The Lyceum not only stands as an invaluable experience to the participants as an introduction to philosophical concepts but provides graduate students with important opportunities to clarify their own thinking about philosophical problems, to become familiar with the institutional and administrative side of their burgeoning careers, and to practice the skills necessary for excellent pedagogy. Inspired by the work of philosopher Mary Midgley, Ellie Robson writes: "When we do philosophy, we should not operate as 'isolated intellectuals', taking part in a sterile enterprise—rather, we are part of a collaborative, living process of shared human development."[2] Properly done, philosophy is obligated to reach beyond the scope of academia and engage with broader communities. Public programs like the Lyceum are at the forefront of philosophical community engagement which focuses on exposing pre-college students to philosophy.

The Purpose of a Lyceum

In this section, we argue not only for the instrumental value which a philosophical education provides to pre-college students, but for the more fundamental essence of philosophy as a transformative endeavor rooted the development of tools for open-ended inquiry, self-reflection, and charitable engagement with ideas. It is from the latter which any practicality in philosophical education arises; rather than explicitly aiming to be a program which teaches "critical thinking,"[3] we strive to cultivate an intellectual environment conducive to the imaginative exploration of ideas and one's place in the world. The practical skills which result from this space of inquiry are of course valuable and useful beyond the context of the Lyceum, but it is important to emphasize that these skills are contingent upon the more holistic presentation of philosophy as a foundational approach to interacting with the world. We aim to provide an experience through which participants begin to develop the skills and dispositions necessary for stepping back, identifying,

---

[2] Robson, *The Philosopher Queens*. 116.

[3] For this paper, we use literature which emphasizes the importance of "critical thinking" as a means of acknowledging the social and practical benefits of a philosophical education. "Critical thinking" is an ill-defined, yet centrally appreciated, concept in education—in order to meaningfully make use of this term, we roughly follow the American Philosophical Association Committee for Pre-College Instruction in Philosophy's 1989 account of critical thinking as: "purposeful, self-regulatory judgment which results in interpretation, analysis, evaluation, and inference, as well as explanation of the evidential, conceptual, methodological, criteriological, or contextual considerations upon which that judgment is based."

and carefully evaluating the stream of information and problems with which they will have to engage throughout the rest of their lives.

Of course, mere exposure to philosophical content does not properly constitute philosophical engagement; the central problem (discussed by Annis and Annis (1979) as cited in Phillips (2019)) is without opportunities to study philosophy, high school students are missing out on a distinctly philosophical approach to the development of critical thinking skills.[4] A lack of philosophical education is not simply a lack of information about philosophy; it is the absence of space to develop the ways of interacting with the world which are unique philosophical inquiries. Considering K-12 schooling does not emphasize the role of free exploration and problem-raising (as opposed to problem-solving, which is often the emphasis of K-12 education) in students' development, the Lyceum is a unique progression in participants' education. By aiming for a holistic and transformative educational experience with philosophy, the skills consequently developed are directly and importantly applicable to social and democratic values. As Abrami *et al.* explain, "most philosophers within the Western tradition have emphasized critique, but by philosophical standards, at least, the emphasis on the development of the critical faculties of individual citizens is relatively recent and linked to the rise of liberal democracy" (2015: 276). An emphasis within education, therefore, should be the development of reflective, careful thinkers capable of understanding and thoughtfully engaging with their social and political milieu.

Although the Iowa Lyceum is not *aimed* towards cultivating "critical thinking, related literature affirms the similar benefits of the Lyceum's pedagogical approaches to philosophical education. In other words, the methods employed by the Lyceum are similarly conducive to the development of skills that other programs, which prioritize practical outcomes, emphasize. Both the Iowa Lyceum and more practically-oriented programs highlight the role of dialogue and active engagement with the presented material and other interlocutors. Dialogue and interactive activities are primary means for *doing* philosophy, rather than just learning *about* philosophy. A meta-analysis by Abrami *et al.* finds,

> "[T]wo general types of instructional interventions are especially helpful in the development of generic CT [Critical Thinking] skills. Notably, the opportunity for dialogue (e.g., discussion) appears to

---

[4] See Phillips, Kristopher G. "The Kids are Alright: Philosophical Dialogue and the Utah Lyceum"; Cherry, Myisha, "Liberatory Dialogue". Phillips discusses at length the lack of clarity in discussing "critical thinking" as a primary outcome or skill developed through philosophy.

improve the outcomes of CT skills acquisition, especially where the teacher poses questions...Similarly, the exposure of students to authentic or situated problems and examples seems to play an important role in promoting CT, particularly when applied problem solving and role-playing methods are used" (2015: 302).

In other words, pedagogical interventions focused on facilitating discussion are fundamental features of a philosophical education and the philosophy classroom. These activities can take the form of posing puzzles or introducing texts which students discuss, for instance. Students are encouraged to participate in the dialogue by asking questions about the material, proposing interpretations or examples of the arguments, and raising critical objections. While instructors serve as guides, the bulk of discussion is open to students to raise points which push the conversation in various directions, according to their curiosity and questions on the subject.

Like the philosophy classroom, the Iowa Lyceum involves a dynamic, back-and-forth teaching style. One way of implementing instructional interventions is through an introductory logic section focused on fallacies and basic argument forms. An introductory logic portion is a central component to the Lyceum structure; participants are often taught through examples "from the wild" in order to reaffirm the purpose of *doing* philosophy as a way of life rather than as an isolated, abstract discipline. As an exercise, the students are shown specific examples of fallacies and argument forms before being tasked with finding or creating their own examples. Through a variety of internet resources, students have easy access to various philosophically interesting, yet fallacious, arguments. Participants tend to be enthusiastic about sharing memes, cartoons, and videos for further critique. We then ask them to articulate why these errors in reasoning are flawed, yet nonetheless tempting. This is one of the most important elements of a philosophical education—namely, students are doing philosophy, in this case, through actively identifying and critiquing the examples which show up in daily life. Regardless of whether participants pursue a career in academic philosophy, the experiences of engaging with the world through activities such as this are invaluable to not only the participants' educational development, but to their engagement with the world as a whole.

In order to facilitate effective communication and interactions with one another, Lyceum organizers, and presenters, participants must feel confident exploring and analyzing arguments. In order to produce comfort in engaging with philosophical dialogue, we lower the stakes by not expecting or requiring participants to come to the Iowa Lyceum with robust knowledge of—or even justified beliefs about—philosophy. This allows us to increase the possibilities for creative and imaginative exploration, so participants are willing to fully consider a greater range of ideas and take greater relative risks in their contributions. Beyond some curiosity and perhaps minimal prior exposure, participants have very little explicit philosophical training. By expanding the possibilities which participants consider, we encourage the students to move beyond limited ways of thinking in order to entertain and explore ideas which they may not have otherwise considered. We meet the students where they are and allow them to pursue ideas to the furthest logical extent.

As opposed to focusing directly on skill-based learning for participants in the Lyceum, we emphasize the Lyceum as a space for developing intellectual virtues. Epistemology and philosophy of education intersect in discussions of education as a tool for cultivating intellectual virtues.[5] Rooted in Aristotle's *Nicomachean Ethics*, becoming a virtuous person does not come from purely theoretical understandings, but rather, through the practical application of virtuous activity to life. To become an intellectually virtuous person requires practice in being curious, open-minded, intellectually courageous, interested in truth for its own sake, and engaged in effective inquiry. Lani Watson argues that learning how to effectively ask questions is a fundamental practice in the development of intellectual virtues, saying:

> "Questioning...is an essential component of our collective, social, and intellectual endeavors... [T]he intellectual skill of good questioning plays two important and closely related roles in the formation of intellectual character. Firstly, good questioning stimulates intellectually virtuous inquiry. Secondly, good questioning contributes to the development of several of the individual intellectual virtues. As such, the skill of good questioning contributes to the formation of intellectually virtuous character as a whole." (2018 : 354)

Accordingly, the discussions and presentations are largely focused on encouraging students to ask questions. Thus, the Lyceum is structured in order to foster the participants' intellectual development by facilitating discussions and encouraging the asking of questions. To best accomplish this, a space must be established for students to feel comfortable engaging with and exploring the ideas introduced to them.

A central thesis to pre-college philosophical training is the concept of a "community of inquiry" (See for example Hagaman (1990); Lipman, Sharp, and Oscanyan, (1980); and Gregory and Laverty (2017). Establishing a community of inquiry is a critical step in facilitating the cultivation of intellectual virtues. Developing open-minded, curious, intellectually courageous participants

---

[5] See Baehr, Jason. *Intellectual Virtues and Education: Essays in Applied Virtue Epistemology.*

requires organizers to model these characteristics in order to develop a safe space for exploration. As Ashby Butnor writes,

> "An intellectually safe place ought to be established with the recognition that vulnerability is a central component of the epistemic mission. We are vulnerable whenever we willingly put our ideas and positions at risk—risk of being challenged, revised, defeated, or elevated in the course of conversation. In some sense, we are putting our very selves at risk" (2012: 29-30).

Given most high school students' lack of exposure to philosophy, combined with the limited timeframe of the Lyceum, immediately fostering an intellectually safe environment which is charitable, encouraging, and validating is absolutely essential. In order for students to benefit from philosophical dialogue, they need to feel confident enough to participate.[6] We communicate with students from the beginning that philosophical arguments can escalate our emotions quickly, and we emphasize that part of the process of skill development within philosophy is learning how to have those arguments without the maladaptive patterns that can come with emotional escalation. Lyceum organizers attempt to avoid emotionally triggering topics, but having a discussion regarding appropriate interpersonal communication of philosophical ideas towards the beginning of the camp establishes a safe community of inquiry.

The Iowa Lyceum aims to create an experience which introduces philosophy to individuals as a fundamentally transformational approach for engaging with the world. This aligns with the ideas presented in Wright's article, "On the benefits of philosophy as a way of life" (henceforth PWOL). In contrast with ordinary philosophy courses which focus on conveying information or even passing on skills, PWOL "often focuses on broader themes of the good life and how one ought to live in pursuit of one's own good life."[7] The general idea behind PWOL courses is that they have a set of interconnected philosophical questions which require the students to not only understand the material, but also employ self-reflection in order to see how philosophical questions are able to apply to their lives or what sort of impact various answers to these philosophical questions have on their lives.

One paradigmatic PWOL course is Notre Dame's "God and the Good Life" which is, at its root, a course in philosophy of religion but has the students

---

[6] See Phillips, Kristopher G. "The Kids are Alright: Philosophical Dialogue and the Utah Lyceum"; Cherry, Myisha, "Liberatory Dialogue."

[7] Wright, Jake. "On the Benefits of Philosophy as a Way of Life in a General Introductory Course." 435.

asking themselves whether they should believe in God and whether they can know anything about God. The end goal is that the students not only develop the skills one typically intends to develop in introductory courses, i.e., the ability to reconstruct and interpret specific canonical philosophers' arguments, but also cultivates actual impacts on the students' lives. The purpose of "God and the Good Life" is to introduce the students to hard-hitting questions in order to inspire thinking more deeply about their beliefs and values, as well as their implications on other aspects of their lives. In a similar vein, the Lyceum encourages participants to critically evaluate and explore their own ideas and values to facilitate self-reflection.

Co-founder and former Iowa Lyceum President, Kristopher G. Phillips, has written on the value of pre-college philosophy, emphasizing that it ought to be valued more as an end in itself, rather than in terms of instrumental value. As Phillips says:

> "The value of philosophy is neither exhausted nor primarily constituted by the instrumental value the field has as an academic discipline—that is, in terms of helping college students enroll in medical, law, or post-graduate programs, or find gainful employment. I believe that philosophy can provide a truly life-changing experience for people who come to it with an open mind. I also believe that philosophical instruction is too valuable to wait until college...Programs such as the Lyceum are, I argue, uniquely situated to help students *do* philosophy, rather than merely learn *about* philosophy" (Phillips 2019: 2).

Clearly the focus of philosophy is not on quantitative learning outcomes— indeed, the very nature of philosophy places import on the critical examination of diverse positions and arguments, which we hope to encourage both within the context of the Lyceum and beyond. There is of course practical value to be gained from a philosophical education, but more importantly, the aims ought to emphasize the intrinsic value of philosophical exploration, from which various skills will follow.

The intention of the Iowa Lyceum is for participants to develop a new approach to life. This consequently entails skills which the students can apply to their day-to-day life when encountering news, politics, and arguments. Of course, while we hope to sow a love of philosophy, so all of our participants will continue pursuing it beyond the program, the influence of a pre-college introduction to philosophy is invaluable in and of itself. The Lyceum does not aim for mere familiarity with philosophical materials and "critical thinking" skills; we aim to facilitate the self-reflection and inquiry necessary for participants to understand their place in, and interactions with, the world.

Bibliography

Abrami, Philip C., Robert M. Bernard, Eugene Borokhovski, David I. Wadding-
ton, C. Anne Wade., and Tonje Persson."Strategies for Teaching Students to
Think Critically: A Meta-Analysis." *Review of Educational Research* 85 no 2
(2015).: 275-314.

Annis, Linda., and David Annis. "The impact of philosophy on students' critical
thinking ability", *Contemporary Educational Psychology* 4 no 3 (1979): 219-226.

Aristotle., Robert C. Bartlett., and Susan D. Collins.. *Aristotle's Nicomachean
Ethics.* Chicago: University of Chicago Press. 2011.

Aristotle. *Aristotle's Physics.* Oxford: Clarendon P., 1970.

Baehr, Jason. *Intellectual Virtues and Education: Essays in Applied Virtue Epistemology.* Routledge. 2016.

Butnor, A. "Critical Communities: Intellectual Safety and the Power of Disagreement", *Education Perspectives* 44 (2012): 29-31.

Cherry, Myisha. "Liberatory Dialogue", *pre-college Philosophy and Public Practice* 1
(2018).: 4-15.

Gregory, M., and Laverty, M. (Eds.). (2017). *In Community of Inquiry with Ann
Margaret Sharp: Childhood, Philosophy and Education.* Routledge.

Hagaman, S. (1990). The Community of Inquiry: An Approach to Collaborative
Learning. *Studies in Art Education, 31*(3), 149-157.

Lipman, M., Sharp, A., and Oscanyan, F. (1980). *Philosophy in the Classroom.*
Temple University Press.

Phillips, Kristopher G. "The kids are alright: philosophical dialogue and the
Utah Lyceum", *pre-college Philosophy and Public Practice* 1 (2019): 42-57.

Phillips, Kristopher G., and Gracia Allen. "The Utah Lyceum: Cultivating "Reasonableness" in Southwest Utah" from *Growing Up With Philosophy Camp.* (2020).

Robson, Ellie. "Mary Midgley" from *The Philosopher Queens.* Unbound Publishers,
edited by Buxton, Rebecca and Lisa Whiting. (2020).

Watson, Lani. "Educating for Good Questioning: a Tool for Intellectual Virtues
Education". *Acta Analytica* 33, (2018): 353-70.

Wright, Jake. "On the benefits of philosophy as a way of life in a general introductory course", *Metaphilosophy* 51 nos. 2-3 (2020): 435-454.

Chapter 3

P4C & Community-Engaged Pedagogy

Erik Kenyon

Friends Academy in Dartmouth, MA

Abstract

P4C facilitators often say that they learn just as much as the children do. What would it look like to harness P4C's potential as a means of *adult* education? At Rollins College, I developed a series of General Education courses which sent both traditional and nontraditional undergraduates into local schools to lead P4C lessons with children from ages 3 to 13. Through collaborations with the campus lab school, first-year seminar program, office of community engagement and center for career and life planning, these P4C courses became a vehicle for broad and meaningful integration of students into the general education curriculum and campus resources. As the college moved into revising the curriculum for its evening undergraduate program, my P4C became the model for a new *Intro to the Pragmatic Liberal Arts* program, which uses community-engagement projects from a range of disciplines to align students' thinking with the College's approach to the applied liberal arts. In this chapter, I use a P4C program I developed for Rollins' program as a case study in backwards course design, drawing attention to campus resources that do not typically make their way into philosophy curricula. My own training is in Greek and Roman philosophy. I argue that the capacity for P4C programs to integrate across the curriculum and co-curriculum provides a mode of rigorous instruction that is grounded in philosophy's Classical roots yet flexible enough to keep up with changing demands upon higher education.

Keywords: civic engagement, community engagement, undergraduate general education, ethics across. the curriculum

***

Adults who lead philosophy for children (P4C) programs routinely comment that they learn just as much as the children do. Yet, what would it look like to harness this potential as a means of adult education? In this chapter, I will discuss the P4C program I developed at Rollins College, a small liberal arts college near Orlando, Florida. Through it, undergraduates were introduced to philosophy by way of primary texts from Plato to Gilligan. They then developed lesson plans and led discussions with children, ages 3 to 13, at local schools. These courses were housed in the College's two general education curricula, serving traditional residential students in the College of Liberal Arts (CLA) and non-traditional, non-residential students in Rollins' Hamilton Holt School. The P4C program grew out of a revision of the CLA curriculum and helped shape revisions to the Holt curriculum when a community engagement (CE) requirement was introduced a few years later. The program has been productive, leading to several articles, a book-length pre-K ethics curriculum and a couple of spots on cable news. The current chapter is written for college or high school faculty looking to develop P4C programs, bringing older students and younger students together. I will use Rollins' program as a case study in backwards course design and draw attention to campus resources that do not typically make their way into philosophy curricula, i.e., offices of career and life planning, community engagement, instructional design and campus lab schools. Through all this, I suggest a mode of instruction that is grounded in philosophy's Classical roots yet flexible enough to keep up with changing demands upon higher education.

From Plato to Picture Books: An Exercise in Backwards Course Design

The move from my graduate research to developing a P4C program made sense only in retrospect. In grad school at Cornell University, I focused on ancient philosophy with a dissertation on Augustine of Hippo's philosophical dialogues; *Against the Academic Skeptics, On the Teacher* and *On Free Choice of the Will* are the most widely known. The questions I pursued were fairly 'academic': Why do these works contain so many bad arguments? So many seemingly random shifts in topic? Why do most of them end with speeches? The answers I came to added up to a pedagogical method which combines elements from the history of philosophy up to that point: Socratic "un-learning" of problematic assumptions, Plotinian reflection on rational activity and a Ciceronian willingness to trade in provisional answers.[1] Meanwhile, through my work on Augustine, I had come into frequent contact with Gareth Matthews, a leader in analytic approaches to ancient and medieval philosophy and a pioneer in the P4C movement. While Gary passed away before I started my own P4C work, he planted the seed through the many stories he told at conference receptions. The final piece is that the father of American Pragmatism, John Dewey, and I share an alma mater, the University of Vermont,

---

[1] For an overview, see my "Platonic Pedagogy in Augustine's Dialogues" *Ancient Philosophy* 34:1 (2014) 151-168. For fuller treatment, see my *Augustine and the Dialogue* (2018).

even if at my time there people tended to name buildings after him rather than actually read his work. It was only once I started teaching that I began to connect these parts of my own education.

In my second year as Visiting faculty at Rollins, I was conscripted to develop courses for CLA's new Gen Ed curriculum. My supervisor strongly encouraged me to develop a community engagement course. My first response was, "What do you want me to do: save the whales? I work on ancient skepticism and the dialogue genre. What pressing social problem could possibly need my skill set?" This was in the wake of the 2012 election cycle, however, and civic discourse in the U.S. was already on the decline. Politicians and citizens alike seemed incapable of engaging in useful dialogue across the aisle. At the same time, I was realizing that my own students, particularly the first-years, were very good at answering questions but not at asking them. Eventually, I came to see schools, colleges and politics as parts of one big problem: as our world was becoming increasingly complex, our ways of thinking were becoming increasingly simplistic. What we needed was a way to help people ask better questions and engage meaningfully with those who see things differently. Here was something I could help with.

In the spring of 2015, I taught my first P4C course, *Socrates and the Art of Living*, which fulfilled a Humanities requirement in CLA's new curriculum. Our Center for Leadership and Community Engagement helped me prepare through a process of backwards course design. The basic idea, as developed by Wiggins and McTighe, *Understanding by Design* (Association for Supervision and Curriculum Development, 2005), is to begin course planning from what you want students to *do* and then work backwards to figure out what content is needed to accomplish that. In this case, learning outcomes (the doing part) were specified by the course's place in the new curriculum. At the 100-level, student work would be assessed for information literacy and written communication as defined by rubrics from the Association of American Colleges and Universities.[2] Given that this was a CE course, the second step was to identify a need outside the College that students could meaningfully address while doing some writing and thinking about information in the process. With this task laid out, I started putting my insights from Gary Matthews to use. While Gary mostly worked with children directly, his friend and colleague, Tom Wartenberg, had developed a course at Mount Holyoke which sent undergraduates to a local charter school to lead groups of 2nd-graders through philosophical discussions using picture books. That was a model that fit my needs. Our Office of Leadership and Community

---

[2] https://www.aacu.org/value-rubrics

Engagement connected me with a gifted class at a nearby elementary school.[3] I thus got to work building a syllabus around Tom's book, *Big Ideas for Little Kids* (Rowman and Littlefield, 2014) and a whole bunch of Plato.

In sum, the world needed more thinking in its K12 schools; my students could help by leading a picture book philosophy program at a local school, and they could work on writing and information literacy in the process. All I needed was to figure out content. For this, I looked to Plato's *Euthyphro* and *Apology* for an opening unit on the examined life. This was followed by units exploring the point of education (*Laches, Charmides* and *Protagoras*) and the pursuit of virtue (*Republic* 1, *Meno* and *Symposium*). For each unit, students would write essays and engage in a peer review process, challenging ideas in each others' drafts and then responding to each other by name in their revised versions. By treating the course as a scholarly microcosm, they would practice and reflect on the nature of information literacy. Having grappled with philosophically rich questions, they would then turn to picture books and develop lesson plans to use with children. With the transition into CE work, I planned for students to split their time between leading lessons at the elementary school and reading the rest of Plato's *Republic* with me. The course would culminate in a take-home essay exam where students used *Republic* as a framework to reflect on their work at the school, to set it within a bigger discussion of happiness, politics and education, and to apply all of this to their own education up to that point and moving forward. In short, they would do a lot of writing.[4]

Collaborating Across Disciplines: Campus Lab Schools

With these elegant plans laid out, it took half a term for things to go off track. Shortly after we started work with children, the school informed us that, due to scheduling conflicts, they would have to back out of 2 of the 6 weeks we planned to work together. This was a rather big problem. At the time, my colleague in Philosophy, Lisa Ryan Musgrave, had a son enrolled in Rollins Child Development and Student Resource Center (CDC). She suggested we try working with them. The

---

[3] For a school its size, Rollins has made substantial investments in CE work. At other schools, similar help could be found through Teaching Centers and/or offices of Instructional Design.

[4] I've found that the biggest challenge in designing CE courses is working out the timing. For a deeper dive into the logistics of P4C and backwards course design, see my "Bringing Undergraduates to Preschool: An Ethics Course for the Very Young," *Big Students, Little Kids, and Picture Books*, ed. Thomas Wartenberg (Rowman and Littlefield, 2019) 1-16. For more detailed discussion of CLA's curriculum review, see Claire Strom and Tricia Zelaya-Leon, (2017). "Creating a Curriculum for the 21st Century and Beyond: From the Academic Side." *Source for College Transitions* 14(2), 14. https://sc.edu/about/offices_ and_divisions/national_resource_center/publications/search/details.php?id=1452

CDC is a lab school, following the model Dewey set up at the University of Chicago. It serves as a functional preschool, a lab space for developmental psychology courses and an incubator for faculty from any discipline looking to work with young children. I conferred with Diane Terorde-Doyle, who was then head teacher at the CDC. She was up for trying things out, so on short notice, we took lesson plans designed for gifted elementary students and used them with 3- and 4-year-olds. The first lesson was pretty much a disaster. The lesson plans, which had been working great with elementary students, overtaxed pre-K attention spans. The questions undergraduates asked were generally too abstract. The sessions were a struggle to get through for children and undergraduate alike.

So we improvised. We reworded questions, streamlined our lesson plans and tried to meet the children in a more developmentally appropriate way.

By the end of that first term, we'd made enough progress at the lab school that we decided to continue the project the next term. I worked closely with Diane to design courses for what ended up being the next two terms, housed in the College's first-year seminar and Gen Ed programs, respectively. With these, we set out to experiment with adapting Wartenberg's methods for use with 4-year-olds. Through much trial and error, students in those classes made significant progress on two fronts. The first was to distill Wartenberg's nine 'philosophy rules' to 3 --we listen, we think, we respond-- and to help children practice them through games such as red light green light.[5] The other was to make the lesson plans more embodied. While lessons still revolved around picture books, we came to open each with a game, hold mini-discussions *while* reading the book and end with an art project to scaffold discussion of an open-ended question.[6] A lesson on bravery, for instance, might open with a game involving blindfolding in which we ask children whether they are afraid, in danger, brave. This would be followed by a dialogical reading of Arnold Lobel's story "Dragons and Giants" in which Frog and Toad attempt to climb a mountain but end up running away from several threats. Children would then be asked to draw a time they were brave, and we would spark discussions by talking with them about their pictures while they draw. In this, we explored Aristotle's definition of bravery as "a mean of fear and confidence aimed at the fine" in ways that 4-year-olds could meaningfully engage with.

By the Fall of 2016, we were ready to put what we'd learned at the CDC to the test. I developed another Gen Ed course, *Virtue In Civic Education*, in

---

[5] Erik Kenyon and Diane Terorde-Doyle, "The Three R's of Thinking: Nurturing Discussion in Preschools," *ASCD Express*, 12:10 (2017).

[6] For fuller discussion of the methods we developed, see Erik Kenyon and Diane Terorde-Doyle, "Art and Dialogue: An Experiment in Pre-K Philosophy," *Analytic Teaching and Philosophical Praxis*, 37:2 (2017) 26-35.

collaboration with the Winter Park Day Nursery. This Voluntary Pre-Kindergarten (VPK) provides free childcare to parents from a broad range of economic backgrounds, many of them minorities. Our main task this term was to find whether methods developed at a campus lab school would be of any use in a more typical pre-K environment. In terms of content, we focused on questions of ethics, first, because we had found that 4-year-olds relate more readily to such questions than they do other areas of philosophy. Second, as a 200-level Gen Ed, this particular course was assessed for critical thinking and ethical reasoning. I thus traded Plato for a more rounded survey of ethical theory, drawing from the works of Aristotle, Kant, Mill and Gilligan.[7]

Philosophy and Internships

As this process of experimentation and refining continued, we found ourselves generating a lot of lesson plans. Eventually, Diane, who was now Director of the CDC, and I joined forces with Sharon Carnahan, Executive Director of the CDC and Professor of Psychology, to turn all this work into a book. As part of that process, I took discreet lesson plans that students had developed and started integrating them into a curriculum paced for pre-K development. Diane compiled years of teachers' reflections on our P4C lessons and Sharon grounded what we were doing in current work in Developmental Psychology and Early Childhood Education. In order to get feedback, we hired nine of our best undergraduate P4C 'alumni' as interns to run lessons at the CDC as fast as we could write them. Among this group was Lexi Tomkunas, a double major in Philosophy and Psychology, who with Carnahan as her adviser developed an assessment scheme for our curriculum. In the process, she arranged lessons at another local VPK, recruited her student peers to work as interns for her project, recorded, coded and analyzed their lessons.

The product of all this, apart from Lexi's excellent thesis, was our book: Kenyon, Terorde-Doyle and Carnahan, *Ethics for the Very Young: A Philosophy Curriculum for Early Childhood Development* (Rowman and Littlefield, 2019). At this point, our work with pre-K philosophy was starting to get attention. We were chosen to host the 2019 meeting of the Philosophy Learning and Teaching Organization (PLATO), which showcased our lab school. In terms of undergraduate learning, hosting a 90-person conference gave ample opportunities for our undergraduates to pitch in and network with P4C practitioners from around the country. We also welcomed back two Rollins

---

[7] While we are still in the process of developing an assessment for our program, anecdotally, the main difference we noticed between the lab school and the VPK was simply the former had more distraction-free environments. Groups at the VPK, when brought outside and separated from each other, engaged quite well with our lessons.

alumni, Alex Earl (Religion '14) and Mollie Jones (English and Philosophy '15), both of whom had written senior theses with me, to present the P4C work they had developed in their own careers as teachers.

Once our P4C program had been going for a while, undergraduates were starting to use it as a talking point as they applied for jobs and graduate programs. If a goal of an interview is to stand out from the crowd, then teaching Kantian ethics to 4-year-olds appears to be a memorable way to show out-of-the-box thinking. It also embodies the applied liberal arts ethos places like Rollins pride themselves on, as students use academic disciplines to address real-world problems. Seeing the opportunity, I tweaked my first-year seminar so that students would meet with the Office of Career and Life Planning, find an internship they would actually be interested in having and then write an application in which they reflect on their P4C. Whether they actually applied, I left up to them. The first time I tried this assignment, 3 students landed internships before the assignment was even due.

Internships are a relatively new must-do for undergraduates. It's easy for those of us who made it through school without thinking about such things to dismiss them as a form of unpaid labor. Whatever the truth about that, a study conducted by Purdue University and the Gallop Corporation has shown the lasting benefits internships can have. "Great Jobs Great Lives" (2014) surveyed over 30,000 college graduates to determine what factors in one's college career would best predict later workplace engagement and an overall sense of (self-reported) well-being in one's life. Of the six that rose to the top, three are embodied in the later iterations of our P4C project:

- An internship that allowed students to apply what they learn in the classroom.
- A project that took a semester or more to complete.
- A mentor who encouraged students to pursue goals and dreams.[8]

While philosophy might not be the most obvious discipline to host internships (recall my initial reaction to the prospect of teaching a CE course), our P4C program has created a number of opportunities for meaningful work and competitive cover letters.

---

[8] https://www.luminafoundation.org/wp-content/uploads/2017/08/galluppurdueindex-report-2014.pdf. Of the remaining three factors "a professor who cared about students as people" and "a professor who made students care about learning" could certainly apply to a P4K project, though that likely has more to do with the individual instructor rather than the structure of the course.

P4C & Purpose Exploration: Intro to the Pragmatic Liberal Arts

Up to this point, I've discussed only Rollins' residential program for traditional students. In the Fall of 2015, Ryan Musgrave, who first introduced me to the CDC, asked me to co-teach a course in the Hamilton Holt School for adult learners. The particular course, Intro to the Liberal Arts, was a required Western Civ survey added to the curriculum in the 1980s. It was typically co-taught, in an effort to foster interdisciplinary thinking. Since Musgrave and I were both philosophers, we went 'meta-disciplinary' and developed a course exploring the nature and value of liberal education. Students worked through ancient and medieval materials with me, while Ryan led them through Pragmatism and the development of liberal education in the U.S. Along the way, we invited the College historian, Jack Lane, to speak about the development of Rollins' curricula, tracing how changes in American society had shaped higher education and vice versa. Central to this was the Holt School's namesake, Hamilton Holt, who was College President from 1925 to 1949. A journalist, activist and educational reformer, Holt organized a conference of leading educators in 1931, headed by John Dewey, to explore ways of adapting Pragmatic approaches to education to the undergraduate level. The result was a spirit of experimentation and applied, student-centered learning that shapes the College to this day.

In the Spring of 2018, our colleague in Humanities, Patricia Simmons, took over from Ryan. Together, we recast the course yet again, bringing back elements of the Western Civ survey (literature, art, music and politics) but framed all of this around the College's Mission to educate students for global citizenship, responsible leadership, productive careers and meaningful lives. In effect, we used Western Civ to help students get a handle on what it was they were supposed to be getting out of college. Along the way, I bent the co-teaching rule and carved out individual sections that I taught as P4C courses in collaboration with an after-school program down the street. To be honest, I did this mostly because people said it was a bad idea. Some faculty thought that CE courses were only for traditional students: "Adult students are already part of the community," this line of thinking went, "they don't need to engage with it." Given the high quality of work my students produced and the course evaluations at the end of each term, which were practically gushing, we quickly shot down these assumptions about adult students' needs.

All of this work reshaping the Intro course proved critically valuable as the Holt School set about its own curriculum revision. The most concrete task was to pull Holt's curriculum into line with CLA's new curriculum, by systematically introducing learning outcomes, yet accommodating the large number of transfer credits most Holt students bring to the program. This meant tweaking rather than replacing the existing distribution model in which students checked off categories, identified by letters, for Social Science, Humanities, Math, etc. (hence its common name, "Alphabet Soup"). The less concrete but more interesting challenge was to confront the transactional mentality that often goes along with box-checking curricula. To this end, we tweaked distribution requirements. We recast courses around desired learning outcomes in information literacy and critical thinking. And we looked to the Intro to the Liberal course as the lynchpin for all of this.

Renewing the College's historic connection to American Pragmatism, we renamed the course, *Intro to the Pragmatic Liberal Arts*. We dropped the co-teaching requirement. And we used my P4C course as a model to develop multiple sections, led by faculty from diverse disciplines and designed to help students engage with the College mission through a community engagement project. At this point, I was both teaching and working for the Holt Dean, mostly organizing professional development for adjunct faculty. Under that umbrella, I joined Meredith Hein, Director of the Center for Leadership and Community Engagement, to recruit and lead faculty through a series of course design workshops. The result was a suite of courses working in partnerships with local schools, retirement homes, wellness centers, land trusts and refugee aid organizations. Each section, meanwhile, met with the Center for Career and Life Planning to help students connect their CE work to their career aspirations. This new Intro to the Pragmatic Liberal Arts program went live with the new Holt curriculum, Fall of 2019.

Students taking a transactional attitude toward the curriculum, particularly the Gen Ed curriculum, is hardly unique to Rollins. Arum and Roksa's study, *Academically Adrift: Limited Learning on College Campuses* (University of Chicago Press, 2011) have identified problems of student motivation hindering learning. According to their analysis, U.S. undergraduates fall into four roughly equal groups of the unengaged, dabblers, unrealistic dreamers and the motivated but directionless. Former Yale Professor, William Deresiewicz, has explored this last group in *Excellent Sheep: The Miseducation of the American Elite and the Way to a Meaningful Life* (Free Press, 2014). Tim Clydesdale, *The Purposeful Graduate: Why Colleges Must Talk to Students about Vocation* (University of Chicago Press, 2015) presents an effort to counter this problem. Through a joint project of Lumina and the Lilly Foundation, 85 schools were each given $2M to develop programs in "Purpose Exploration." The framework is borrowed from developmental and positive psychology. As William Damon puts it, purpose is "a stable and generalized intention to accomplish something that is at the same time meaningful to the self and consequential for the world beyond the self" (*The Path to Purpose: How Young People Find Their Calling in Life*, Free Press, 2009). All 85 schools in the Lumina / Lilly study were Christian and thus dipped into their own particular traditions for language of "vocation," "calling," etc. The Network for Vocation in Undergraduate Education (NetVUE) is a direct result of the Lumina / Lilly study. It is expanding rapidly and providing rich resources to address the gap in student motivation. The trouble is that it's all still tied up in Christianity.

In reaffirming Rollins' historic connection to Pragmatism, we sought a religion-neutral framework for a NetVUE style program. As we scaled up our Intro to the Pragmatic Liberal Arts from my P4C course to a suite of sections spread across disciplines, we looked to Positive Psychology for guidance. As part of our course design workshops, each faculty member read the chapter on "Purpose" from Duckworth's book, *Grit* (Scribner, 2016), along with an essay from our College president, Grant Cornwell, "On Purpose: Liberal Education and the Question of Value." As positive psychology puts it, if interest is what we like doing and strengths are what we're good at doing, then we should try to align those with a purpose, i.e., find a need out in the world that we could use our strengths and interests to address. What do global citizenship, responsible leadership, productive careers and meaningful lives all have in common? They all provide ways for the individual to relate to the needs of the broader world. In effect, Rollins' Mission provides four lenses through which to explore purpose. While the sections of our Intro drew content from different disciplines --urban planning, international relations, art history, leadership studies-- each section *used* that content to help students explore purpose through the four lenses of the college mission. While students in various sections may or may not be reading philosophical texts, they are all thinking about their studies in self-reflective ways which reflect the role of P4C in the program's development, and they are all engaging in philosophical questions of what makes a career "successful", what is a meaningful life, etc.

Pivoting: CE & Natural Disasters

While it took half a term for my original P4C class to be disrupted, we were through a full term and a half of Holt's new curriculum before COVID-19 hit. With multiple sections to choose from, we found that students had started sorting themselves out. I got all the Psychology majors. Since this group was unusually well attuned to issues of child development, I decided to try again with 3-year-olds. We reached out to Winter Park Day Nursery and set out to work with their after-school program. We basically adapted our methods for 4-year-olds to make them even more embodied and fast-paced, e.g., lessons on self-control which passed quickly between Simon Says, Red Light Green Light and Freeze Tag with a bit of commentary ("were you using self-control") sprinkled throughout. It was going really well. Once we made our way up to picture books, one group held the children's attention for 25 minutes. This is an eternity for a group of 3-year-olds. Then COVID got serious. Within a week, the

Nursery asked us not to come back and, with Spring Break looming, the College also then asked us not to come back but to finish the term virtually. This was a rather big problem for a class that was built around hands-on work in the community.

So we improvised again. At this point, in Spring 2020, I had joined the PLATO education committee, which was developing teacher training resources for an OER site housed by the Library of Congress. My particular role was to augment our pre-K lesson plans by showing videos of pre-K philosophy in action, modelling techniques for leading discussion, pointing out philosophically rich comments made by actual children, etc. To this end, Diane had been using our curriculum to lead lessons at the CDC, which I had been recording. We had hours and hours of footage that neither of us had found time to edit. Meanwhile, I had a class of Psychology majors in need of meaningful work. So, midway through term, we fundamentally changed the nature of our CE project. I brought in Sharon and Diane to help us collectively figure out a coding scheme. Small groups of students chose different lessons to watch and code for useful material. They then divvied up tasks as some of them taught themselves video-editing and others wrote short discussions of what was happening in these edited videos.

I'll be honest: editing videos of lessons with children is nowhere near so engaging as leading lessons in person. That said, my students poured themselves into the work, learned new skills, and produced new and useful resources. While I've never seen the word "bittersweet" turn up so much in course evaluations, my students appreciated that, despite everything else going on, they were still contributing to something useful, in this case, on a national scale. When we launched the new Holt curriculum, Anne Stone, Professor of Communication, undertook a Scholarship of Teaching and Learning (SoTL) project, studying the effectiveness of our various CE projects. Her initial results showed that the more direct hands-on work in the community, the more transformative our adult students found the course. Which is to say, students got more out of getting down on the floor to work with 4-year-olds than they did from indirect community service, e.g., research projects conducted for the benefit of local non-profits.

Conclusion: P4C and Pragmatism Today

One technique for beginning the process of backwards course design is to ask faculty: what do you want students to retain from your class 20 years later? This forces instructors to look beyond the details of content and articulate the fundamental value of their subject: what Education departments refer to as "learning outcomes". In my case, it's usually something like a sense of epistemic humility and agency in the face of difficult problems, the skills to engage in useful dialogue and, ideally, taking pleasure in the process. This is particularly the case, when we're talking about general education. If a student is going to take one philosophy course in college, this is what I want to stick to. Yet, there was one learning outcome to our P4C program I didn't see coming. Over 5 years of teaching such courses I never once uttered the word "empathy" in class. But it comes up in course evaluations all the time, as undergraduates reflect on how they have developed a better sense of empathy through their work with children and on the need for P4C, or something like it, to nurture a sense of empathy in children.

With this, we're back to where we started: my dismay at the decline in civic discourse and looking to P4C as a way of doing something about it. In one sense, my P4C courses have proceeded as very traditional philosophy classes. Students read, discuss and write about a hefty selection of philosophical texts. But their work with children raises these discussions to a new level. It also, as I learned when I actually read some Dewey, embodies the ethos of American Pragmatism. To my mind, at least, the Pragmatists returned philosophy to its Classical roots as a force for improving human life, crossing disciplinary boundaries, engaging the world and being responsive to its changing needs. This sums up our CE work pretty well. While all of this takes time away from traditional classroom approaches, I've found that undergraduates in my P4C courses ended up with a more sophisticated grasp of the material than when I've taught the same material in non-CE courses.

Another thing I didn't see coming was the role of my own personal purpose in all this. According to Damon, a key factor in students developing a sense of purpose is to be around purposeful people: by interacting with people who have built their lives around meaningful work, students are encouraged to do the same. As I've tried to make clear above, I didn't start P4C work with any grand plan in mind. I tried something out, much of it really didn't work, so I tried again the next term. With each new class, I explained where they fit into this larger process and how they would move the work forward.[9] Along the way, I put to use aspects of my own education that I had previously not given much thought to. I collaborated with faculty colleagues in Psychology, English and Education to develop new courses and worked closely with staff colleagues in Community Engagement and Career and Life Planning to find organic connections between

---

[9] This lines up with best practices as set out in Yamamura et al., *Place-Based Community Engagement in Higher Education: A Strategy to Transform Universities and Communities* (Stylus, 2018), who advocate cultivating community partners over several terms.

the curriculum and co-curriculum.[10] In sum, as I helped my undergraduates align their own skills, interests with needs in the world, I was able to model how someone who had spent seven years in grad school geeking out over the intricacies of ancient philosophical dialogues was able to find pressing needs for such a skill set and engage in meaningful work within the Academy and beyond.

Bibliography

Arum, Richard., and Josipa Roksa. *Academically Adrift Limited Learning on College Campuses.* University of Chicago Press, 2011.

Clydesdale, Timothy T. *The Purposeful Graduate: Why Colleges Must Talk to Students about Vocation.* University of Chicago Press, 2016.

Damon, William. *The Path to Purpose How Young People Find Their Calling in Life.* Free Press, 2009.

Deresiewicz, William. *Excellent Sheep: The Miseducation of the American Elite and the Way to a Meaningful Life.* Free Press, 2015.

Duckworth, Angela. *Grit.* Vermilion, 2019.

Fournier@aacu.org. "VALUE Rubrics." Association of American Colleges and Universities. April 29, 2021. https://www.aacu.org/value-rubrics.

Gallup, Inc. "Great Jobs, Great Lives." 2014. https://www.luminafoundation. org/wp-content/uploads/2017/08/galluppurdueindex-report-2014.pdf.

Kenyon, Erik. *Augustine and the Dialogue.* Cambridge University Press, 2018.

Kenyon, Erik. "Platonic Pedagogy in Augustine's Dialogues." *Ancient Philosophy* 34, no. 1 (2014): 151-68. doi:10.5840/ancientphil20143419.

Kenyon, Erik., and Diane Terorde-Doyle. "The Three R's of Thinking: Nurturing Discussion in Preschools." *ASCD Express,* 12:10 (2017).

Kenyon, Erik., and Diane Terorde-Doyle. "Art and Dialogue: An Experiment in Pre-K Philosophy." *Analytic Teaching and Philosophical Praxis,* 37:2 (2017) 26-35.

"Tools and Resources." University of South Carolina. https://sc.edu/about/offices _and_divisions/national_resource_center/publications/search/details.php?id= 1452.

Wartenberg, Thomas E. *Big Ideas for Little Kids: Teaching Philosophy through Children's Literature.* Rowman and Littlefield Education, 2014.

Wartenberg, Thomas E. *Philosophy in Classrooms and Beyond: New Approaches to Picture-Book Philosophy.* Rowman and Littlefield Publishers, 2019.

---

[10] In a follow-up study to "Great Jobs Great Lives", the Gallop foundation found (a) that students who had useful interaction with their college career centers were 33% more likely to secure a "good job" upon graduation than those who did not and (b) that first-generation students were dramatically less likely than their peers to make use of career centers. Together, these findings suggest the use --if not the necessity-- of faculty integrating career services within the academic curriculum. "The Value of Career Services, Inclusive Experiences and Mentorship for College Graduates" (2016) https://acue.org/wp-content/uploads/2018/11/ Gallup-Purdue-Index-Study-Year-3-2016.pdf.

Wiggins, Grant P., and Jay McTighe. *Understanding by Design Study Guide*. Association for Supervision and Curriculum Development, 2000.

Yamamura, Erica K., and Kent Koth. *Place-based Community Engagement in Higher Education: A Strategy to Transform Universities and Communities*. Stylus Publishing, LLC, 2018.

Chapter 4

Philosophy In & By the Community

Marisa Diaz-Waian

Merlin CCC

Abstract

Merlin was born of two things – love and sorrow; For me, the two are inextricably intertwined. On the one hand, Merlin is a natural (albeit non-traditional) extension of my academic training in philosophy; on the other, it's a very personal (albeit public) way to philosophically navigate my father's death. But more than anything, Merlin - at its core - represents a way of doing philosophy in the community together. It's a platform for rigorously exploring and playing with ideas and perspectives, of learning from and with one another, and of putting *philosophy to task*. Over the years, and with the help and support of community, the organization has taken shape in interesting, delightful, and unexpected ways. In this chapter, I'll highlight this evolution by laying out my approach to philosophy, the kind of public philosophy that I do, and some of its chief attributes. Then I'll focus on two of our programs and their methodologies, and some of the benefits and challenges of philosophizing in the way that we do. Finally, and woven more generally throughout, I will discuss the significance and beauty of community and place.

Keywords: beauty, community, community philosophy, critical and creative thinking, dialogue, nature, non-profit, pedagogy, people, philosophical sensitivity, place, practice, process, public philosophy, street philosophy, way of life

***

My father died in 2010. It was a Sunday. I remember this distinctly because the neighborhood farmer's market was the day prior. There, I would gather our favorite treats so that, come Sunday, we could enjoy a feast together. This became a ritual of ours. On that afternoon, I had prepared a lunch for him, kissed him on his forehead, and promised I would come back in shortly to check on him. It was sunny, and warm, and he was content.

I, on the other hand, was a bit frantic. I was working on a final paper for a philosophy class on personal identity and had not yet found my stride. That day my stride found me. Three hours later, in the midst of describing how my father's identity seemed to stretch beyond his physical self, something shook me. "Crap!," I gasped, "I lost track of time!" I pushed my chair out and rushed into the house (from the garage studio) to find my father resting exactly where I had left him – with his treats fully eaten, a ray of sunshine beaming across his chest, and peaceful. I exhaled a sigh of relief and walked toward him. Within a second, however, I realized, that he was not asleep; it was something else. I called his name, "Poppa? Poppa?!" Nothing. I ran toward him. "Poppa?!" I screamed. I struggled to get him out his lounge chair. As I pulled him toward me, I heard an exhale – long and final. It was his last breath, still warm on my cheek. Try though I did, my CPR attempts were futile and I was left howling in despair, with his lifeless body in my arms.

The details of that day, the next few hours, and all of my experiences with him, really—*from the day he adopted me at age 12, through our wanderings into the great wide open and conversations over the years, to my evolving role from daughter-student-friend to daughter-caregiver-student-friend*—have continued to shape me and the trajectory of my life. Eventually, they led me to where I am now—here in Montana, living on a nature preserve and directing Merlin CCC, a public philosophy non-profit that I founded in 2014 (*Merlin*, for short).[1]

Ultimately, Merlin was born of love and sorrow. Love as a motivator is easy enough to grasp. But sorrow is more opaque. For me, the two are inextricably intertwined. On the one hand, Merlin is a natural (albeit non-traditional) extension of my academic training in philosophy, which sees the discipline in its most robust form as a "hands in dirt" activity rooted in the joys, sorrows, and challenges of everyday life. On the other hand, it is a very personal (albeit public) way for me to philosophically navigate my father's death—of grieving his loss, of honoring his life, and (as I have come to discover) of remaining open to the lessons he continues to teach.

This latter sentiment is in keeping with my position in that philosophy paper I wrote, on that last Sunday in 2010. *What is death if we have lived well? What is death if we still inspire? What is death if we are still part of the dialogue?* It also speaks to the practice of philosophy which—as Grace Lockrobin notes—is "not restricted to the canon of great philosophical ideas suspended in text" but

---

[1] Merlin is a Helena-based 501(c)(3) public philosophy non-profit dedicated to enriching lives and strengthening the community and environment through philosophy. Merlin CCC, "Our Mission," accessed February 1, 2021, https://merlinccc.org/about-us/our-mission/. All activities or resources from our website that are referenced in this chapter are included in footnotes where applicable, and (for sake of reader ease) included in bulk by activity grouping in the Supplementary Material section of this chapter.

rather "an ongoing and open-ended exchange."[2] That is to say, philosophy is not meant to be closed away in some book on a shelf, but to be *lived*.

At its core, Merlin is our way of doing this—of *living* philosophy, of rigorously exploring and playing with ideas, of gaining new and enriched perspectives, of learning from and with one another, and of *putting philosophy to task*. Merlin is, in the purest and simplest of terms, *street philosophy*.[3] It is a way of doing philosophy in the community together, as members of the symposium.

Marisa Diaz-Waian

Over the years, with the help and support of community (and continued inspiration from my father), Merlin has taken shape in interesting, delightful, and unexpected ways. In this chapter, I will illustrate this evolution by laying out my approach to philosophy, the *kind* of public philosophy that I do (via Merlin), and some of its attributes. I will also outline some of the specific characteristics (or "flavors") of our philosophy in the community activities. Then I will focus on two of our programs and methodologies in detail, as well as some of the benefits and challenges of philosophizing in the way that we do.

---

[2] Grace Lockrobin, "Relocation and Repopulation: Why Community Philosophy Matters," In *Philosophy and Community: Theories, Practices, and Possibilities*, ed. Amanda Fulford, Grace Lockrobin, and Richard Smith (London; New York: Bloomsbury Academic, 2020), 17.

[3] "The academic department was not always the home of philosophy," notes Lockrobin, "nor were philosophers themselves always academics. Plato famously described Socrates, in the Athenian marketplace [i.e., "the streets"], engaging the public in conversations that connected to their everyday concerns." Ibid., 18-19.

Finally, and woven more generally throughout, I will discuss the significance and beauty of community and place.

Hands in Dirt

As the director of a public philosophy non-profit, I have to be prepared to respond to questions about philosophy succinctly – What is it? What do you do? Why philosophy? And, *inevitably*, how do you make money (i.e., survive)? These are all, of course, legitimate and important inquires. But they are also very *different* questions, and not ones to which any "elevator pitch" could do reasonable justice. Answering these takes time, just as philosophy does.

That said, the ability to capture the "essence" of a thing pithily has value – not only for inquirers but also for its practitioners. What exactly *is* this enterprise in which we are engaged? In this section, I'll attempt to address *the what's* and *the why* of philosophy by discussing my conception of philosophy, the kind of work that I do in the community, and some of its features. Then, in a separate section, I will lay out some of the specific characteristics (or "flavors") of our programming. (I'll come back to the survival question later, i.e., when I talk about benefits and challenges.)

My Approach

I love the outdoors. I like wandering and thinking. I like exploring and observing, and more generally, just communing with and in nature. For this reason, perhaps, I am drawn to metaphors about philosophy that conjure up images of deep exploration, curiosity, play, attunement, and connectivity. Gardening metaphors are particularly well-suited for this and, as a fan of ancient philosophy and Socrates, Plato's *Phaedrus* and *Theaetetus* naturally come to mind. In *Phaedrus*, Socrates compares philosophy to the growing of plants from soil,[4] which extends into *Theaetetus* by way of a discussion about midwifery.[5] At first blush, these might seem like odd analogies. But by thinking about philosophy in these terms, several things become clear:

- First, the seeds of philosophy are in all of us (i.e., *we are all philosophical beings*).[6]

---

[4] *Phaedrus* 276b-277a in *Plato: Complete Works*, ed. J. M. Cooper and D.S. Hutchinson (Indianapolis: Hackett Publishing Company, 1997). *All further Plato citations in this chapter will come from this source, unless otherwise noted.*

[5] *Theaetetus* 149a-151d.

[6] Jana Mohr Lone makes reference to this idea in "The Philosopher as Teacher: Philosophical Sensitivity," *Metaphilosophy* 44, no. 1-2 (2013): 171-186. She says: "We

- Second, seeds grow and flourish in relation to their environment. Gardeners cultivate soil in order to help seeds sprout and thrive. Philosophy operates similarly (i.e., in order for the seeds of philosophy to take sprout and thrive, we must cultivate the ecosystem of ourselves in particular ways).[7]

- Third, cultivation in gardening involves removing obstacles (like weeds) and breaking up crusty soil to create an optimal environment for the retention and penetration of water, air, and nutrients. Philosophical cultivation is analogous. It, too, involves removing obstacles (like flawed reasoning or "harmful" habits of "body and mind) and breaking up crusty "soil" (like rigidity of thought or perspectival narrowness) to create an optimal environment for philosophical growth and transformation.

- Fourth, gardening is a practice that involves skill, knowledge, being in tune with one's surroundings, and responding accordingly. The seasoned gardener, for example, will know when to protect her crops based on perceived changes in her environment and how to do so based on skills that she has acquired over time. She will also have a healthy amount of humility; Mother Nature has a way of keeping us on our toes. The practice of philosophy also involves skill, knowledge, humility (especially of the epistemic sort), and attunement to certain things (e.g., good and bad reasoning, similarities, distinctions, context), which together help to inform how she might respond to the world.

- Fifth, gardening is hard work and a labor of love. You cannot expect the garden to plant, prune, stake, weed, stave off predators, water, nourish, and pick its fruits for you.[8] To be successful at gardening requires committed and active engagement. Philosophy is kindred. The seeds are there. But you have to put in the work (physically, intellectually, and emotionally) if you want them to take root and blossom.

- Finally, being in a garden, playing around with soil, watching plants bloom, and butterflies and bees bop about from flower to flower is *fun*.

---

traditionally recognize as important the development of children's physical selves, intellectual selves, moral selves, and social and emotional selves, but we pay little attention to the cultivate of the *philosophical* self. Consequently, the philosophical selves of most children remain undeveloped," 173. For more detail, see my "Big Ideas by Little Philosophers (BiLP)" discussion later in this chapter.

[7] Implicit here is also the claim that growth and flourishing are desired ends or aims of both activities. While I have yet to meet a gardener who deviates from this position, it's not as clear-cut in philosophy.

[8] Of course, nature is pretty handy and has some built-in mechanisms for these processes. Gardens don't "need" us per se and often do much better on their own without our meddling.

So, too, is enjoying and sharing the smells and fresh tastes of a garden's bounty; these experiences spark our sense of wonder, imagination, and curiosity, and help us acknowledge and embrace our deep interconnectivity. Philosophy does this as well. Playing with ideas, stretching our imaginations, following reason where reason guides, and seeing how we – as living beings – are connected in unique, beautiful, and unexpected ways is *exhilaratingly fun* and a source of great *delight*. One only need watch a child engage in either activity to appreciate this.

More could be added to this list. But this is a good start and, hopefully—at least from my perspective—helps to highlight the nature of philosophy and its assorted aims,[9] some of the virtues that philosophizing cultivates (and necessitates),[10] and the ways in which I think about and practice philosophy in the community. These track well, too, with some more traditional definitions of philosophy that I hold dear: Philosophy is the art of critical (and creative) thinking; the love of wisdom;[11] a preparation for death;[12] the craft of crafts, and the science of sciences,[13] and; the greatest kind of music.[14] It is also, as many thinkers in the ancient philosophical traditions claim, and as Pierre Hadot and John M. Cooper articulate[15]—not just a thing to be studied, but something that we *do* as a *practice* and *a way of life.*[16] This last conception of philosophy, perhaps, most closely describes my approach and gives wings (and footing) to

---

[9] E.g., truth, goodness, freedom, wellness, flourishing.

[10] Lockrobin, "Relocation and Repopulation: Why Community Philosophy Matters," 19.

[11] Attributed to Pythagoras in Diogenes Laertius, Book 1, proem. 12 in *Diogenes Laertius: Lives of Eminent Philosophers*, ed. R.D. Hicks (Creative Commons), accessed February 1, 2021, http://www.perseus.tufts.edu/hopper/text?doc=Perseus%3Atext%3A1999.01.0258.

[12] Plato, *Phaedo* 64a.

[13] Aristotle, *Metaphysics*, Book 1.2 (982a) (Creative Commons), accessed February 1, 2021, http://www.perseus.tufts.edu/hopper/text?doc=Perseus%3Atext%3A1999.01.0052%3Abook%3D1%3Asection%3D982a.

[14] Ibid., *Phaedo* 61a. Thank you to friend and colleague, David Nowakowski, for bringing this beautiful definition of philosophy into my wheelhouse.

[15] Pierre Hadot, "Philosophy as a Way of Life," in *Philosophy as a Way of Life: Spiritual Exercises from Socrates to Foucault.* Edited by Arnold I. Davidson. Translated by Michael Chase (Maldan, MA; Oxford, UK: Blackwell Publishing Ltd., 1995), 264-276; John M. Cooper, "Ancient Philosophies as Ways of Life" (The Tanner Lectures on Human Values presented at Stanford University, Stanford, CA, January 25-26, 2012), https://tannerlectures.utah.edu/Cooper%20Lecture.pdf.

[16] For greater details about philosophy as a way of life and teaching resources, see Notre Dame's philosophy as a way of life website (https://philife.nd.edu/). See also: https://merlin ccc.org/resource-center/pwol-philife-public-philosophy-resources/.

my unabashedly passionate proclamation that philosophy, like gardening, is a "hands-in-dirt" activity that bears the most beautiful of fruits.

The *Kind* of Philosophy I Do

Philosophy can be done in many ways. I practice 'philosophy in the community,' which is an umbrella term for a wide range of related practices,[17] and a unique form of public philosophy. Broadly construed, *public philosophy* can be thought of as "Philosophical work done by professional philosophers outside the '"walls"' or domain of the academy, *or* philosophical work done by professional or non-professional philosophers for/with an audience of non-professional philosophers."[18] Typically, and for numerous reasons, public philosophy is discussed in contrast to academic philosophy. But this is deceiving as the two are not mutually exclusive and can have significant overlap.[19] Moreover, as philosophy *qua* philosophy, both academic and public philosophy share, at least in the most *fundamental* of senses, similar aims (e.g., improved understanding about x or y) and similar methodologies (i.e., the use of philosophical reasoning). Although it's beyond the scope of this chapter, there is an interesting history behind the public-academic distinction (and what counts as "real" philosophy) that parallels the evolution of philosophy from its earlier forms of practice (and foci), to the academy (and its subsequent specializations), to the present-day revival of philosophy as a way of life (and, more generally, of public-facing philosophical work).[20]

---

[17] "Philosophy in communities groups have different views and expressions concerning the place of practical and political action, about their relationship to academic philosophy traditions, about their purposes, about how they should be characterized as well as about the meaning and value of philosophy itself." Steve Bramall, "Understanding Philosophy in Communities: The Spaces, People, Politics and Philosophy of Community Philosophy," in *Philosophy and Community: Theories, Practices, and Possibilities*, ed. Amanda Fulford, Grace Lockrobin, and Richard Smith (London; New York: Bloomsbury Academic, 2020), 5.

[18] This definition of public philosophy is provided by Brian J. Collins in his article, "The Broad Nature and Importance of Public Philosophy," *pre-college Philosophy and Public Practice* 2 (2020), 72.

[19] Collins argues makes a compelling argument for teaching "being a form of public philosophy" because "it introduces philosophy to an audience of non-professional philosophers (i.e., students). In most cases this type of instructional work is done within the confines of the academy and the goal is to get the students to think more like philosophers, but...this does not diminish the public nature of such an act." Ibid., 72-87.

[20] Hadot, "Philosophy as a Way of Life," 264-276.

In truth, I have always found it challenging to think about philosophy *without* thinking about its public face. Of course, I *can* envision it, but I *really* have to stretch the boundaries of my imagination and conception of the discipline in order to do so. And even then, if successful, I do it "in brackets," never fully separating the public domain and its affairs from the larger enterprise of philosophy. Some of this can simply be chalked up to personal temperament and proclivities; as much as I am a "solo bird" who "digs her some elbow room and alarmingly lengthy periods of isolation,"[21] I love community and tend to lean heavily toward it. Plus, thinking about ideas detached from the ways in which they inhabit the world and play out in its domains is tricky. The boundaries between theory and practice, between private and public, have always been blurry to me.

More of my challenge with thinking about philosophy *sans* its public side, however, is attributable to the kind of philosophical training I received as a youth (informally) and a student (formally). I feel fortunate to have been introduced to philosophy as something that is meant to be *lived*, not in ways that remove or divorce one from the world and its problems, but as active agents within it. Here, philosophy is just as much an activity that involves careful and rigorous thinking as it is a mechanism for thriving and becoming the best possible versions of ourselves,[22] individually and communally. To me, such an approach grounds philosophy in everyday life and *puts philosophy to task*—theoretically and practically.[23] Moreover, it reveals something fundamental about the practice. As Darien Pollock notes "All rich philosophical inquiries, even our traditional ones, are products of…"the street disposition." This disposition is anchored in a general inclination to make sense of existential puzzles that haunt the human experience."[24] That is, philosophy

---

[21] My friend, Kathleen O'Brien-Thompson, refers to these as my "going dark" phases – like a moon.

[22] *Euthyphro*, 16a ("…and that I would be better for the rest of my life.")

[23] Lockrobin refers to the union of theory in practice in terms of restoring Bertrand Russell's *ancient philosophical project*, which has as its aims "seeking knowledge of the natural world along with the wisdom required to use it in pursuit of the good life," as cited in "Relocation and Repopulation: Why Community Philosophy Matters," 26-27. This marriage also benefits the discipline itself and the people for whom it serves.

[24] Darien Pollock, "Philosophizing in the Streets," Blog of the APA (blog). *American Philosophical Association*, November 8, 2018, https://blog.apaonline.org/2018/11/08/philoso phizing-in-the-streets/. Pollock goes on to say that, unfortunately, "many professional philosophers neglect the universal disposition from which philosophical inquiries emerge. As a consequence, philosophy has evolved into a set of competing ideological frameworks and lost its grounding in the genuine compassion for bringing truth to bear on the countless

"presupposes a particular kind of civic engagement."[25] Its questions are the questions of *life*.

Needless to say, all of this has informed the kind of public philosophy that I do, the most fitting category of which seems to be *Community Philosophy*, as described in *Philosophy and Community: Theories, Practices and Possibilities*.[26] Steve Bramall and Grace Lockrobin offer thoughtful accounts. Community Philosophy, says Bramall, is a "mode of participatory public engagement"[27] with deep Socratic roots. It is "*a philosophy of street and marketplace rather than of the academy*,"[28] and is "powered by the energy of purposeful community engagement."[29] It also, points out Lockrobin, *relocates* philosophy—from the academy and more traditional places of learning into non-standard places—and "*repopulates* it with new voices, including some who have been historically marginalized."[30] Unlike some forms of public philosophy like *Popular Philosophy*,[31] where professional philosophers strive

---

frustrations, worries, and problems distinctive to the human condition. This detachment not only harms the discipline but it also damages the public insofar as it limits the philosophical standpoints that can contribute and be taken seriously."

[25] Ibid.

[26] Amanda Fulford, Grace Lockrobin, and Richard Smith, eds., *Philosophy and Community: Theories, Practices and Possibilities* (London; New York: Bloomsbury Academic, 2020).

[27] Bramall, "Understanding Philosophy in Communities: The Spaces, People, Politics and Philosophy of Community Philosophy," 6.

[28] Ibid. *My emphasis*. This does not mean, says Bramall, that Community Philosophy is anti-academy or "philosophy lite." Rather, "it is a particular, complex, embedded social philosophical practice."

[29] Ibid.

[30] Lockrobin, "Relocation and Repopulation: Why Community Philosophy Matters," 33. *My emphasis*. Prison initiatives are great examples of relocating and repopulating philosophy. Some programs that stand out here are University of Wyoming's *Wyoming Pathways from Prison program* (http://www.uwyo.edu/gwst/wpfp/) and The Center for Public Philosophy's *Prison Ethics Bowl* program (https://publicphilosophy.ucsc.edu/philosophy-inside/) in collaboration with Mount Tamalpais College's *Prison University Project* (https://www.mttam college.org/).

[31] *Popular Philosophy* is characterized by a desire to facilitate "broader access to philosophy for non-professional philosophers and the creation of forums for additional, valuable philosophical discourse." It frequently takes the form of "philosophical translation" – i.e., magazine articles, blogs, op-eds, podcasts, etc. written or conducted by professional philosophers for the general public.

to make philosophy more accessible, or *Field Philosophy*,[32] where professional philosophers cross-pollinate with other disciplines to distribute the benefits of philosophy more broadly, Community Philosophy has a "different objective achieved by different means."[33] Community Philosophy is not philosophy *for* the wider community but philosophy *by* the community.[34]

Of course, not all manifestations of Community Philosophy look the same. Each group, notes Bramall, must take a position somewhere along at least four dimensions—space, action, people, and philosophy itself.[35] Where they fall along these spectrums, as well as how much (if at all) they cross-over with other forms of public philosophy, will result in different expressions of Community Philosophy. Despite its possible variants, however, there are some general features which all groups share. Community Philosophy:

- Sees philosophy as a living praxis[36] and as something that can be done *by any, and all, people*[37]
- Tends to seek out spaces and opportunities for diverse groups of people to meet, think, and do philosophy together[38]
- Views community from the dual perspective of people and place[39]
- Is committed to fostering philosophical discussion about topics that matter to its participants
- Draws on the democratic engagement practices of transformational community work[40]

---

[32] According to Lockrobin's account: "Field Philosophers think within organizations on particular projects, assimilating the insights of those they find there. The products of their philosophical thinking are disseminated within those organizations—as well as to fellow academics—and are designed to be useful to those grappling with those problems, while enriching the academic philosopher with a more vivid sense of real-world philosophical problems." Lockrobin, "Relocation and Repopulation: Why Community Philosophy Matters," 25.

[33] Ibid.

[34] Bramall, "Understanding Philosophy in Communities: The Spaces, People, Politics and Philosophy of Community Philosophy," 27.

[35] Ibid., 11-12.

[36] Lockrobin, "Relocation and Repopulation: Why Community Philosophy Matters," 27.

[37] Bramall, "Understanding Philosophy in Communities: The Spaces, People, Politics and Philosophy of Community Philosophy," 7. *My emphasis.*

[38] Bramall, "Understanding Philosophy in Communities: The Spaces, People, Politics, and Philosophy of Community Philosophy," 10.

[39] Lockrobin, "Relocation and Repopulation: Why Community Philosophy Matters," 15.

[40] Bramall, "Understanding Philosophy in Communities: The Spaces, People, Politics, and Philosophy of Community Philosophy," 9.

- Sees the practice of philosophy as educative, transformative, and (often) as a form of self-care[41]
- Emphasizes and values engaged, open dialogue

This last point requires additional attention. Dialogue plays an important role in philosophy *in general*. As Amanda Fulford notes, in addition to writing, "the practice of philosophy has, from its ancient roots" been "marked by dialogue."[42] In addition, the actual *doing* of philosophy is dialogic, as is philosophy *itself*.[43] This latter point is particularly relevant to Community Philosophy.

> To posit the idea of philosophy-as-dialogue, as co-constructed through encounter and conversation with others, changes our view not only of who does—or can do—philosophy, but also the very nature of philosophy itself. In this sense, the emphasis on philosophy as a body of knowledge to be attained, or a set of texts to be read, shifts towards an idea of the love of wisdom that is developed through conversation (our turning together) with others.[44]

Moreover, "the craft of dialoguing with anyone and everyone is the very stuff of philosophy," claims Adam Briggle.[45] To follow reason where reason guides, to follow the path toward wisdom together,[46] is part of the gig. The idea of *togetherness* is significant here. Similar to Socrates' "midwife," professional philosophers in Community Philosophy are like facilitators "in the service of the philosophical development of *others*."[47] As such, they "meet people where they

---

[41] Amanda Fulford, "Philosophy, Dialogue and the Creation of Community," in *Philosophy and Community: Theories, Practices, and Possibilities*, ed. Amanda Fulford, Grace Lockrobin, and Richard Smith (London; New York: Bloomsbury Academic, 2020), 94-97.

[42] Amanda Fulford, "Philosophy, Dialogue and the Creation of Community," 92.

[43] Ibid.

[44] Ibid., 93.

[45] Adam Briggle, "Dialogue and Next Generation Philosophy," *pre-college Philosophy and Public Practice* 1 (2019): 78.

[46] Ibid., 77.

[47] Lockrobin, "Relocation and Repopulation: Why Community Philosophy Matters," 25. *My emphasis*. Not all Community Philosophy groups have trained philosophers, nor need they in order to exist (as groups) and philosophize (as people). That said, "Community Philosophy can benefit from the support and guidance of professional philosophers, particularly when they are able to facilitate the development of necessary skills and strategies required to investigate the questions that people find curious," 20.

are" and think together *with* them, dialoguing, and providing philosophical guidance (when needed) along the way.

Of course, not *all* dialogue is philosophical. Asking you about what you had for breakfast, for example, is less likely to result in deep philosophical exchange in a way that questions about beauty or love might (though, to be sure, philosophical conversations about breakfast *can* be had).[48] In fact, while not breakfast *per se*, there is a hilarious video by David Corbel that ponders the meta-question *What Makes Soup Soup?*[49] But I digress. My point here is less about subject matter and more about the nature of dialogic exchange. In *Plato's Literary Garden*, Kenneth Sayre refers to philosophical dialogue as a kind of "horticultural tool" that has as one of its aims pollinating the mind of its interlocutors "with the vital discourse conducive to learning" so that these seeds might germinate and become "'tender growths.'"[50] Here philosophical dialogue is central to the cultivation and development of ideas, ourselves, and others.

This sentiment is in keeping with Myisha Cherry's claim that not all dialogue is created equal:[51] "What is often disguised as dialogue may actually be a monologue that excludes and dehumanizes others, blocks knowledge production, promotes self-interests, and normalizes inaction. Intellectual work should resist these activities."[52] I agree. In my opinion, any philosophical dialogue that does this is—in a very important sense—*not* really philosophical (even if its subject matter happens to be, even if professional philosophers are involved). Honest philosophical exchange requires humility, openness, courage, and a certain kind of "relinquishment"[53] wherein the parties involved have an opportunity to experience mutual transformation[54] and the "deconstructive and transformative power of the question itself."[55]

---

[48] For example, if you told me that you had pickles and horseradish for breakfast, I would likely follow this with a *"Why?"* From there, things could get philosophical very quickly, e.g., maybe you desired such a combo because it represented the perfect harmony of flavors—which could then lead to an exploration of why harmony is desirable and what makes something harmonious.

[49] BBC Scotland, "What Makes Soup *Soup*?" a comedy short by David Corbel on YouTube video, 1:54, February 1, 2019, https://youtu.be/Y1HVTNxwt7w.

[50] Kenneth Sayre, *Plato's Literary Garden: How to Read a Platonic Dialogue* (Notre Dame: University of Notre Dame Press, 1995), xv.

[51] Myisha Cherry, "Liberatory Dialogue," *Precollege Philosophy and Public Practice* 1 (2019): 5.

[52] Ibid., 13.

[53] Briggle, "Dialogue and Next Generation Philosophy," 77.

[54] Amanda Fulford, "Philosophy, Dialogue and the Creation of Community," 96.

[55] Ibid., 98.

Flavor: Dimensions, Fit & Spice

Even though Community Philosophy groups share these basic features, every group has its own flavor. To better appreciate this, let's return first to Bramall's four dimensions of Community Philosophy—space, action, people, and philosophy itself. According to Bramall, every group must take a stance on these and will fall somewhere along the spectrum, ranging from more to less formal places of learning (*space*), more to less politically and practically engaged (*action*), more to less traditional participants (*people*), and more to less conventional practices, conceptual approaches, and methodologies (*conceptions of philosophy*).[56]

With respect to the first dimension, our programs tend to take place in less formal learning spaces, with hiking trails, pubs, parks, theaters, outdoor meeting spots, convention centers, and other such venues being home to our philosophical gatherings. However, this depends on the program. Some of our activities—like our philosophy symposiums and forums—take place in more traditional places of learning, e.g., colleges, universities, libraries. We also offer several online programs. Here "space" becomes more nebulous. Generally speaking, however, philosophy in "atypical places" is kind of our *jam* (and our preference).

As it concerns the second dimension of *action*, Bramall appears to treat political and practical engagement as equivalents. But, I'm hesitant to characterize them this way. While certainly related, I think they are different kinds of engagement, and not mutually exclusive. From this vantage point, I would say that we are less politically engaged (in the sense of activism) and more practically engaged (in the sense of applied philosophy), though overlap can (and has) occurred. If I were to treat them as identical—with the spirit in which I think Bramall maintains—then I would characterize Merlin as less radical in its activism (e.g., less likely to spearhead a campaign), though still involved in social and political change (via the cultivation of skills and virtues important to civic engagement).[57] Broadly

---

[56] Bramall, "Understanding Philosophy in Communities: The Spaces, People, Politics and Philosophy of Community Philosophy," 11-12. With respect to the fourth dimension, Bramall does not explicitly connect the dots between practice, methodology, and conception of philosophy. However, I think it is reasonable (based on his overall discussion) that these are implied. I go into greater detail on this later in the body of this chapter.

[57] A good example of this would be our community conversations series on homelessness. See: https://merlinccc.org/merlin-think-and-drink-archive/august-2018-philosophy-think-drink-moral-dimensions-homelessness/, https://merlinccc.org/merlin-think-and-drink-archive/september-2018-philosophy-think-drink-moral-dimensions-homelessness-part-two/, and https://merlinccc.org/merlin-think-and-drink-archive/october-2018-philosophy-think-drink-moral-dimensions-homelessness-part-three/.

speaking, all of our activities are structured to encourage active engagement and the application of philosophical thinking to matters of everyday living. This has taken shape in numerous ways, some of which are more political than others.

In regard to the third dimension, i.e., *people*, our span is wide-ranging and inclusive. All kinds of people participate in our activities—from young to old, with diverse life experiences and backgrounds, and with varying levels of familiarity with philosophy or philosophizing together (at least in an organized, community sense). Generally speaking, while *some* of our participants have had formal training in philosophy, *the majority have not.* People that take part in our activities identify as students, artists, teachers, ranchers, musicians, farmers, retirees, hunters, hikers, fisherfolk, bikers, waiters, authors, lawyers, homemakers, and more. Our programs are also inter-generational. Though some programs lend themselves more naturally to this (due to topic or venue, for example), an underlying design principle for all of our activities is that they are structured in ways that encourage people of all ages to come and think together, and learn from one another. Even in cases where programs are designed for youth, adults and elders are invited and encouraged to participate. Because of my life experiences, especially those I had with my father, I am a big believer in the value of intergenerational relationships and dialogue. The diverse contributions and enriched understandings that come from these sorts of pairings is beautiful.

Finally, with respect to the fourth dimension, while my discussion earlier about 'philosophy as gardening' illustrates the *conception* of philosophy upon which Merlin rests, it does not speak to the conventionality of practices and methodologies that we employ. Although Bramall does not overtly mention this, I think it's relevant to bring up here. To me, one's conception of philosophy is intimately bound up with her practice and methodology. These, too, are connected—to greater and lesser degrees—with the practices and methodologies of academic philosophy. This connection seems implicit in Bramall's claim, especially given his explicit acknowledgments that "philosophy in communities relies on academic philosophy,"[58] and that Community Philosophy is "*nourished* by academic philosophy, but at the same time a critical friend"[59] of it. Jules Evans echoes this sentiment: "Without street philosophy, academic philosophy becomes irrelevant. Without academic philosophy, street philosophy becomes

---

[58] Bramall, "Understanding Philosophy in Communities: The Spaces, People, Politics and Philosophy of Community Philosophy," 12. Bramall also points out that the same can be said in reverse (a sentiment with which I whole-heartedly agree).
[59] Ibid., 6-7. *My emphasis.*

incoherent."[60] And Lockrobin adds that although asking questions is an important part of philosophizing, that's only one piece of the pie.[61] Philosophizing also entails "*answering* questions by *means of appropriate methods of investigation.*"[62] Here, methodology is part and parcel of philosophical thinking. Simply put—just like other disciplines, philosophy has its own way of doing things. And a considerable amount of this "way" has been influenced and shaped by the academy.

With this in mind, where does Merlin fall along the spectrum? On the one hand, we share with the academy the rigor, depth, and general investigatory methods of philosophy (e.g., analysis, synthesis, making distinctions and comparisons, identifying complexities, nuances, and subtleties, employing reasoning and logic). We also refer to and use many of the same classic texts that are used in classrooms, as well as current research, writing, and other scholarly contributions from academicians in the field. Our relationship with the academy and the *discipline* of philosophy is friendly and respectful.

On the other hand, in terms of some of the structure, practices, and foci of traditional classroom pedagogy, we have less in common with the academy. One obvious reason for this is because grades and departmental objectives are not things that we typically need to consider.[63] As such, our activities can be shaped differently. By design and necessity, our programs tend to be more flexible, playful, experimental, and modular (though we do have some programs that are segmental) than those that take place in traditional academic institutions. Moreover, as discussed earlier, our programs take place in unconventional settings. This opens up the door for very different kinds, modes, and ways of investigating and philosophizing together than a traditional classroom setting

---

[60] Jules Evans, "Connected Communities: Philosophical Communities," (A Report for the Arts and Humanities Research Council presented at University of London, London, UK, November 12, 2012), 35, http://static1.squarespace.com/static/5c8bd3835239589598cac07e/5caeecaf0c f24e366c39d10a/5caef0370cf24e366c3a72f4/1554968631713/Connected-Communities-Philosophical-Communities1.pdf?format=original.

[61] Lockrobin, "Relocation and Repopulation: Why Community Philosophy Matters," 20.

[62] Michael Hand as cited in Lockrobin, Ibid.

[63] Of course, I recognize that there are some departments who utilize non-traditional forms of grading or no grading at all. Further, while we don't have departmental objectives to consider, we do have organizational objectives to consider. It seems reasonable to suggest that at least some of these aims are similar to a philosophy department's aims. However, there are also some that would simply be inapplicable for our organization and the kind of work that we do in the community. One notable exception to this is any programming that we offer *in conjunction with* a particular university or institute of learning. In such cases, departmental objectives would need to be considered.

might afford. Another reason for the variance has to do with the fact that Community Philosophy *qua* Community Philosophy is largely driven by the interests of its participants. Although some classroom courses may be designed this way—I have been a student in at least one and taught a couple of institutional courses in this fashion myself—that is *not* the norm. Classroom curriculum typically has various things that need to be taught in a certain timeframe for various reasons.

Additionally—as a form of public philosophy in the broad sense—Community Philosophy typically asks questions of practical and applicable importance that go "*beyond* the "'conceptual walls'" of abstract academic investigation."[64] This is not to imply that practical-oriented questions do not take place in the academy (e.g., applied ethics courses do this all of the time),[65] nor is it to say that abstract theorizing is impractical, inapplicable, or unimportant. It is simply to suggest that the kinds of questions that are asked and focused on in Community Philosophy are often very different than those that are asked and focused on in the academy.

As a final point of mention, to the extent that a philosophy department and its instructors see philosophy as a "hands in dirt" activity and a living praxis that can be done by all people, then at least some of the variances listed above will become audibly muted.

Fit-Stretch-Spill

Another component of a group's unique flavor has to do with whether or not it fits squarely into only *one* category of public philosophy, or spills over into others. At Merlin, our feet are planted firmly in the Community Philosophy category. *However,* our work also stretches across and into some other domains, including *Field Philosophy*[66] and *Popular Philosophy*[67] (mentioned earlier), and *Activist Philosophy*, which Collins describes as public philosophy that has a focus on "creating and deploying philosophical methods that brings philosophy to bear on pressing societal and political concerns."[68] Some examples of programs or activities that we've done that exemplify this sort of crossover include: Collaborative research and community programs, with

---

[64] Collins, "The Broad Nature and Importance of Public Philosophy," 73.
[65] Some of this will also depend on the teacher. I have had many professors who, as a matter of practice, always cast abstract theory into practical terms by raising questions about its applicability and more.
[66] See footnote 32.
[67] See footnote 31.
[68] Collins, "The Broad Nature and Importance of Public Philosophy," 74.

professionals from different disciplines and backgrounds, on issues of land management and conservation (*Field* and *Activist*); Op-eds, publications, and presentations (*Popular* and *Field*), and; community discussions on the moral dimensions of homelessness (*Activist* and *Field*).[69]

"Guess the Spices!?"

Last but not least, when reflecting upon flavor, one must never overlook the importance of spice. I recall with great fondness my father's amusing affinity for cooking things, and then asking me, with utter sincerity (and always a hilariously animated grin), to "*Guess the Spices!?*" He would give me no clues other than what I could pick up with my senses; I was on my own. And, of course, inevitably, he would always sneak in one spice that was so random and unexpected that unless you were *really* paying attention, would go unnoticed. That was the one—if you guessed it—that he would go "bananas about." So, of course, that is always the one for which I aimed. I mention this in part because it makes my heart smile; I miss that man. He was such a wonderful human being. But I also mention it because he's *right*. Flavor and spice go hand in hand. A bland soup might be lovingly prepared and nourishing, while still…"*meh!*" But a flavorful one?!? *Fuggedaboutit!* (as Donnie Brasco would say).[70]

With this in mind, Merlin has a veritable list of seasonings in its philosophical soup which, when mixed together, give rise to our particular expression of Community Philosophy. Some of these spices include:

- *Experiential Spice* – Bringing ideas to life is joyful, challenging, and rewarding. Our activities typically involve a multi-modal "embodied" approach that allow ideas themselves to "breathe," and for participants to "breathe them in" in various ways. My conception of philosophy as a "hands-in-dirt" activity reflects some of this idea—*you have to get in there and get your hands dirty, to play with ideas, and experience them from as many angles and perspectives as possible.*

- *Community-Centered & Organic Spice* – We're committed to follow people's musings where they lead, in general (via reasoning together) and more concretely (via creating activities and programs inspired by those musings). In other words, our programming is homegrown and

---

[69] See footnote 57.

[70] Kader Be Haci, "Donnie Brasco—Forget About It," YouTube Video, :50, accessed April 17, 2017, https://youtu.be/FV9y0nySqMg. *Note: Some explicit words are used in this video clip.*

responsive.[71] It is designed around people, not the other way around. What transpires is a *direct result* of the unique members in the community.

- ***Sense of Place Spice*** – People exist not just in spaces but in *places*, which have their own unique histories and charm. Helena (where our activities primarily occur) has an inviting landscape with meandering hiking trails and breathtaking views, an abundance of iconic architectural character, and a delightfully unusual mix of people. All of this contributes to Helena's distinctive sense of place, i.e., a "fingerprint" that's informed by its constituent parts and processes, and packed with meaning. Our programs honor this in at least three ways: by philosophizing together in various spaces throughout the community, by bringing philosophical thinking to bear on local issues, and by intentionally reflecting upon and thinking about Helena's unique sense of place. Our "Thinking About Place"[72] project, inspired by community member Dennis McCahon, is a prime example of a program that focuses on each of these aspects of "place;" our other activities tap into the spirit of this more generally.

- ***Outside of the Box & Experimental Spice*** – We love doing things outside of the box and finding fun ways to do philosophy together. In addition to utilizing many unusual (or at least unexpected) venues for

[71] In reflecting on the notion of "responsiveness", Briggle cites the work of Thomas More when he says that there is a type of philosophy that "recognizes the play that's being staged, adapts itself to playing a part in it, revises what it has to say as the drama unfolds, and speaks appropriately for the time and place," "Dialogue and Next Generation Philosophy," 77.

[72] Our "Thinking About Place" program is an experimental and community-wide invitation to explore Helena afoot while considering questions about "place." Aims of this project include: (a) creating opportunities for people to explore, observe, and reflect upon Helena's unique sense of place; (b) facilitating new ways of seeing and moving through the town; (c) promoting discussion and enhanced understanding about the relationship between place and community; (d) generating a working list of specific attributes identified by walkers that are important to "place;" (e) bringing the insights of community members to bear by dialoguing with various city officials and planners relative to Helena's future plans for growth and preservation. Insofar as it has the additional aims of social and political change and works with professionals form other fields, the program is also an example of activist philosophy and field philosophy. You can access this program on our main Philosophy Community Endeavors page here: https://merlinccc.org/conferences-and-events/helena-community-endeavors/.

Programs that are completed (in these sense that they were designed as stand-alone activities or a series of activities that have since expired), reside on our Philosophy Community Endeavors *archive* page which can be accessed here: https://merlinccc.org/category/merlin-community-endeavors-archive/.

philosophizing, we take great delight in transforming spaces to create unique experiences. Our "Philosophy Drive-In's"[73] are a good example. We also love experimenting and don't shy away from "trying things out."[74] Sometimes we knock it out of the park; other times we don't.

- ***Collaborative & Cross-Disciplinary Spice*** – Many voices make for a rich and diverse learning environment. It also helps build and foster community. In light of this, we strive to create programs that are cross-disciplinary (relative to the kinds of guest thinkers we bring in and participants we draw) and collaborative (in terms of our various partnerships with businesses, organizations, schools and other learning centers, and people in the community).

- ***Holistic Spice*** – Thinking of philosophy in holistic terms might sound strange, but it's very much in keeping with our practice. From our experience, philosophy involves more than just the mind (intellect); the heart (emotion) has a role, too. A visual might help here: Imagine a person walking on a tightrope. On one side of her balancing stick is a brain, and on the other side a heart. *Philosophical thinking and living is a matter of balance that involves both of these.* As Martha Nussbaum writes in *Upheavals of Thought: The Intelligence of Emotions*: "If emotions are suffused with intelligence and discernment, and if they contain in themselves an awareness of value or importance, they cannot, for example, easily be sidelined in accounts of ethical judgment, as so often they have been in the history of philosophy. Instead of viewing morality as a system of principles to be grasped by the detached intellect, and emotions as motivations that either support or subvert our choice to act according to principle, we will have to consider emotions as part and parcel of the system of ethical reasoning." [75] Our programs

---

[73] Our drive-ins involve short or full-length films, followed by lively philosophical discussion. In these activities, we transform the inside of the Reeder's Alley Convention Center to look and feel like drive-in movie theater, replete with a big movie screen and a star machine. See: https://merlinccc.org/category/merlin-drive-in-archive/.

[74] I recognize that many teachers inside the academy might want to experiment with various (and more radical) program designs but, due to institutional or departmental limitations, may not have that option available to them. I am grateful that I have this flexibility through Merlin.

[75] Martha Nussbaum, *Upheavals of Thought: The Intelligence of Emotions* (Cambridge, UK; New York: Cambridge University Press, 2003), 1. Nussbaum goes on to say: "We cannot plausibly omit [emotions], once we acknowledge that emotions include in their content judgments that can be true or false, and good or bad guides to ethical choice. We

are designed to honor this robust way of "making sense of the world" and foster *philosophical poise* across the poles of the human experience. Activities like these help cultivate what Jana Mohr Lone refers to as "philosophical sensitivity"[76] and other important philosophical virtues, like humility, courage, and compassion.

Program Highlights

In an attempt to bring some of the things that I've been talking about together, I'll focus on two of our philosophies in the community programs. While a synopsis will be provided for both, I am also including URL links (via endnotes) in the instance that you would like to peruse these programs at a more leisurely pace, and, with much more information at your fingertips. My aim here is to give you a basic picture of *how* my approach to philosophy, the *kind* of work that we do, and the *characteristics* and *spices* at play in our program design, translate and manifest into *philosophy on the ground* (for us).

Big Ideas by Little Philosophers (BiLp)[77]

The familiar utterance "from the mouths of babes" is rife with meaning. There is a certain and undeniably "truth-facing" landscape that young people inhabit. What we can learn from them and what they contribute to philosophical thinking and dialogue is important. As such, finding ways to cultivate these natural faculties is not only worthwhile but imperative. As Lone eloquently articulates:

---

will have to grapple with the messy material of grief and love, anger and fear, and the role these tumultuous experiences play in thought and the good and the just."

[76] According to Jana Mohr Lone, 'philosophical sensitivity' is a kind of a natural faculty (in the Aristotelian sense) "that can be developed over time and with training" that involves a particular way of seeing the world. It is a sort of "perceptual capacity that facilitates our awareness of the philosophical dimension of experience" and, like other natural faculties, can be cultivated. "The Philosopher as Teacher: Philosophical Sensitivity," 171-172.

[77] You can view the inter-workings of this segmental program over the course of 2019 and 202 here: https://merlinccc.org/big-ideas-by-little-philosophers-bilp-archive/big-ideas-little-philosophers-spring-2019-2/, https://merlinccc.org/big-ideas-by-little-philosophers-bilp-summer-2019/, https://merlinccc.org/big-ideas-by-little-philosophers-bilp-archive/big-ideas-by-little-philosophers-bilp-fall-2019/, and https://merlinccc.org/big-ideas-by-little-philosophers-bilp-archive/big-ideas-by-little-philosophers-bilp-winter-2019-2020/.

[T]he philosophical dimension of life is natural for most children. They wonder about the significance of being alive, the nature of identity, the meaning of friendship and love, how to live good lives, and whether knowledge is possible. Yet continuing to wonder about these issues does not become part of the fabric of most adult lives. I think that this is a loss, and that encouraging children to engage in ongoing and critical philosophical reflection can be an important gift. Probing the assumptions that underlie what we say and do and critically analyzing the meaning of our experiences involve developing deep reasoning skills. When we engage in philosophical inquiry with children, we provide them with some important faculties for taking control of their future and developing the confidence to build meaningful lives. Thinking about philosophical questions pushes us to remain alive to the profound mysteriousness of the human condition. This awareness can enhance the depth and richness of all of our lives.[78]

Lone talks about nurturing young minds in the context of cultivating philosophical sensitivity. She says: "Sensitivity to the philosophical dimension of experience is a way of perceiving the world, a capacity that can grow over time with training and experience. Philosophical sensitivity heightens our awareness that the way things appear to us does not necessarily reflect the way things really are. Development of this capacity allows us to notice the philosophical facets of questions, beliefs, and situations, which we might otherwise miss. It brings together the reason and imagination."[79]

With this as our backdrop, our *Big Ideas by Little Philosophers (BiLp)* program was hatched. In order to give wings to this idea, we sought out partnerships with local learning centers that might be interested in incorporating philosophy into their curriculum for youth, as well as other organizations who were interested in teaming up. We were grateful to find willing participants with *Cottonwood ALC*[80]—an independent PK-12 organization for self-directed learners—and *Helena Civic Television*,[81] a unique community-based public

[78] Jana Mohr Lone, "The Cultivation of Philosophical Sensitivity," on Merlin website by permission of the author, February 7, 2018, https://merlinccc.org/scholarly-articles/cultivation-of-philosophical-sensitivity/.

[79] Jana Mohr Lone, *The Philosophical Child* (Lanham, MD: Rowman and Littlefield Publishers, Inc., 2012), 23.

[80] *Cottonwood ALC* is a Helena-based agile learning center committed to shifting the way we think about learning, education, and what it means to be in community. They work to empower youth and ignite the fire of curiosity in all people. Cottonwood ALC, "Homepage," accessed December 20, 2020, https://www.cottonwoodalc.org/.

[81] *Helena Civic Television* is a community-based public access station dedicated to

access station that has played an integral role in numerous of our philosophy in the community activities.

To give you a basic lay of the land, I'll describe the demographics of the youth involved in our program first. Ages range from 7 to 17; a class can (and typically *does*) involve *all* of these ages at the same time. It will usually also involve at least one adult from Cottonwood (who helps us co-facilitate discussion and activities). In terms of gender, there has been a relatively balanced mix of boys and girls, as well as some youth who are non-conforming. Finally, as one might suspect, there is a significant variance across our young thinkers in terms of life experiences and cognitive, social, and emotional development.

With this in mind, our BiLP program is designed to be highly adaptive and flexible, and has gone through many evolutions—shifting in shape both as a function of the interests of its young thinkers, as well as in response to thoughtful reflection about what has worked well (and what hasn't). A consistent ingredient through all of these evolutions is our focus on wonder, questioning, and reflection. (Lone and Michael D. Burroughs do a wonderful job outlining this in their book *Philosophy in Education: Questioning and Dialogue in Schools.*[82]) We also emphasize philosophy as *play.* As Erica Preston-Roedder writes, "The power of describing philosophy as *play* is that it calls attention to the motivation which drives a person to philosophize. That is, philosophy can, and often should be, a practice where the activity itself sustains and recruits one's attention."[83] This is not say, however, that play is a frivolous, low stakes, or modest endeavor. Rather, "the critical feature of play is the way that it calls upon a person's intrinsic motivation. While some play is absorbing because it is fun, other play sustains our attention because it is interesting, challenging, gripping, etc."[84]

One activity in our BiLP program—our "Know Thyself" project[85]—reflects Preston-Roedder's sentiment "*to a T,*" as well as Lone and Burrough's discussion about wonder, questioning, and reflection. This semester-long project started

---

sharing stories with, for, and about the Helena community. They develop and produce educational, governmental, and cultural programming and provide an electronic forum for the free exchange of ideas that reflect the talents, interests, concerns and diversity of Helena residents. Helena Civic Television (HCTV), "Home Page," accessed January 2, 2021, https://www.helenacivictv.org/.

[82] Jana Mohr Lone and Michael D. Burroughs. "Wonder, Questioning, and Reflection." In *Philosophy in Education,* 17-27 (Lanham: MD: Rowman and Littlefield Publishers, Inc., 2016).

[83] Erica Preston-Roedder, "What Can Philosophy Learn from Improvisational Theater?" *Precollege Philosophy and Public Practice* 2 (2020): 23.

[84] Ibid., 24.

[85] Access resources from this program here: https://merlinccc.org/big-ideas-by-little-philosophers-bilp-archive/big-ideas-by-little-philosophers-bilp-summer-2019/.

with a (seemingly) simple question: "What do you like and why do you like it?" The aim of the project was to help students come to a better understanding of themselves—i.e., what the things they like reveal about themselves and the values that they hold. It is one thing to be drawn to something; it is another matter entirely to understand more deeply *why* it is that we are drawn to something and *what* that reveals about us.

To begin, students were asked to think about something that they regularly do that brings them joy. Responses ranged from drawing, video gaming, and dancing, to design, photography, music, and more. Every student (not surprisingly) had multiple interests, but for the sake of the reflective work that they were about to embark on (as well as logistical aspects), they were asked to pick the one activity that stood out to them as their the most "beloved." Then the fun began.

Each week our group would embark on a series of philosophical discussions aimed at discovering why each of us liked what we liked. Students were asked to bring in an example of their "what" (e.g., an image, a video, an art piece, a list of specific games, etc.) to share with the group, the objective of which was to (a) help others in the group get a better idea of what brought their classmates joy, and (b) help each thinker begin the reflective and analytic process required for the next steps in the project. By being asked to provide examples of the thing they liked, each student was implicitly engaging in their own selection process. For example, the students who identified video gaming as their activity of choice were asked to come up with a list of their 5 favorite games.

After each student shared their activity, they were asked: "What specifically do you like about that thing you are showing us? What is it about that activity (e.g., game, drawing, dance style, design, photograph) that is compelling to you?" Some responses included:

- I like (these) games because they are challenging and take practice
- I like (these) dance styles because they emphasize 'togetherness,' 'an intergenerational feel,' and flow
- I like (these) games because they are progressive, responsive (i.e., in the sense that doors open based on your prior actions), and have a purpose
- I like spaces because they feel welcoming or have the potential to feel welcoming
- I like doing art that is not "wall-worthy" on the first go-around
- I like (these) games because they are fun, have rules, involve imaginary worlds, and do not involve skill, strength or luck
- I like spaces that serve multiple purposes and allow me to lay things out in a certain way
- I like (this) photograph because it has a lot of contrast and shading, and has multiple layers ("the more you look, the more you see")

Next, each student was asked a series of deeper questions inspired by their personal responses. For example:

- You identified 'challenge' as something you found compelling about video gaming. Think about the relationship between challenge and satisfaction. Are challenges inherent (built-in to) the game itself, unique to the user (the same game can pose different challenges for different users), or both? Can you think of an example of something you have experienced that was not challenging but was still satisfying?

- You identified 'togetherness' and 'intergenerationality' as something you found compelling about certain dance styles. Think more about this. Why are these important to you? Do you think learning to dance from a grandparent is different than learning to dance from a friend your own age? If so, why and how? Is there something special about teaching dance to someone younger than you?

- You identified the 'progressiveness,' 'responsiveness,' and 'purposeful' as things you found about video gaming. Why does this matter? Can you think of a game that does not have these characteristics that you still like? Think about purpose. Can something be satisfying without having a purpose?

- You identified 'potentiality' as something you found compelling about design (spaces). The concept of 'potentiality' is really interesting. Think more about this. Do you see a difference between potentiality and possibility? Or are they the same thing? Do you think there is a relationship between potentiality and hope? Between hope and possibility?

- You identified doing art that is not "wall-worthy" at the outset being important to you. Think more about this. What do you think "wall-worthy" art consists of/must look like or be in order to be "wall-worthy?" Why is not caring about creating "wall-worthy" art right out of the gate important to you?

- You identified rules as something you found compelling about video gaming. You also mentioned that you disagreed with the dictionary's definition of games involving "skill, strength, or luck." Think more about this. Can you think of a situation in your games where skill, strength, and luck are not involved? What are those situations? If rules didn't exist, would "skill, strength, or luck" make sense or even matter?

- You identified 'multi-functionality' as something you found compelling about design (spaces). Why is it important to you for a space to serve numerous purposes? Is purpose "built-in to" a thing (e.g., a chair is for sitting)? Or is a thing's purpose ultimately defined by its user (e.g., a chair is for sitting, standing, hanging things on, using as a flower stand, a place for a cat's bed, etc.)? Both?

- You identified 'contrast' and "multiple layers" as things you found compelling about the photograph you shared. Think more about your statement "the more you look, the more you see." Why is this appealing to you? Are there examples you can think of where you prefer the opposite (e.g., "what you see is what you get")?

This process of "peeling back the layers" continued for weeks, with each student being asked to think more deeply, clarify, and refine their thoughts. The "Know Thyself" project culminated in a showcase at a community block party—in the form of an art exhibition highlighting our young thinkers' philosophical work. Students fielded questions about their projects (and their thought processes) from interested community members and Helena Civic Television filmed the festivities.

Philosophy Walks[86]

Our philosophy walks are, admittedly, one of my *favorite* community activities that we offer. There are several reasons why these "thinky-wanderings" hold a special place in my heart. First, they bring me back to childhood. I have always "loved me a good walkabout," so much so that I have often wondered if my love of wandering is deep-baked into my DNA. More poignantly, though, nature walks were my first introductions to philosophy as a youth. My father and I would frequently set out on long meanderings. The conversations that we shared on those outings helped cultivate and promote my sense of wonder, curiosity, and imagination, as well as contribute to new ways of understanding and being in the world. Our Merlin philosophy walks are directly linked to these transformative experiences and, as a somewhat telling sign of my affection for them, were the first activities that we offered upon opening our doors for business.

Beyond my nostalgic motivations, my love of philosophy walks is deeply connected to my belief in the *pedagogy of nature* and *movement*. Simply put, *thinking and walking go hand in hand*. Ample literature supports this and, of course, many philosophers—as in the case of the Peripatetics, for example— have made walking central to their practice. Graeme Tiffany refers to the subjective experience and value of walking in a "Deweyan sense," in that it becomes "uncertainty-appreciative, which, surely, all good philosophical practice strives to be."[87] This kind of embodied activity can be very

---

[86] Archive pages for our philosophy walks can be accessed here: https://merlinccc.org/category/merlin-philosophy-walks-archive/.
[87] Graeme Tiffany, "Afterword: Thoughts on Moving Philosophy Outside," In *Philosophy and Community: Theories, Practices, and Possibilities*, ed. Amanda Fulford, Grace Lockrobin, and

transformative. There is wisdom in nature, and moving through her can move us. As William Wordsworth said nature is our teacher[88] and something that can, according to John Burroughs, help soothe and heal our souls, and put our senses in tune once more.[89]

Almost every person who has come on a philosophy walk with us has expressed the sentiments to which Tiffany, Wordsworth, and Burroughs aver: walking in nature "helps me see things in a different light," "takes my thinking to a different place," and "puts me in connection with myself and others in unexpected and enlightening ways." I have thought a lot about this and why it is such a common phenomenon. I, too, feel this when I am outdoors. On the one hand, nature is fertile ground for imagination and wonder—two central elements of critical, creative thinking. *Being in* nature and *moving through* her invites us to think deeply, elicits reflection, and tills the soil for inquiry and contemplation. But even more than this, I think, is mother nature's ability to humble us, and force us, ever so gently, into a shared experience of vulnerability. I'm often heard saying that "there are no CEO's on the trail." By this, I mean that when we're in nature, walls drop away. In a structural sense, this is easy enough to see. When we're outdoors, there are *literally* no walls (at least in the buildings or office sense). The horizon is our only "real" boundary, and even that, as we walk, is always in flux. But even more relevant, I think, is the fact that walls fall away *socially*. On the trail, in nature, although we are still "who we are" as individuals (each with our own life experiences and values), we inevitably become something else—something more stripped down, unified, primal, and connected; we are reminded that we are beings who, despite our differences, all cry, love, laugh, feel joy, and grieve. In other words, in nature, the walls of hierarchy and separation that so often present themselves in society settings seem to disappear. This shared experience of vulnerability relates to Tiffany's assertion that when walking and philosophy are combined, the practice becomes "*propositional*—capable of showing us new ways of thinking, acting, being, and becoming."[90]

For all of these reasons, I hold philosophy walks near and dear, and after several years of playing with format—from walk length and logistical structure, to subject matter and modes of investigation—I've landed on a general

---

Richard Smith (London; New York: Bloomsbury Academic, 2020), 251.

[88] William Wordsworth, "The Tables Turned," *The Poetry Foundation*, accessed January 20, 2021, https://www.poetryfoundation.org/poems/45557/the-tables-turned.

[89] John Burroughs, "The Gospel of Nature," In *Time and Change* (Boston; New York: 1912), Project Gutenberg EBook, XIII, no. 1, Posted May 2004, https://www.gutenberg.org/files/5706/5706-h/5706-h.htm.

[90] Ibid., 250. *My emphasis.*

structure that works well within the framework of our operations and mission.[91] Our walks typically run two to three hours, with stopping points along the way for focused discussion. Before embarking, usually at our meeting spot, we'll provide a quick lay of the intellectual landscape that we'll be exploring together, as well as information about what to anticipate relative to structure and flow. Stops are normally organized as stand-alone discussions (e.g., as conversations that revolve around a particular question or area of focus), though we have—depending on the walk topic—also designed them to build on one another. On most occasions, in between stops, we'll incorporate additional questions to ponder, as well as solo or group "tasks," which then serve as springboards for discussion at the next stop (or simply as opportunities for personal reflection or observation). We frequently use touchstone questions, too, so that participants have continual opportunities to "try on" and practice thinking about the concepts we are exploring and apply them to their own lives throughout the walk. Finally, our walks typically (though not always) have some sort of environmental bent, incorporate guest thinkers from a variety of disciplines, and range widely in topics from "Nature and the Humanities[92]" and "Storytelling and Imagination Across Cultures[93]" to "Environmental Ethics, Conservation, and Preservation[94]" and "Leisure & Loafing.[95]"

Our "Virtue and Excellence—From Ecology to Ethics[96]" walk, designed and led by David Nowakowski, is a great example of an outing that incorporates all of these components. In this walk, we invited participants to consider the ancient Greek conception of "flourishing" and "virtue" alongside five basic

---

[91] By "I've" here, I mean 'I' (*with the help and feedback of others*), have landed upon a design that works well.

[92] Access to audio-video and resources related to our "Nature and the Humanities" walk can be found here: https://merlinccc.org/merlin-philosophy-walks-archive/november-2019-philosophy-walk-humanities-nature/.

[93] Access to audio-video and resources related to our "Story and Imagination Across Cultures" walk can be found here: https://merlinccc.org/merlin-philosophy-walks-archive/october-2019-philosophy-walk-story-imagination-across-cultures/.

[94] Access to audio-video and resources related to our "Environmental Ethics, Conservation and Preservation" walk can be found here: https://merlinccc.org/merlin-philosophy-walks-archive/september-2017-philosophy-walk-conservation-preservation-environmental-ethics-fall-series-walk-1/.

[95] This walk was inspired community member Daniel Gardener and designed by David Nowakowski. Access to audio-video and resources can be found here: https://merlinccc.org/merlin-philosophy-walks-archive/june-2020-leisure-loafing/

[96] Access to audio-video and resources for this walk can be found here: https://merlinccc.org/merlin-philosophy-walks-archive/september-2019-philosophy-walk-virtue-ethics-ecology-ethics/.

ecological principles. Our preliminary stop laid the groundwork for our discussion and introduced: the study of physics and ethics historically in Greco-Roman and Indian traditions; the domain of ecology and its investigation of the world as it is; virtue as excellence; and excellence from the perspective of asking—what are the ways in which the world (including me operates), and given these principles, how and I act more/less effectively in the world as it is? The preliminary stop also served as an invitation for participants to get used to thinking in whole system terms (i.e., thinking about and "attending to" in particular ways) and draw practical implications from these ways of seeing (relative to us acting more effectively or excellently in the world). At each of our four main stops, we examined virtue through the lens of a different ecological principle: whole systems, resource flows, dynamic balance, and limits and evolutionary processes. The stops were designed to build on one another so that people could "move through" ideas and experience the layered complexity and interconnectivity of the philosophical and ecological concepts we were exploring. Touchstone questions were also utilized. These included:

- How might patterns of nature provide a guide for living?
- How can an ecological perspective help us to focus and direct our lives— not only as we engage with plants and other animals, wild places, or "the environment," but especially in our human relationships, and in cultivating ourselves?
- How can the tools of ecology help us understand ourselves, and to live a virtuous (excellent, flourishing) life?
- What does it mean to think about human life, and about virtue, as an ecologist would?

This walk ended up being so successful, that elements of its design have made their way into other Merlin activities.

Now, for obvious reasons, while walking is central to these outings, additional modes of transport may also be employed depending on location and aims. Our hayride-philosophy walks are one such example. We usually offer at least two of these per year. These excursions involve stretches of hayriding through Merlin Nature Preserve and Little Falcon Farm, as well as walking and discussion. At least one of the stops takes place at the site of an old homestead where we create a "designated outdoor classroom" with haybale seats arranged in a semi-circle beneath a shaded tree, alongside a pond. Here guest speakers might invite participants to engage in a particular activity or discussion based on what we have observed at previous stops. We might also have props set up there ahead of time (and at various spots throughout the preserve)—that can be used for working through ideas in a specific "hands-on" way.

Our nature preserve outings also include annual Halloween Hayride-Philosophy Walks[97] for youth. These are structured similarly to our other hayride walks on the preserve but also involve costumes, fresh-baked goods, cider, and theme-related goodie bags for continued exploration. Play and imagination are heavily emphasized, as are compassion and teamwork (e.g., scavenger hunts that require kids work creatively together, thought experiments during which children contribute their perspective, and riddles that invite the collective brainpower of youth to solve). We've investigated topics such as: "Exploring the World through our Senses,[98]" "Imagination and Storytelling,[99]" "Planet Hopping and Star Walking: A Journey into Outer Space,[100]" and "What is it Like to Be a Bat?"[101]

Ultimately, our walks are opportunities for people to stretch their minds and legs, and to engage with their surroundings, ideas, and one another in deeply embodied ways. In the spirit of Aldo Leopold's 'land ethic'[102]—our walks are structured to help nurture and facilitate this complex, relational, and widened perspective; to foster an increased appreciation, awareness, and understanding of the topic at hand, and; to enrich and enhance our sense of ethics and community.

---

[97] Our Halloween Hayride Philosophy Walks are geared for youth and explore a range of topics through play, imagination, curiosity, storytelling, and working together toward improved understanding. URL links for specific Halloween Hayride Walks are provided in the footnotes below.

[98] Access resources for our "Exploring the World through Our Senses" Halloween Hayride-Philosophy Walk here: https://merlinccc.org/merlin-philosophy-walks-archive/october-2017-halloween-themed-little-philosophers-walk-exploring-world-through-senses/.

[99] Access resources from our "Imagination and Storytelling" Halloween Hayride-Philosophy Walk here: https://merlinccc.org/merlin-philosophy-walks-archive/october-2016-little-philosophers-walk/.

[100] Access resources from our "Planet Hopping and Star Walking: A Journey Into Outer Space" Halloween Hayride-Philosophy Walk here: https://merlinccc.org/merlin-philosophy-walks-archive/october-2019-halloween-planet-hopping-star-walking/.

[101] Access resources from our "What is it Like to be a Bat?" Halloween Hayride-Philosophy Walk here: https://merlinccc.org/merlin-philosophy-walks-archive/october-2018-halloween-themed-little-philosophers-walk-what-is-it-like-to-be-a-bat/.

[102] In its most distilled form "a land ethic is simply caring: about people, about land, and strengthening the relationships between them." As cited on Aldo Leopold, "The Land Ethic," *The Aldo Leopold Foundation*, accessed January 30, 2021, https://www.aldoleopold.org/about/the-land-ethic/.

Benefits and Challenges

In this section, I'll highlight some of the benefits and challenges of philosophizing in the way that we do. In an attempt to streamline things, I will focus largely on those that may be more unique to Community Philosophy (or philosophy done in n0n-traditional ways), as well as philosophy conducted *as* a 501(c)(3) non-profit.

The first of these challenges has to do with *mixed-age programming.* No doubt, many academic and public-facing philosophy programs involve mixed-age groups. For example, Stephen Kekoa Miller, who teaches at *Oakwood Friends School,* writes about his experiences facilitating mixed-age groups in the context of Community of Inquiry.[103] Among the challenges he points out are varying levels of maturation (within and across age groups), navigating the discussion dynamics of topical issues (e.g., different scaffolding for different age groups), and finding a balance between open-inquiry and teacher-centered discussion.[104] I have experienced many of these same challenges in our programming, especially those with more wildly swinging age variances (like our symposiums and philosophy walks) and our philosophy for youth programs. Despite the challenges, however, I agree with Miller that philosophizing with mixed-age groups is hugely rewarding, and the degree to which participants express that their experience is "informed and improved by having a mix of ages present"[105] is substantial. The soils of mixed-age conversation are rich with perspective, and the directions their dialogue can take are surprising, illuminating, and powerful.

Another challenge we deal with has to do with structure. Typically, our community programs are *modular.* Although we offer a few segmental programs, the majority of our activities are structured as one-off gigs. This has worked well for us in general and has met the needs of most community members, but not without posing some interesting pedagogic challenges. For our more formal programs, like our philosophy workshops,[106] limitations of time and structure have typically made them heavier on theory, with minimal room for lived,

---

[103] Community of Inquiry is a way of doing philosophy that is "committed to bringing out multiple perspectives, critiquing them, and optimally causing all views to gain in precision and nuance through the process of conversation." Stephen Kekoa Miller, "Restoring Wonder: The Benefits and Challenges of Doing Philosophy in Mixed-Aged Groups," in *Philosophy and Classrooms and Beyond: New Approaches to Picture-Book Philosophy,* ed. Thomas E. Wartenberg (London: Rowman and Littlefield Publishers Inc., 2019), 20.

[104] Ibid., 22-23.

[105] Ibid., 24.

[106] Access to audio-video and resources related to our philosophy workshops can be found here: https://merlinccc.org/category/merlin-workshops-courses-archive/.

practical activities. Exercises and "assignments" have mostly been relegated to "things to try at home at your leisure," with no real opportunity to follow up. Meanwhile, our more informal programs (like our philosophy walks or monthly "Think and Drink" conversations) provide a space for peer-to-peer dialogue, but those same limitations of time and structure can make it a challenge to rigorously explore diverse philosophical arguments and theories, and cultivate the development of some of the skills needed to converse on applied, practical questions with depth, precision, and mutual respect.[107]

We have responded to these challenges, first, by trying to make our activities as immersive and multi-modal as possible. This allows for different kinds of "embodied" engagement that can help bring ideas to life and facilitate deep and meaningful connections in (relatively) short periods of time. Second, we try to offer at least *some* segmental activities where, for example, we explore one idea or conceptual theme from a variety of angles over the course of a designated period of time. Our three-part philosophy walk series on "The Environment, Ethics, and Stewardship[108]" is a good example of this. We might also pair these activities with other philosophical activities that overlap in theme but offer different modes of philosophical engagement. The above walk series was programmed in this way—alongside an identically-themed three-part philosophy symposium series,[109] each with several panelists and opportunities for free-flowing dialogue. Third, we continually tweak and refine our programming not from a one-size-fits-all approach, but rather with the view that our program offerings should be as diverse and eclectic as our community members. Some individuals are interested in particular topics;

---

[107] Thank you colleague and friend, David Nowakowski, for your helpful articulation of these challenges.

[108] Access to audio-video recordings from each of the walks in our "The Environment, Ethics, and Stewardship" series can be found here: https://merlinccc.org/merlin-philosophy-walks-archive /september-2018-philosophy-walk-environment-ethics-stewardship-fall-series-walk-1/; https://merlinccc.org/merlin-philosophy-walks-archive/november-2018-philosophy-walk-environment-ethics-stewardship-fall-series-walk-2/, and; https://merlinccc.org/merlin-philosophy-walks-archive/march-2019-philosophy-walk-environment-ethics-stewardship-fall-series-walk-3/.

[109] Access to audio-video recordings from each of symposium in "The Environment, Ethics, and Stewardship" series can be found here: https://merlinccc.org/lecture-library/2018-philo sophy-forums-and-roundtables-environment-ethics-stewardship-part-1-archive/; https://merlinccc.org/lecture-library/2018-philosophy-forums-and-roundtables-environment-ethics-stewardship-part-2-archive/, and; https://merlinccc.org/lecture-library/2018-philosophy-forums-and-roundtables-environment-ethics-stewardship-part-3-archive/.

others prefer a wide range. Some want discussions to involve texts and teacher-centered dialogue while others prefer a different dynamic altogether.

Of course, by maintaining this attitude, I am not saying that the challenges posed by more modular programming disappear. They are still something we must work through, and are. Our recent launch of a pilot program called "Philosophy Night School[110]" is one such attempt. These community offerings, which meet one evening for four to five consecutive weeks, are designed to inspire rigorous and careful thinking about a range of philosophical topics in a manner similar to auditing a college class. Because they are specifically structured so that each session builds upon the previous session, it is easier to integrate exercises and assignments between gatherings, as well as follow-up on these together as a community of thinkers. On the other end of the spectrum lie our more informal gatherings, like our monthly Think and Drinks. Here, clearly articulating conversational guidelines and aims, and establishing group covenants that honor these (and hold each of us accountable) is important both generally, for open, honest, and effective philosophical exchange and, more specifically, when conducting stand-alone activities that may or may not involve the same participants. Across both program extremes, modeling the skills and habits of philosophical thinking (and inviting others to do the same) is also critical. Facilitators play a particularly important role here.

Ultimately, my point about designing programs in this way, has to do with two things—*flexibility* and *inclusivity*. By recognizing that different people want and need different things from our programming, we free ourselves from the mistaken belief that all of our programming must fit the *same mold* and meet the *same ends*. As a Community Philosophy organization, our programming should be responsive to the community members that it serves. This "loose grip" approach has additional benefits, too: (a) it allows room for us to play with and "try on" different ways of philosophizing together, (b) it broadens the field of who might participate in our activities, and (c) it inspires creativity and refinement of our philosophical skills as facilitators and program designers.

Two additional challenges that I will mention only in brief are *replicability* and *funding*. With respect to the first of these, our programs are typically designed *around* people, not the other way around. As such, if I wanted to create an identical program elsewhere with a comprehensive list of checkboxes—other than a program's basic features and structure (which *are* transferable, at least in theory)—this would be difficult. However, I see this as more of a strength than anything. Community Philosophy *qua* Community

---

[110] Information about our Philosophy Night School program can be found here: https://merlinccc.org/philosophy-night-school/.

Philosophy is philosophy *by* the people. Every community is different. If our programs were *completely* replicable (like template punch cards), then we're doing it wrong.

As it concerns funding, as a 501(c)(3) non-profit organization we rely heavily on grants and donations. Although we occasionally charge for programs—though rarely, and always on a sliding scale—most of our philosophy in the community activities are free. This means that income has to be generated elsewhere. (This is where the question of "How do I survive?" posed earlier in this chapter comes into play.)

Funding for all non-profits is a legitimate concern and requires a fair amount of creativity. This is certainly the case for philosophy-specific grant funding, and even more so for those programs that take place *outside* of academia. Merlin has been fortunate to receive funding from the *Philosophy Learning and Teaching Organization* (PLATO)[111] and *Humanities Montana.*[112] We have also been very lucky and are extremely grateful to our many generous donors and sponsors who have continued to support our efforts over the years. Helena is quite an amazing community!

But the grueling work of applying for grants goes on. Applying to organizations *not* familiar with (or focused on) the benefits of engaging in philosophical pursuits is particularly challenging. As one might anticipate, these funding requests require much more explanation about how and why philosophy in the community should be supported, and more specifically, how exactly philosophy and our programs fit in with their mission. They also tend to want things spoken of in terms of hard "deliverables" (which often means figuring out how to reasonably cast qualitative measurements in quantifiable terms). This latter point continues to be a thorn in my side (for a number of reasons that I won't go into). But here is where I think the challenge becomes an opportunity and, if done well, a *strength.*

At the beginning of this chapter, I spoke about my difficulty coming up with an "elevator pitch" for philosophy (what it is, what we do, and why we do it). Unless

---

[111] The *Philosophy Learning and teaching Organization (PLATO)* is an organization devoted to enriching young people's educational experiences by introducing them to the benefits and rigors of philosophy before they graduate from high school. In addition to K-12 programs, they also support philosophy in the community programs that involve people of all ages. Philosophy Learning and Teaching Organization (PLATO), "Homepage," accessed December 16, 2020, https://www.plato-philosophy.org/.

[112] *Humanities Montana* serves communities through stories and conversations. They offer and support a wide-range of experiences that nurture imagination ad ideas by speaking to Montanans' diverse history, literature, and philosophy. Humanities Montana, "Homepage," accessed December 16, 2020, https://www.humanitiesmontana.org/.

that elevator ride moves *very slowly* and covers a substantial number of floors, scratching anything more than the surface is unlikely. However, delivering a pithy explanation replete with aims and benefits has value. This is precisely what an elevator pitch is supposed to do. In the context of grant writing or other funder-related correspondence, it becomes an opportunity to showcase the specific and broad-reaching applicability and value of philosophical thinking and living. It also inspires anyone who might be engaged in funder-related correspondence to refine and articulate their belief in the value of philosophy, and to describe its reach in ways that are unique, comprehensible, and robust, while at the same time easily digestible. *Distillation of this sort is an art.* Not only does it help inquirers (and funders) appreciate the weight of philosophy, it invites its practitioners to engage in an intense meta-dialogue *about* the practice. This creates opportunities to modify and improve existing programs and to develop new programs. It can also pave the way for unique and unexpected community partnerships.

Of final mention, it is worth noting that the kind of philosophy that we do (replete with its challenges and benefits), is deeply connected to our organizational structure. I am often asked why I opted to found Merlin as a not-for-profit entity, as opposed to a for-profit one. My response is in keeping with one of the core characteristics of Community Philosophy. That is, non-profits, like Community Philosophy, are *in the service of others*; And, quite frankly, in the service of others is where I want to be. While personal disposition is a factor, my training in philosophy and my years serving as caregiver to my father as we navigated the wakes of Parkinson's are much bigger players.[113] My life experiences primed me for this kind of work and my gratitude is immense.

Community, Place & Beauty

While I've spoken about community and place at various points throughout this chapter, I would be remiss if I did not return to it here, as a sort of full-circle parting. Recently, I came across a podcast discussion between NPR's Krista Tippet and Nobel physicist Frank Wilzcek. The interview, titled "Beauty as a Compass for Truth[114]" explored the relationship between ideas and reality, complexity, complementarity, and how beauty might be a compass for us all (in

---

[113] Marisa Diaz-Waian, "In Memoriam," Personal Journal Entry (2012). https://merlinccc.org/wp-content/uploads/2015/02/Marisa-Diaz-Waian-A-Dedication-to-her-Father-In-Memoriam-2012-.pdf.

[114] Krista Tippett, "Beauty as a Compass for Truth," interview with Frank Wilczek, *On Being*, podcast audio, January 7, 2021, https://onbeing.org/programs/frank-wilczek-beauty-as-a-compass-for-truth/.

scientific and moral realms). Upon listening to it, I could not help but think of this in terms of community and place.

Every community has its own beauty—beauty that is shaped and informed by its human inhabitants and unique social undercurrents, as well as (and equally by) its landscape, flora, and fauna. All of these contribute to the larger socio-ecological notion of *community* which requires that its inhabitants find (and sometimes stumble or crash into) ways of *being* together. Bramall sheds some light on this when he talks about the history of philosophy:

> [A] history of big ideas and big thinkers is a pretty thin account, and it can give a misleading view of what lived philosophy is like and how it works [...] A thicker history would be a many-tongued history of groups of people finding ways of thinking together. And finding ways of thinking together means finding ways of *being* together...Being together and thinking together, a complex unified practice, is how philosophy in communities is experienced.[115]

Although Bramall focuses on ways of being together *as thinking humans*, his point is still applicable to the larger socio-ecological conception of community to which I am referring. Community—whether meso, micro, exo, or macro—requires finding ways to cohabitate.

To this end, it is not surprising that "Finding Your Way with Philosophy" became a tagline for Merlin upon our inception. As a Community Philosophy organization in the service of the philosophical development of others, it is not *my way* or *any other philosopher's way* for that matter. Instead, it's about creating opportunities for people to find *their own way* with philosophy—ways that, inevitably, require figuring out how *to be* and move through this world together. This brings me back to the idea of beauty as a compass for truth; this has "teeth." Here, 'beauty' is not a matter of simple aesthetics but rather beauty in a deeper and more connective sense. Fulford alludes to this in the context of philosophy when she says that the questions with which it's concerned "are ones that we can, and do, all ask, and where in the most ordinary of places we can find something natural and beautiful."[116] Beauty is a complex and unifying thing; it promotes, nourishes, and reflects the community, and helps us find ways of being and moving through this messy world together. Philosophy is

---

[115] Bramall, "Understanding Philosophy in Communities: The Spaces, People, Politics and Philosophy of Community Philosophy,"3-4.
[116] Amanda Fulford, "Preface: 'In All Things of Nature There is Something Wonderful'," in *Philosophy and Community: Theories, Practices, and Possibilities*, ed. Amanda Fulford, Grace Lockrobin, and Richard Smith (London; New York: Bloomsbury Academic, 2020), xii.

analogous. For ages, thinkers have spoken of philosophy *in terms of what is beautiful* and *what is good.* This is not a coincidence. That's exactly what philosophy is—she is a trusty steed, a lighthouse in the storm, and a thing which can inspire, direct, and "lead out" what is beautiful in all of us.[117]

Bibliography

Aristotle. *Metaphysics*, Book 1.2 (982a). Creative Commons. Accessed February 1, 2021. http://www.perseus.tufts.edu/hopper/text?doc=Perseus%3Atext%3A1999.01.0052%3Abook%3D1%3Asection%3D982a.

Bramall, Steve. "Understanding Philosophy in Communities: The Spaces, People, Politics and Philosophy of Community Philosophy." In *Philosophy and Community: Theories, Practices, and Possibilities*, edited by Amanda Fulford, Grace Lockrobin, and Richard Smith, 3-14. London; New York: Bloomsbury Academic, 2020.

Briggle, Adam. "Dialogue and Next Generation Philosophy." *Pre-college Philosophy and Public Practice* 1 (2019):75-88.

Burroughs, John. "The Gospel of Nature," In *Time and Change* (Boston; New York: 1912), Project Gutenberg Ebook, XIII, no. 1, Posted May 2004, https://www.gutenberg.org/files/5706/5706-h/5706-h.htm.

Cherry, Myisha. "Liberatory Dialogue." *Pre-college Philosophy and Public Practice* 1 (2019): 4-15.

Collins, Brian J. "The Broad Nature and Importance of Public Philosophy." *Pre-college Philosophy and Public Practice* 2 (2020): 72-87.

Cooper, John M. "Ancient Philosophies as Ways of Life." The Tanner Lectures on Human Values presented at Stanford University. Stanford, CA. January 25-26, 2012. https://tannerlectures.utah.edu/Cooper%20Lecture.pdf.

Corbel, David. "What Makes Soup *Soup*?" A Comedy Short on YouTube Video. 1:54. Posted by BBC Scotland, February 1, 2019. https://youtu.be/Y1HVTNxwt7w.

Cottonwood ALC. "Homepage." Accessed December 20, 2020. https://www.cottonwoodalc.org/.

Diaz-Waian, Marisa. "In Memoriam." Personal Journal Entry (2012). https://merlinccc.org/wp-content/uploads/2015/02/Marisa-Diaz-Waian-A-Dedication-to-her-Father-In-Memoriam-2012-.pdf.

Evans, Jules. "Connected Communities: Philosophical Communities." A Report for the Arts and Humanities Research Council presented at University of London. London, UK. November 12, 2012. http://static1.squarespace.com/static/5c8bd3835239589598cac07e/5caeecaf0cf24e366c39d10a/5caef0370cf24e366c3a72f4/1554968631713/Connected-Communities-Philosophical-Communities1.pdf?format=original.

---

[117] Thank you to Roberta Israeloff for your encouragement, guidance, and keen eye; to Stephen Kekoa Miller for your editorial support and amazing display of patience, and; to all those who have (and continue) to shape Merlin in such delightful ways.

Fulford, Amanda, Grace Lockrobin., and Richard Smith, eds. *Philosophy and Community: Theories, Practices and Possibilities.* London; New York: Bloomsbury Academic, 2020.

Fulford, Amanda. "Philosophy, dialogue and the creation of community." In *Philosophy and Community: Theories, Practices, and Possibilities,* edited by Amanda Fulford, Grace Lockrobin, and Richard Smith, 91-102. London; New York: Bloomsbury Academic, 2020.

Fulford, Amanda. "Preface: 'In all things of nature there is something wonderful'." In *Philosophy and Community: Theories, Practices, and Possibilities,* edited by Amanda Fulford, Grace Lockrobin, and Richard Smith, xii-xv. London; New York: Bloomsbury Academic, 2020.

Hadot, Pierre. "Philosophy as a Way of Life." In *Philosophy as a Way of Life: Spiritual Exercises from Socrates to Foucault.* Edited by Arnold I. Davidson. Translated by Michael Chase, 264-276. Maldan, MA; Oxford, UK: Blackwell Publishing Ltd., 1995.

Helena Civic Television (HCTV). "Homepage." Accessed January 2, 2021. https://www.helenacivictv.org/.

Humanities Montana. "Homepage." Accessed December 16, 2020. https://www.humanitiesmontana.org/.

Kader Be Haci. "Donnie Brasco—Forget About It." YouTube Video,:50. April 17, 2017. https://youtu.be/FV9y0nySqMg.

Laertius, Diogenes. *Diogenes Laertius: Lives of Eminent Philosophers,* ed. R.D. Hicks. Creative Commons. Accessed February 1, 2021. http://www.perseus.tufts.edu/hopper/text?doc=Perseus%3Atext%3A1999.01.0258.

Leopold, Aldo. "The Land Ethic." *The Aldo Leopold Foundation.* Accessed January 30, 2021. https://www.aldoleopold.org/about/the-land-ethic/.

Lockrobin, Grace. "Relocation and Repopulation: Why Community Philosophy Matters." In *Philosophy and Community: Theories, Practices, and Possibilities,* edited by Amanda Fulford, Grace Lockrobin, and Richard Smith, 15-37. London; New York: Bloomsbury Academic, 2020.

Lone, Jana Mohr. "The Cultivation of Philosophical Sensitivity" on Merlin website by permission of the author. February 7, 2018. https://merlinccc.org/scholarly-articles/cultivation-of-philosophical-sensitivity/.

Lone, Jana Mohr. "The Philosopher as Teacher: Philosophical Sensitivity" *Metaphilosophy* 44, no. 1-2 (2013): 171-186.

Lone, Jana Mohr. *The Philosophical Child.* Lanham, MD: Rowman and Littlefield Publishers, Inc., 2012.

Lone, Jana Mohr., and Michael D. Burroughs. "Wonder, Questioning, and Reflection." In *Philosophy in Education,* 17-27. Lanham: MD: Rowman and Littlefield Publishers, Inc., 2016.

Merlin. "Our Mission." Accessed February 1, 2021. https://merlinccc.org/about-us/our-mission/. *All activities or resources from this website that are referenced in this chapter are included in bulk by activity grouping in the Supplementary Material section.*

Miller, Stephen Kekoa. "Restoring Wonder: The Benefits and Challenges of Doing Philosophy in Mixed-Aged Groups," in *Philosophy and Classrooms and Beyond:*

New Approaches to Picture-Book Philosophy, ed. Thomas E. Wartenberg (London: Rowman and Littlefield Publishers Inc., 2019), 17-33.

Nussbaum, Martha. *Upheavals of Thought: The Intelligence of Emotions.* Cambridge, UK; New York: Cambridge University Press, 2003.

Plato. *Plato: Complete Works.* Edited by J. M. Cooper and D.S. Hutchinson. Indianapolis: Hackett Publishing Company, 1997.

Philosophy Learning and Teaching Organization (PLATO). "Homepage" Accessed December 16, 2020. https://www.plato-philosophy.org/.

Pollock, Darien. "Philosophizing in the Streets." Blog of the APA (blog). *American Philosophical Association.* November 8, 2018. https://blog.apaonline.org/2018/11/08/philosophizing-in-the-streets/.

Preston-Roedder, Erica. "What Can Philosophy Learn from Improvisational Theater?" *pre-college Philosophy and Public Practice* 2 (2020): 18-35.

Sayre, Kenneth. *Plato's Literary Garden: How to Read a Platonic Dialogue.* Notre Dame: University of Notre Dame Press, 1995.

Tiffany, Graeme. "Afterword: Thoughts on Moving Philosophy Outside." In *Philosophy and Community: Theories, Practices, and Possibilities*, edited by Amanda Fulford, Grace Lockrobin, and Richard Smith, 248-253. London; New York: Bloomsbury Academic, 2020.

Tippett, Krista. "Beauty as a Compass for Truth." Interview with Frank Wilczek. *On Being.* Podcast audio. January 7, 2021. https://onbeing.org/programs/frank-wilczek-beauty-as-a-compass-for-truth/.

Wordsworth, William. "The Tables Turned," *The Poetry Foundation.* Accessed January 20, 2021. https://www.poetryfoundation.org/poems/45557/the-tables-turned.

Further Reading

Diaz-Waian, Marisa. "Navigating the Wakes of Loss: How Philosophy Can Help Us Grieve." *International Journal of Applied Philosophy* 28:1 (2014): 19-48.

Dudok de Wit, Michaël. "Father and Daughter." *CinéTé and Cloudrunner* short film on YouTube video, 9:22. March 3, 2013. https://youtu.be/CvA4Gn5OudI.

Kenyon, Erik, Diane Terorde-Doyle., and Sharon Carnahan. *Ethics for the Very Young: A Philosophy Curriculum for Early Childhood Education.* Lanham, MD: Rowman and Littlefield, 2019.

Nehamas, Alexander. *The Art of Living: Socratic Reflections from Plato to Foucault.* Berkeley, CA; Los Angeles, CA: University of California Press, 1998.

Patrick Eudaily, Seán. "The Right to (a Public) Philosophy: Renewing the Civic Purposes of Democratic Justice and Responsibility in the Post-Secondary Public Education "to Come."" *The Good Society* 14, no. 3 (2005): 24-28.

Philosophy as a Way of Life. "Homepage." Notre Dame University and The Andrew W. Mellon Foundation. Accessed January 3, 2021. https://philife.nd.edu/.

Prison Ethics Bowl. "Homepage." *The Center for Public Philosophy.* Accessed January 28, 2021. https://publicphilosophy.ucsc.edu/philosophy-inside/.

Prison University Project. "Homepage." Mount Tamalpais College. Accessed January 28, 2021. https://www.mttamcollege.org.

Wyoming Pathways to Prison Program. "Homepage." *University of Wyoming.* Accessed January 28, 2021. http://www.uwyo.edu/gwst/wpfp/.

Supplementary Materials

All activities or resources from the Merlin website that are referenced in this chapter are included below by activity grouping.

Big Ideas by Little Philosophers (BiLP)

- https://merlinccc.org/big-ideas-by-little-philosophers-bilp-archive/big-ideas-little-philosophers-spring-2019-2/.
- https://merlinccc.org/big-ideas-by-little-philosophers-bilp-archive/big-ideas-by-little-philosophers-bilp-summer-2019/.
- https://merlinccc.org/big-ideas-by-little-philosophers-bilp-archive/big-ideas-by-little-philosophers-bilp-fall-2019/.
- https://merlinccc.org/big-ideas-by-little-philosophers-bilp-archive/big-ideas-by-little-philosophers-bilp-winter-2019-2020/.

Halloween Hayride-Philosophy Walks for Youth

- https://merlinccc.org/merlin-philosophy-walks-archive/october-2017-halloween-themed-little-philosophers-walk-exploring-world-through-senses/.
- https://merlinccc.org/merlin-philosophy-walks-archive/october-2016-little-philosophers-walk/.
- https://merlinccc.org/merlin-philosophy-walks-archive/october-2019-halloween-planet-hopping-star-walking/.
- https://merlinccc.org/merlin-philosophy-walks-archive/october-2018-halloween-themed-little-philosophers-walk-what-is-it-like-to-be-a-bat/.

Philosophy Community Endeavors

- https://merlinccc.org/conferences-and-events/helena-community-endeavors/.
- https://merlinccc.org/category/merlin-community-endeavors-archive/.

Philosophy Drive-In's

- https://merlinccc.org/category/merlin-drive-in-archive/.

Philosophy Night School

- https://merlinccc.org/philosophy-night-school/.

Philosophy Symposiums

- https://merlinccc.org/lecture-library/2018-philosophy-forums-and-roundtables-environment-ethics-stewardship-part-1-archive/.
- https://merlinccc.org/lecture-library/2018-philosophy-forums-and-roundtables-environment-ethics-stewardship-part-2-archive/.
- https://merlinccc.org/lecture-library/2018-philosophy-forums-and-roundtables-environment-ethics-stewardship-part-3-archive/.

Philosophy Think and Drink Conversations

- https://merlinccc.org/merlin-think-and-drink-archive/august-2018-philosophy-think-drink-moral-dimensions-homelessness/.
- https://merlinccc.org/merlin-think-and-drink-archive/september-2018-philosophy-think-drink-moral-dimensions-homelessness-part-two/.
- https://merlinccc.org/merlin-think-and-drink-archive/october-2018-philosophy-think-drink-moral-dimensions-homelessness-part-three/.

Philosophy Walks

- https://merlinccc.org/category/merlin-philosophy-walks-archive/.
- https://merlinccc.org/merlin-philosophy-walks-archive/june-2020-leisure-loafing/.
- https://merlinccc.org/merlin-philosophy-walks-archive/november-2019-philosophy-walk-humanities-nature/.
- https://merlinccc.org/merlin-philosophy-walks-archive/october-2019-philosophy-walk-story-imagination-across-cultures/.
- https://merlinccc.org/merlin-philosophy-walks-archive/september-2017-philosophy-walk-conservation-preservation-environmental-ethics-fall-series-walk-1/.
- https://merlinccc.org/merlin-philosophy-walks-archive/september-2019-philosophy-walk-virtue-ethics-ecology-ethics/.
- https://merlinccc.org/merlin-philosophy-walks-archive/september-2018-philosophy-walk-environment-ethics-stewardship-fall-series-walk-1/.
- https://merlinccc.org/merlin-philosophy-walks-archive/november-2018-philosophy-walk-environment-ethics-stewardship-fall-series-walk-2/.
- https://merlinccc.org/merlin-philosophy-walks-archive/march-2019-philosophy-walk-environment-ethics-stewardship-fall-series-walk-3/.

Philosophy as a Way of Life

- https://merlinccc.org/resource-center/pwol-philife-public-philosophy-resources/.

Philosophy Workshops

- https://merlinccc.org/category/merlin-workshops-courses-archive/.

Chapter 5
Philosophical Horizons:
P4/WC and Anti-Racism in Memphis, TN

Christian Kronsted

University of Memphis

Jonathan Wurtz

University of Memphis

Abstract

Memphis, Tennessee is the Blackest city with a Philosophy for/with Children (P4/WC) program in the United States, making it a unique site of engagement for practitioners. The city faces deeply historically rooted structural problems that continue to manifest themselves, in housing, food security, hate crimes, police brutality, workplace inequality, and segregation; all of which are present in our classrooms where we practice P4C. In this chapter, we illustrate some of the challenges we have faced while practicing P4/WC in Memphis, and the ways in which these obstacles have transformed the practice and mission of the Philosophical Horizons (PH) outreach program. We have found that many of the methods and assumptions of traditional P4C can sometimes be harmful or alienating to some of our students if not properly reformed.

We here outline the history of our program Philosophical Horizons (PH) and discuss some of the obstacles we have faced teaching in our specific context. We further provide a discussion of why the typical methods and assumptions of P4C do not serve us well in the context of Memphis. Additionally, we describe our own approach to philosophy for/with children and our primary mission within the city as an anti-racist practice. Finally, we discuss two case studies that exemplify some of the dynamics that we outline in this chapter.

Keywords: Philosophical Horizons, Philosophy for/with Children, Anti-racism, Community of Inquiry, Memphis

***

In this chapter, we want to illustrate some of the challenges we have faced doing Philosophy for/with children (P4/WC) in Memphis, Tennessee, as well as the ways in which these obstacles have transformed our practice and mission. From our research, Memphis is statistically the blackest city with a P4/WC program in the United States, making it a unique site of engagement for practitioners. The city faces deep historically rooted structural problems that continue to manifest themselves in avenues like housing, food security, hate crimes, police brutality, workplace inequality, segregation, all of which are present in our classrooms. Consequently, as practitioners of philosophy for/with children in non-traditional P4C environments, we simply cannot Socratize as usual. In fact, we find that many of the methods and assumptions of traditional P4C can sometimes be harmful or alienating to our students if not properly reformed.

Given the lack of resources that we have encountered, we hope that this essay can serve as a steppingstone for other P4/WC practitioners who wish to start programs in cities that are relevantly similar to Memphis. At the same time, we also want to encourage practitioners who do not practice in majority-minority cities to reflect on the ways their organization may face similar challenges or reaffirm harmful norms.

We here outline the history of our program Philosophical Horizons (PH) and discuss some of the obstacles we have faced teaching in our specific context. We further provide a discussion of why the typical methods and assumptions of P4C do not serve us well in the context of Memphis, TN. Additionally, we describe both the theoretical and practical moves that we have had to make to transform philosophy for/with children into an anti-racist practice. We then end with a discussion of two case studies that exemplify some of the dynamics that we will be outlining below.

Philosophical Horizons–A Short History

Since its inception in 2008, racial diversity, intellectual plurality, and social justice have been at the core of Philosophical Horizons' identity. Indeed, early in its life, PH would specifically define itself around the racial diversity of Memphis, TN, and the intellectual plurality of its philosophy department. As Dr. Deborah Tollefsen and Dr. Bill Lawson write in a 2008 grant proposal for the Tennessee Board of Regent (TBR), their goal was "to recruit qualified students from underrepresented groups to TBR schools and provide students with the skills they need to succeed in the college classroom" (Tollefsen and Lawson 2008). Memphis is not only the city with the largest percentage African American population in Tennessee but also the 10th city in the US with the highest percentage of African Americans with 64.2% of the total 651,073 people living in Memphis (US Census, 2019). It, therefore, makes sense that the program would emphasize questions of race when defining its own boundaries and goals. These are simply unavoidable for us.

Race and racism are an inescapable element of Memphis' historical and contemporary identity. Our students come face to face with them on a daily basis, not merely because the majority of them are not White, but also because the city itself is a significant site of racial injustice and civil rights advocacy, dating all the way back to post-civil war USA. From places like Beale Street to historical events like Martin Luther King Jr's assassination, the streets of Memphis are marked by a long racial-laden history. Consequently, questions about race and racism inevitably become a major part of our sessions since they partly contribute to our student's (and our) everyday experience as Memphians. As our first program coordinator Dr. Michael D. Burroughs recalls during his time with Hickory Ridge Middle School students (in which roughly 80% of students are African-American):

> There are differences between myself and group members at Hickory Ridge—in age, race, and socio-economic background to name a few. But it is a virtue of philosophical engagement as open space that these differences can be considered without determining the limits of our discussion before we start. Thus, differences which have played a large role in the historical and contemporary social climate of Memphis (such as race and social class) are discussed in our group at Hickory Ridge. We discuss the experience of racism; we explore what it means to respond to bigotry as a child and as an adult. We have had and continue to have different life experiences—I have not been a frequent victim of racism, nor do I see the world as a child—but when taken seriously in philosophical engagement we give the child a space to share her privileged perspective. (Burroughs 2009, 10-11)

As part of our mission, PH believes that it is critical to examine the nature and value of Western philosophy; especially considering that we are teaching P4/WC in a majority Black city. We did not start PH because we believe philosophy is valuable in itself. Rather, there is a specific niche for the program to fill in Memphis. Part of the reason for starting this program was to help mitigate the pedagogical deficits our public education system is experiencing. In 2008 Memphis began defunding its public schools (Baker 2008). Simultaneously, Memphis had an "under 18" poverty rate of above 35% (Delavega 2017) and suffered from widespread segregation—especially in its public schools where Black students typically make up close to 90% of the classroom (Kiel 2008). Combined with the consequences of test-based culture, Memphis public schools—especially those that serve underrepresented minorities—lacked both the time and support to emphasize "the development of critical thinking and analytic skills that allow one to formulate positions with clarity, precision, and

depth and to critically and respectfully evaluate the positions offered by others'"
(Tollefsen and Lawson, 2008). One of the first High Schools PH worked with after
receiving the TBR grant was Booker T. Washington High School. The program
would specifically help underrepresented youth enroll in college by offering
philosophy classes for college credit. The graduation rate of Booker T.
Washington High School in 2008 was approximately 55% but jumped to 82% by
2011. Furthermore, the number of students going to college also increased from
7% to 70% in the same amount of time. Both of these facts won the school the
"Race to the Top" challenge and prompted then-President Obama to give a
commencement speech to the graduating class that same year. Obviously, we are
not claiming that PH is solely responsible for this increase, but that one of the
program's priorities was to help underserved and underrepresented students
graduate and enter college. There was a clear need for philosophical dialogue in
Memphis' educational infrastructure. The department of philosophy merely did
its part in alleviating the pedagogical stresses faced by the city. Simply put, for PH,
the value of public philosophy has always originated from the communities
within which it is practiced. In Memphis, this meant, and still means, recognizing
the implicit racial structures that condition our everyday.

Today, Philosophical Horizons continues to uphold its commitments to
helping underserved and underrepresented pre-college students in the
Memphis area. But over the last twelve years of operations, many things have
changed. For example, we are no longer funded by grants, and an unexpected
loss of faculty meant that extra-curricular activities could no longer be
prioritized to the same extent by the department. For these reasons, over the
last three years, PH has increasingly become student-driven. As a P4/WC
program, this means that outreach, lesson planning, ordering of new materials,
putting together games and activities are all done exclusively by graduate
students (on top of their regular responsibilities). Furthermore, due to the lack
of funding, the program is also mainly "funded" by graduate students. From
books to transportation, the program runs thanks to the dedication and
initiative of our graduate community. While we are striving for high levels of
professionalism, our success is largely dependent on graduate students
believing in the value of our mission and the value of P4/WC. As a result, we are
currently less equipped to help underrepresented pre-college students become
college-ready than we used to be.

This shift in the program's infrastructure, however, has pushed us to look at
other needs that P4/WC could address in the Memphis youth community. While
we still seek to help underrepresented students become college-ready, we have
also realized that college is often a non-reality for many of our students. College
can mean entering into debt, balancing a full-time job on top of schoolwork,
having to find childcare, or it can be an impossibility due to a lack of resources or

uncared for learning disabilities. This is further demonstrated by the fact that only around one in two high school students (57% on average between 2014 and 2017) in Memphis will enter into a higher institution of learning (Anderson et al., 2016; Anderson et al. 2017, Anderson et al. 2018). As a result, PH has since broadened its horizons and mission. While we still hope to help our students enroll in post-secondary education, our practice and curriculum is now mainly informed by our attempt to epistemically empower underrepresented minority youth in Memphis.

To this end, Philosophical Horizons is currently made up of seven graduate student volunteers and one faculty advisor, and we are working with three different institutions in the Memphis area: Leadership Preparatory Charter School, The University of Memphis Campus School, and Memphis Rox Climbing Gym. On average, we hold four sessions a week across our three partner institutions. We typically hold sessions with anywhere between five to fifteen students, and two facilitators. This is done for contingency reasons (in case one of the volunteers cannot make it to a scheduled session) and to help get the discussion rolling with multiple perspectives. This is also done to pair less experienced volunteers with more veteran practitioners. Every semester we also train new volunteers by holding mock P4/WC sessions where experienced grad students act as the children and new volunteers lead the sessions. Additionally, we also hold a meeting at the beginning of every academic year where we explain the philosophical background, mission, and style of the program.

On the more institutional side of the program, PH has also become a registered student organization with The University of Memphis which has opened access to funding and institutional support for the program. This also means that some of our program volunteers take on leadership roles with the university, which include two co-coordinators, one secretary, and one treasurer. Finally, while we have a general curriculum available for all our volunteers, most of our facilitators work with their students in real-time to create their syllabi. For example, if students are particularly interested in questions of justice, then our volunteers are encouraged to plan accordingly rather than following the planned curriculum.

The Limits of P4C for a Critical Discussion of Race and Racism

Like most other P4C programs, PH was inspired by Mathew Lipman's work in the '60s and '70s. One particular idea that originated in Lipman's philosophy and continues to inform the majority of P4/WC practice today is the idea of a Community of Inquiry (CI). This is not a new idea, and in fact, most P4/WC practitioners in the US and Europe will have some familiarity with the concept. However, one of our biggest challenges here in Memphis has been to re-adapt and rethink traditional P4/WC teaching practices for our audience. For while the CI has been an immensely influential idea, it can also be risky and potentially alienating to our own community members. Furthermore, very little exists in terms of P4/WC literature that offers exercises and strategies specifically designed to address problematic racial dynamics, either philosophically speaking or in our practice as facilitators. Race and racism are, in fact, often depicted as "no go areas" because of the sense of discomfort, and tension, these concepts tend to bring with them (Chetty and Suissa 2016). However, as pointed out above, these questions are unavoidable for us. As a result, P4/WC practitioners in Memphis can often find themselves lost and unprepared to deal with the needs of our pre-college students (at least when they first begin). This is not to say that the P4/WC literature has not been useful or productive for us. But rather that the lack of lesson plans and teaching strategies with regards to race and racism has left a hole for PH to fill in for itself.

Before proceeding to the philosophical background of Philosophical Horizons, we, therefore, want to start by highlighting how the CI, while being particularly important for P4C programs across the world, has fallen short of expectation here in Memphis. For Lipman, philosophy for children has a very specific goal; to produce critical thinkers. In other words, it is meant to create individuals who can protect themselves "from being coerced or brainwashed into believing what others want us to believe without our having an opportunity to inquire for ourselves" (Lipman 2003, 47). Thus, P4C is seen as a sort of "defensive" training regimen for children's minds, and the CI is the means through which a society can create such critical thinkers. According to Lipman, such a community is defined by features like: "Inclusion," "participation," "shared cognition," "a quest for meaning," "feelings of social solidarity," "deliberation," "impartiality," "modeling," "thinking for one self," "challenging as a procedure," "reasonableness," "reading," "questioning," and "discussing" (Ibid., 95-100). Let us take a closer look at three specific features—reasonableness, impartiality, and feelings of social solidarity—of the CI so that we can see how they can fail us in minority-majority classrooms.

For Lipman, reasonableness is a "fundamental" element of any CI (Ibid., 97). It refers to both the capacity to employ reason in one's own thought and the ways in which one is acted upon by others. In other words, a reasonable person not only uses reason to think about how they act in the community but also uses rational thinking to actively listen to other's arguments. A reasonable community of inquirers is, therefore, largely conditioned by the relative reasonableness of its participants; it assumes that everyone in the community is similarly reasonable. And as such, it entails that one cannot practice P4C with unreasonable people or address unreasonable topics. While this may not be an issue in itself, it becomes clearly problematic when we are asked to delineate the boundaries of reasonableness. For example, when Christian taught the prisoner's dilemma to a classroom of African American students in Chicago, no one in his group rationalized the same conclusion that the traditional western game theory model predicts. When asked why the students did not vote in their own rational self-interest they responded, "It's Chicago, ... we don't snitch!"

In the history of western philosophy, questions regarding race have often been cast as unreasonable or not philosophically relevant. This is, in fact, a common occurrence that we still find today, for example, in defenders of Kant, Hegel, or Heidegger who argue that their views on race do not have any effect or relationship to their philosophy. Even to this day, many philosophers hold and affirm the idea that "race is not philosophically interesting – whereas 'differences is'" (Chetty 2018, 11). A point which is too often echoed by P4/WC curriculums and teaching manuals. But when the race is seen as unreasonable and non-philosophical, then questions of race and racism that so many of *our* students desperately want to discuss fall outside the scope of P4/WC. Consequently, students, like the ones from Hickory Ridge Middle school or Christian's session in Chicago, must also be considered unreasonable or unphilosophical.

In Memphis, however, race is always in the background, and our students often racialize non-racialized discussions and exercises. What this entails, according to the normative epistemic norm of P4C, is that our students cannot form a community of inquiry as long as race is a prominent (unreasonable) element of their thinking. If we want to cultivate a community of inquirers a la Lipman, our only solution would be to hold "color blind" sessions that actively erase questions regarding race and racism. However, by making race a non-topic, or philosophically uninteresting one, we are also reaffirming certain racist norms. As Daren Chetty further elaborates:

> In a classroom where children are engaged in a philosophical inquiry structured by norms of 'reasonableness', the constitution of certain contributions as 'unreasonable' may serve to exclude perspectives offered by pupils from racialised minorities, and in so doing, to both mask and perpetuate racialised structures of domination. (Ibid., 12)

As a result, it is clear that using the criteria of reasonableness–especially as it is defined by much of canonical western philosophy–can constitute a very legitimate harm to our students by silencing them and managing their thinking. This is especially the case when reasonableness hides its own normative assumptions behind the concept of impartiality.

For Lipman, impartiality represents the CI's capacity to investigate a question by accounting for all different "considerations and points of view, as well as the interests of everyone" (Ibid., 96). Impartiality assumes that all members of the

CI are equally invulnerable to inquiry. However, considering all points of view often means that those students whose situation is the most precarious can become the intellectual petri dish of more privileged students or facilitators. For example, in one of our sessions at the University of Memphis' Campus School (a White majority school), a Black student shared that they were adopted; at which point a White student jumped at the opportunity to *interrogate* the Black student about why they didn't have biological parents. So, while P4C is meant as a form of intellectual "defense" training, not everyone is in the same starting position to come out of sparring without injury. Teaching P4/WC in a city like Memphis means that volatile topics will quickly come up in discussions. However, the impartiality approach can quickly lead to the most precarious of our students having to put their life experiences on display for all to scrutinize. Needless to say, not only can this be an invasive practice, but also one that compounds the harm of everyday racism they already experience. This is not just an issue that practitioners in Black majority cities face, of course, but something that anyone working with underrepresented and underserved youth will have to face. For example, Hell Rainville, who works with indigenous peoples in Canada, describes how she worries "that our purportedly neutral approach to philosophical inquiry may unwittingly contribute to the marginalization of Indigenous peoples in North America and around the world" (Rainville 2000, 67). As a result, while we cannot stay silent on these topics, their very nature can lead to harmful and/or even triggering situations. This means that, as practitioners, we cannot remain agnostic/impartial in how we address these situations without becoming "the best ally of the status quo" (Kohan 1995, 30). If impartiality means openness to all points of view, then, in order to mitigate the harm that can occur in these classrooms from both students and instructors, we cannot remain impartial. On the contrary, we must take great precautions to recognize the history of oppression that is acting in the background and lead our sessions accordingly. We must become knowledgeable of the community within which we are practicing and use this knowledge to help us direct our sessions.[1]

Finally, feelings of social solidarity represent a kind of "friendship" between all the members of the community. The CI is, in other words, supposed to be a classroom in which everyone sees each other as a person worth caring for and listening to. It is supposed to express the sense that everyone is in this together. However, what does social solidarity look like in a segregated space of control

[1] For an excellent example of this being done with Latinx students see Chávez Leyva Yolanda, and Amy Reed-Sandoval. 2016. "Philosophy for Children and the Legacy of Anti-Mexican Discrimination in El Paso Schools." *APA Newsletter on Hispanic/Latino Issues in Philosophy* 16, no.1: 17–22.

and discipline like a Memphis classroom? Especially solidarity between young Black students and older White authorities? There is an entire history undermining social solidarity between P4/WC practitioners and their Memphian students—from the history of race and racism in Memphis to western philosophers' tendency to white-wash philosophical thinking. This is not to say that it is impossible, but that for us, social solidarity cannot be a feature of our CI by virtue of these very specific socio-historical conditions. It is presumptuous to think that we can begin from a point of solidarity in such a deeply racialized space. Especially since graduate student volunteers come and go, and that most of them come from outside Memphis. As a result, rather than a feature, cultivating feelings of social solidarity is a goal of our community of inquiry. Echoing what was said earlier, PH is primarily interested in producing and practicing pedagogical strategies and exercises that can overcome some of these racial barriers—both in the city itself and the field.

So it is clear from what has been said so far that the CI, as presented by Lipman and many contemporary P4C practitioners, does not properly fit our needs, and in fact may be more harmful than beneficial in some cases. In the next section, we address some of the theoretical and practical moves we have made to create spaces conducive to philosophical dialogue in Memphis, TN.

Philosophy for/with Children as a Force for Anti-Racism in Memphis, TN

While we share sympathies with P4C, the ingrained systemic racism that permeates through Memphis, TN, means that we had to go beyond P4C's mission, methodology, and philosophy to properly address the needs of our community. This means that as a P4/WC program, we are not, strictly speaking, in the business of creating critical thinkers. While it may be a by-product of our practice, the majority of our members mainly see Philosophical Horizons as a platform for promoting and cultivating racial justice by exposing underrepresented and underserved minority students to the practice of philosophical thinking and questioning. Some of the time, this does mean helping our students develop the skills required for a successful college career, like critical thinking or analytic reasoning. However, more often than not, it means operating as a platform from within which Memphis youth can have a space to address their most existentially pressing questions and worries. As our second program coordinator, Dr. John Torrey, put it: "Particularly for underserved and underrepresented minorities that are not given access to this kind of engagement, being exposed to different ways of describing and analyzing one's self and one's relation to the world can be invaluable" (Torrey 2020, 408). It is invaluable because it exposes "them to alternative ways of processing and describing their world [which] gives them more chances to be able to speak" (Ibid., 409). Our approach, in other words, allows underserved students to do "introspective work about who [they] are as individuals and as part of a community," and provides them with "a language and a set of theoretical tools to engage our communities and try to make them the best that we can" (Ibid.).

This aspect of the program makes PH more akin to Philosophy *with* Children (PwC) programs than P4C:

Now philosophy *for* children becomes philosophy *with* children. The change in the preposition is an important index of difference: it betokens a still greater emphasis on dialogue as fundamental and indispensable to the pedagogy of philosophy, which is no longer understood as the modelling and coaching of an ideal of analytical reason, but as what generates communal reflection, contemplation and communication. (Vansieleghem and Kennedy 2011, 178)

To do philosophy *with* children rather than philosophy *for* children means focusing less on the analytic and democratic goals established by Lipman, and more on the existentially pressing issues that children and teenagers want to address but find no space within which to do so. Rather than dictating to our students what counts as philosophical or not, we simply derive our inquiries from their own experience. In other words, to facilitate fruitful philosophical discussion, we try not to steer our students towards the topics we find "philosophical." We rather try to emphasize what our students find meaningful to pursue. From our experience, our students are mainly preoccupied with questions concerning the metaphysical nature of race, the dynamics of racism, religious metaphysics, religious hermeneutics, as well as the nature of morality, and justice. All of which, as discussed above, are deeply entrenched topics in the city's history. Most of our students are Black, religious, have experienced racism, know about MLK Jr. and the civil rights movement, and have been affected by the high crime rate and systemic discrimination of the city. It is, therefore, understandable that these are the kinds of questions our students raise when given the opportunity to philosophize.

In this sense, we see PH as fulfilling an important role for Memphis youth, especially with regards to how they come to make sense of themselves, others, and the world. It is a program from within which our underrepresented and underserved students can gain epistemic recognition as knowers and thinkers. PH aims to expand their epistemic tool bag, and affirm their epistemic agency. It is important, however, to emphasize that we are not counselors, nor are we psychiatrists; we are philosophers. We are not attempting to console students or guide them in any normative direction. That is not our job. As philosophers, we are engaging with other philosophical minds who have questions and seek answers. Our task is to offer our students a platform within which they can practice "philosophizing," and ask their most existentially pressing questions.

Part of doing this work in a city like Memphis requires that, rather than being impartial teachers, we become culturally responsive teachers. As Burroughs and Jana Mohr Lone put it, culturally responsive teaching involves:

1. Developing a knowledge base about cultural diversity, which includes understanding the cultural characteristics of various ethnic groups;
2. Designing culturally relevant curricula;
3. Building a learning community conducive to learning for diverse students;
4. Accommodation of the communication styles of different ethnic groups by developing classroom interactions that reflect these styles; and
5. Providing a wide range of instructional strategies to meet the needs of a diverse student body (Gay, 2002, 106–14). (Burroughs and Lone 2016, 213)

To promote a culturally responsive form of teaching, we not only have become versed in the history of Memphis, but our program also approaches philosophy with children as a pluralistic, intersectional, and immanent practice. By pluralistic, we mean that philosophy is not, in itself, enough to inspire philosophical thinking and dialogue. We take it for granted that the best philosophical practices are complemented by other disciplines like history, religious studies, sociology, politics, biology, psychology, cognitive science, physics, and many others. In this sense, being knowledgeable of philosophy is only a part of doing philosophy for/with children. Secondly, insofar as PH's mission is to mitigate racial structural norms through epistemic empowerment, it approaches philosophical dialogue with special attention to our student's identities as well as that of its facilitator. We do not believe that we can create a philosophically productive space of dialogue without being aware of who is practicing philosophy and where they are practicing it. Finally, by immanent, we mean that what we consider to be philosophically rich and interesting is directly derived from the material conditions from within which we are operating. As we have stated above, we find that the value of philosophy comes directly from the community which it serves. Consequently, we view philosophical insights and truth as emerging out of the concrete lived experiences and struggles of philosophical thinkers rather than some transcendental ideal.

These are skills that all our graduate student facilitators come to learn by virtue of our pluralistic department, our diverse graduate student population, and our involvement in the city. We are lucky enough that our philosophy department has been a power-house in diversifying the profession. We not only have a diverse faculty and student body (at least compared to the rest of the US), but a departmental culture that pushes for pluralistic and intersectional thinking as well. Just like our pre-college students cannot avoid issues of race and racism, the graduate students in the department of philosophy at The University of Memphis cannot avoid thinking about the racial dimensions of their own research. This does not mean that every philosopher graduating from our department is automatically a critical race theorist. However, Memphis has a particular intellectual style and reputation that we use to our advantage. Even grad students working on metaphysics and mathematics come to better understand issues around racism and social justice.

From all that has been said above, PH is a P4/WC program committed to mitigating the racial power dynamics that our students are subject to on a daily basis. We not only try to give them space within which they can practice thinking about themselves, others, and the world, but one where they can also be recognized as epistemic agents. However, one of the difficulties we face in this commitment is the fact that most P4/WC practices are intended to be used in *classroom* settings. Schools are so laden with power dynamics that it is impossible for students to express their own views and experiences free from the gaze of authority figures. This is especially important when we highlight strategies used to discipline and regulate Black bodies. For example, many schools employ police officers who propagate the school-to-prison pipeline or implement dress codes that specifically disallows non-White aesthetics. But these elements are not only alienating but counterproductive to PH's mission. As Burroughs and Lone argue:

> To ensure that every child's approach to philosophical thinking is valued requires a clear awareness of the dangers of setting up any "voice of authority" (whether that voice be adult, White, male, middle class, etc.) that can shut down a student's ability to be heard and/or inhibit a student's willingness to express honestly his or her point of view. Educational institutions often mirror the power dynamics of the larger society, and it is imperative that part of philosophical inquiry includes questioning those dynamics and the perspectives of those who benefit from them.
>
> Children's questions and ideas can be powerful opening points for examining issues of race, class, gender, ethnicity, and political and social inequalities. Too often, the adults in their lives are uncomfortable having such exchanges, and end up shutting down children when they initiate these exchanges. (Ibid., 210)

To mitigate the obstacles and potential harms that come with a classroom setting, PH has had to reach beyond schools and into less official and regulated spaces. As a result, in 2018, we partnered with the nonprofit rock-climbing gym and community center Memphis Rox. Memphis Rox is a unique space from within which to practice P4/WC because of how different it is from a typical classroom. First and foremost, our students are not mandated to be in a session, nor are they required to stay for the whole time. It may be the case that they drift in and out during the hour-long period we typically get with them. This also means that students come to our sessions entirely of their own volition. We have to convince them that this is something they want to do and want to keep doing, which is a hard sell when there is an entire rock-climbing gym to compete with. Secondly, our students do not uphold the same "classroom etiquette" that we typically see in school settings. There are no teachers, grades, security guards, principals, or permanent files acting as disciplinary mechanisms. The gym membership itself is on a donation basis and so entirely open to the public. Hence while the gym does have a code of conduct and some authority figures, it is significantly less of a disciplinary space than the public-school classroom. As part of our next section will highlight, this shift outside the classroom has resulted in some very unique and engaging philosophical discussions.

Two on the Ground Cases from Memphis

While this essay has not provided a clear-cut teaching manual for practicing P4/WC in majority-minority cities, we would like to end our discussion with two recent insightful anecdotes. We hope that these cases can at least provide some context as to what practitioners can expect in a pedagogical environment like Memphis. The first story details Jonathan's first day at Memphis Rox and highlights the differences between practicing P4/WC in classroom and non-classroom settings. The second story details one of Christian's sessions in which the underlying racial dynamics of the city suddenly emerged. Together, we hope that these two examples will illustrate the theoretical points argued above.

First Day at Memphis Rox

Jonathan's first day at Memphis Rox perfectly demonstrates the limits of traditional P4C practice in upholding PH's anti-racist commitments. From the moment Jonathan stepped into the gym, it was clear that this would not be like any other classroom experience. First, they had to recruit their own students rather than having a classroom ready to philosophize. Furthermore, the program had not been particularly well advertised. In fact, the only advertisement was a small print-out mentioning philosophy drowning between other flashier advertisements on a large board at the entrance. As a result, Jonathan had to go around and ask students to join, which, at first, they were fairly unsuccessful at.

As discussed above, being an unfamiliar White adult entering into a majority African American space meant that social solidarity remained to be established. Thankfully, the gym manager, who was obviously a lot more acquainted with the students, was able to pull in roughly seven students between the ages of 13 to 17.

Jonathan then made their way to a room in the back of the gym where the newly recruited students were now hanging out. The room itself was fairly spacious and had a big glass wall separating it from the rest of the facility. This meant that the student could see what was happening outside and did not *have* to focus on philosophy. For example, sometimes, other students would show up looking for their friends. At other times, students had to leave in the middle of a session because their parents had arrived to pick them up. There were no clear boundaries or restrictions between the room and the rest of the gym. This marked the second major difference from a typical classroom session. There was nothing tying the students to the session. The students had to come to us and come back every single week for these to be more than just a taste of philosophy. The classroom makes it easy for practitioners since students are essentially "forced" to attend. However, at Memphis Rox, no one forced our students to attend or participate. If they showed up, it was because they wanted to be there and had a thirst for philosophical inquiry. Those that did not want to be there would either leave in the middle of the session or start another activity with their friends in the same room. We can see already how the dynamics in such a space are radically different from those practitioners typically encounter in a classroom. Students had more power to self-determine and greater freedom of movement than they would ever be allowed to have in a school environment.

The benefits of this unique environment for practicing P4/WC became evidently clear on the first day. For as soon as Jonathan was about to open the door, a Black female student excitedly opened it for them and asked, "are you the philosopher?!" to which they promptly replied, "that's me!" Hearing their response, she looked at them very seriously and asked, "Why do Black people believe in Christianity when Christianity was used to enslave Black people?" While Jonathan had already prepared a lesson plan for the day talking about distributive justice, they were suddenly thrown into a new topic of conversation. One that couldn't be passed over, at least not without some undesirable consequences. The session, therefore, proceeded with this young Black woman's question and other students began to chime in, asking their own questions about the bible and their own identity: how much should they live by it? Is it harmful or useful for them? Where do they fit in this ideological system? Furthermore, the students did not merely ask questions but also took the time to lay out some of the bible's arguments, pointing to inconsistencies, outdated norms, and epistemic gaps. The session had now been changed to an inquiry about blackness and its relationship to Christianity, and Jonathan was a new resource they could use to explore these topics.

There is a lot that we could unpack from this one encounter, but it will be more useful to focus on two elements that specifically highlight some of the insights discussed above. First and foremost, these kinds of questions typically would not have shown up in a traditional classroom, and especially not with such determination. This is primarily because the US's liberal constitution (specifically the first amendment) prevents public institutions from promoting a particular set of moral norms. As such, public school teachers cannot really tackle questions of religion and identity without the possibility of summoning either the wrath of parents or administrators—something which PH also fears and therefore why its members typically avoid religious topics in general. However, the lack of disciplinary measures combined with the freedom experienced by the students meant that they could ask questions that well-meaning liberal Christian teachers or even P4/WC volunteers in Memphis often suppress. In fact, while Jonathan had years of experience teaching P4/WC in Memphis, they had yet to encounter such an explicit question, let alone of the first day. It was clear from the beginning that these students were much more comfortable and open to philosophical dialogue than students in the classroom would be. This was further proved by the fact that they were the ones to take charge of the session. They did not allow Jonathan to ever mention distributive justice; they had questions, and they wanted to use this space to think about and discuss them. Without really knowing what philosophy was and without the facilitator's guidance, they had created a rich and insightful space of philosophical inquiry in the first couple of minutes.

Secondly, it is important to note that the session was not only about learning and practicing philosophical conversation. In fact, the students seemed to care very little about "philosophy" at first. What was important to them was what this philosophy session *allowed them to do*. While we do not know what exactly they thought philosophy was, or how the gym manager got them interested in it; there are two things that Jonathan recognized from the beginning. First, this was a space within which these high schoolers could practice and affirm their epistemic agency. Second, this was a space in which the students could become involved in the production of their own subjectivities. In other words, the students were driving the session with questions that mattered to them, and in doing so, began to formulate an understanding of themselves in relation to their community, history, and world.

As articulated by Torrey (2020), part of the value of public philosophy's in a majority-minority city comes from its capacity to provide a platform within which underserved and underrepresented groups can practice introspection, dialogue, and argumentation. The students at Memphis Rox were already eager to engage in this kind of practice. Unfortunately, due to the racial (and sexual) systemic inequities that continue to flourish in the contemporary United States, much of Memphis' youth will most likely never be given an opportunity to practice these skills in a philosophical fashion. Even in classrooms where P4C sessions are taking place, disciplinary mechanisms and racial norms mean that students are never really given the capacity to enact their epistemic agency, and by extent, participate in their own subject production. There is always a higher authority that can, at some point, undermine or veto student's choices. But Memphis Rox, however, was a different kind of place in which the student could disclose their questions without fear of rejection or discipline. If anything, it was Jonathan who was constantly being evaluated by the students.

Some Parents Don't Love Their Kids, and I Bet That Woman Was White

When teaching at the Campus School, Christian led a session on rights and how they frequently clash with moral intuitions. As part of the session, Christian had prepared a story of a boy who buys a basketball but leaves it behind for all to play with at the community court. The boy simply forgets his ball after playing with it, and after six weeks, it is now a de facto community ball. However, one day the boy suddenly remembered his basketball went back to the court to reclaim it at the expense of the community.

At first, the story produced the expected result, a discussion regarding rights, ownership, and community. However, the proposed solution to the problem seemed to be split down racial lines. Overwhelmingly the White students *assumed* that the boy had "worked *very* hard to earn money for the ball" and therefore had the right to reclaim it. As a young girl said quite explicitly: "He probably worked really hard for that ball. Do you know how many allowances it takes for me to afford a basketball?" In contrast, the students of color in the room tended to fall into a shared or cooperative solution such as "taking turns having the ball at home and at the court," thus prioritizing the community over the rights of the individual. Already at this juncture in the story, we see how the idea of the CI being a space of solidarity is endangered by the fault lines that students bring with them into the classroom from the outside world. This was made even more apparent when one of the White students admitted that "My dad says that if you want something, you just have to work for it."

Next, Christian told the students of a real-life example from his own country that was much like the story of the boy with the ball. A rich woman, who was a local religious leader in his hometown, bought a property in the middle of the city and "forgot about it." Over the years, the abandoned property became a community center and shelter inhabited and run by youth. However, one day the "rich woman" realized that she suddenly wanted the building back and decided to tear it down. Christian asked the students to consider if their opinions were the same in this case as the case with the boy and his basketball. Since the two cases were very similar structurally speaking, Christian had hoped that the students would use a method of comparison.

However, here the conversation took an unexpected turn. A Black student asked "Was that lady White? I bet she was White!" Almost simultaneously, a White student said, "Why were those young people living there? Is it because so many parents don't love their kids?" all the while intensely looking at a Black student. These questions were also accompanied by comments such as "If they [the young people] are not staying at home they probably did something to deserve it" and "I think she can do what she wants with the house, it's her house, she paid for it." Not only was the classroom again divided down racial lines regarding the right to property versus human concerns, but many non-White students saw the story as a continuation of trends in their own life. Memphis has a well-known problem of predatory property practices in which White landlords force Black and Brown renters from their homes (Franklel and Keating, 2018; Sells, 2019). Moreover, the White students assumed that the displaced youth in the story were Black or Brown (even though this story took place in Denmark). Coming into the classroom, Christian thought that telling a story taking place in a land "far, far away" would encourage the students to consider the questions more abstractly. He was wrong. Instead, the students took the story as a direct continuation of their reality. A reality deeply rooted in race and class tensions in Memphis.

The student who asked why parents do not love their kids further elaborated by referring to an anecdote with his father explaining why homelessness occurs in American cities. According to him, his father strongly insinuated that parents of color typically do not love their kids (why else would there be homelessness?). As a middle schooler, the student had already been fed the myth that Black and Brown families are dysfunctional, and this assumption operated unchallenged in the student's network of beliefs.

Additionally, the student who suspected that the "rich woman" was White had already internalized the tense history between White women and people of color in the United States. A history of White women being willing to sell out people of color for a seat at the table. Racial tension was certainly on everyone's mind, even in middle school.

The reactions to the story not only took the instructor by surprise; they underscored how early students understand and are subject to volatile topics at the intersections of race and class. Race relations are often expressed both directly and indirectly, as in some of the White student's insistence on property rights trumping human concerns. Further, pervasive myths about ownership, hard work, equality, and entitlement are often ingrained into many of our White students while being directly at odds with the reality of our Black and Brown students. As the story shows, teaching in Memphis means needing to be ready to confront hard truths as they pop up from behind the most seemingly non-volatile stories.

As we discussed above, many of Lipman's criteria for the CI do not work neatly in Memphis classrooms because of the tensions that are ingrained into the history and daily life in the city. Solidarity is not a point from which we can start our discussion because many of our students, young or older, inherit these tensions before they enter the CI. Even in a classroom consisting of generally more well-off children like the one at the Campus School, the fault lines still lurk in the background and present themselves at unpredictable times.

If we do not confront these questions of race and racism as they occur in our classroom, the invisible divide between our students will continue to fester and perhaps grow stronger and become more implicit. One of the realities we have faced teaching in Memphis classrooms is that if we do not address questions of race and racism head-on, we, in turn, do a disservice to our students who want to and need to discuss these questions at a non-abstract level.

Christian's classroom had for a few weeks seemed like it did, in fact, encompass the type of solidarity and friendly impartiality promoted by Lipman. However, continuing forward incidents like the rich lady versus community story made it clear that this was not the case. In fact, having assumed solidarity and impartiality from the beginning, Christian had not foreseen the racialized turn of the discussion. Furthermore, having had already established a practice of impartiality in that specific classroom meant that racialized comments like "I bet she was White" and "so many parents don't love their kids" had to be examined. While examining those assumptions is not in itself a bad thing, in this case, it led to a potentially harmful and alienating environment. As an instructor, the concept of impartiality should have been handled differently to mitigate its potential harms. This is especially so since the Campus School, despite being in Memphis, is one of the most racially segregated schools in the city (Kebede, 2018). As discussed above, Christian had to drastically change his facilitation style in order to both have conversations about race and racism and avoid creating an alienating classroom environment for his Black and Brown students. Teaching in Memphis has taught us many things, amongst them that discussing race and racism with kids is difficult, risky, but deeply important.

Conclusion

What can our experience in Memphis, Tennessee, contribute to other P4/WC programs across the world? Part of the value of our work here in Memphis is that it is in a unique space to practice P4/WC, and as such, we cannot say for certain that our difficulties or strategies can be applied everywhere. In fact, part of our point is that each P4/WC program should build their curriculum with special attention to their local history. So, when Jonathan was met with the question, "why do Black people believe in Christianity when Christianity was used to enslave Black people?" he was better able to navigate the tensions in the question thanks to his local knowledge of Memphis. Jonathan and his students did not only talk about the ways in which Christianity's universalism could easily fall into racist rhetoric but also about how local churches and religious ideology were important platforms during the civil rights movement. Similarly, Christian's anecdote shows us that Memphis students will often racialize particular situations that were racially neutral to begin with. For example, when one of the students asked whether the Danish lady in question was White, his knowledge of the local history allowed him to relate the student's own experience with the thought experiment presented. Rather than saying just yes, he pushed his students to contemplate why they could assume that she was White. It was because he understood the racial dynamics present in the classroom, and the city more broadly speaking, that he could use his student's statement to his advantage.

Secondly, as practitioners of philosophy for/with children, we ought to become knowledgeable of other disciplines so that we can better address our student's questions. Jonathan's knowledge of history, politics, religious studies, and developmental psychology all contributed to his ability to promote a philosophical conversation. As stated above, the students at Memphis did not want to be taught philosophy; they wanted to inquire and think through existentially pressing questions. To properly answer these questions, we need more than just philosophical knowledge. Similarly, to understand the philosophically relevant elements to his student's question, Christian needed to know and understand the history and politics of race and racism, both locally and in the United States. In general, we believe that some of the most fruitful and meaningful philosophical conversations emerge out of discussions that are pluralistic in nature.

Finally, we recommend that P4/WC practitioners, especially those practicing in minority-majority cities, expand beyond the classroom and into less disciplinary spaces. This becomes clear when we compare Christian's anecdote to Jon's. In Christian's case, a school administrator (a White woman) was sitting in the back of the room doing paperwork, silently monitoring the conversation. In that conversation, Christian wanted to acknowledge the student's distrust of White women given the extremely contentious history between White women and Black people in Memphis and the United States. However, given the disciplinary nature of the space, he was reluctant to validate the student's experience. Many parents and school officials are often under the impression that schools are not spaces to address such controversial topics. In contrast, at Memphis Rox, Jonathan had the freedom to fully explore the racial tensions of the questions he received without the looming presence of disciplinary power. If the students (or their parents) didn't like what was discussed, they didn't have to come back. If we want to address topics as complex and controversial as race and racism in P4/WC sessions, it is important that we consider the possibility of also operating outside of the highly disciplinary environments of the school.

Bibliography

Anderson, J., G. Bhagat, A. W. Garrison, A. James-Garner, A. Jordan, J. Lotz., and M. Sell (2017). Destination 2025 Annual Report 2017. Shelby County Schools. https://www.scsk12.org/2025/files/2017/Annual%20Report%202017-18.pdf.

Anderson, J., J. Hester, A. James-Garner, A. Jordan, J. Lotz, M. Sell., and C. Shirley (2018). Destination 2025 Annual Report 2018. Shelby County Schools. http://www.scsk12.org/2025/files/2017/Annual%20Report%202017.pdfBak er, Jackson. 2008. "Council Votes 10-3 to Cut School Funding." Memphis Flyer. June 3, 2008. https://www.memphisflyer.com/TheDailyBuzz/archives/2008/06/03/council-votes-10-3-to-cut-school-funding.

Burroughs, Michael D. 2009. "Reconsidering the Examined Life: Philosophy with Children." 1–13. University of Memphis: https://squirefoundation.org. https://squirefoundation.org/files/2018/10/burroughs_2009.pdf.

Chetty, Darren. 2018. "Racism as 'Reasonableness': Philosophy for Children and the Gated Community of Inquiry." *Ethics and Education* 13 (1): 39–54.

Chetty, Darren., and Judith Suissa. 2016. "'NO GO AREAS' Racism and Discomfort in the Community of Inquiry." In *The Routledge International Handbook of Philosophy for Children*, edited by Karin Murris, Gregory Maugh, and Haynes Joanna, 11–18. Routledge.

Delavega, Maria Elena. 2017. "Memphis Poverty Fact Sheet," 13. University of Memphis: Memphis, TN. https://www.memphis.edu/socialwork/research/2017 povertyfactsheetwebversion.pdf.

Frankel, Todd., and Dan Keating. 2018. "Eviction filings and code complaints: What happened when a private equity firm became one city's biggest homeowner". *The Washington Post.* https://www.washingtonpost.com/business/economy/eviction-filings-and-code-complaints-what-happened-when-a-private-equity-firm-became-one-citys-biggest-homeowner/2018/12/25/99567 8d4-02f3-11e9-b6a9-0aa5c2fcc9e4_story.html.

Kebede, L. F. (2018, November 7). University of Memphis runs the most segregated elementary school in the city. Will its middle school be more diverse? Chalkbeat Tennessee. https://tn.chalkbeat.org/2018/11/7/21106161 /university-of-memphis-runs-the-most-segregated-elementary-school-in-the-city-will-its-middle-school.

Kiel, Daniel. 2008. "Exploded Dream: Desegregation in the Memphis City Schools." *Law and Inequality: A Journal of Theory and Practice* 26 (2): 261–303.

Kohan, Walter O. 1995. "The Origin, Nature and Aim of Philosophy in Relation to Philosophy for Children." *Thinking: The Journal of Philosophy for Children* 12 (2): 25–30.

Lipman, Matthew. 2003. *Thinking in education*. 2 edition. New York: Cambridge University Press.

Lone, Jana Mohr., and Michael D. Burroughs. 2016. *Philosophy in Education: Questioning and Dialogue in Schools*. Rowman and Littlefield.

Rainville, Hell. 2000. "Philosophy for Children in Native America. A Post-Colonial Critique." References.

Sells, Toby. 2019. "Dream Denied: Corporations Buying Up Memphis Homes, Destabilizing Neighborhoods." *The Memphis Flyer*. https://www.memphisflyer.com/memphis/dream-denied-corporations-buying-up-memphis-homesdestabilizing-neighborhoods/Content?oid=21933012 *Analytic Teaching* 21 (1): 65–77.

Tollefsen, Deborah., and Bill Lawson. 2008. "2009-2010 Access and Diversity Grant Application". Tennessee Board of Regents. https://www.plato-philosophy.org/wp-content/uploads/2017/04/Memphis-Pre-College-Philosophy-Access-and-Diversity-Grant-Proposal.pdf.

Torrey, John. 2020. "Reaching Out to the Underrepresented: An Interview with John Torrey." In *The Routledge Handbook of Philosophy of the City*, edited by Joseph S. Biehl and Samantha Noll, 407–11. New York, NY: Routledge Handbooks in Philosophy.

United States Census Bureau. 2019. "U.S. Census Bureau QuickFacts: Memphis City, Tennessee." https://www.census.gov/quickfacts/memphiscitytennessee.

Vansieleghem, Nancy., and David Kennedy. 2011. "What Is Philosophy for Children, What Is Philosophy with Children-After Matthew Lipman?: What Is Philosophy for Children?" *Journal of Philosophy of Education* 45 (2): 171–82.

Yolanda, Chávez., and Amy Reed-Sandoval. 2016. "Philosophy for Children and the Legacy of Anti-Mexican Discrimination in El Paso Schools." APA Newsletter on Hispanic/Latino Issues in Philosophy 16, no.1: 17–22).

Chapter 6

Overcoming Barriers: Pre-college Philosophy Programs in Neoliberalism

Sarah Vitale

Ball State University

Abstract

Through the Philosophy Outreach Project, university students engage in philosophical dialogue with high school students across Indiana. They create resources for students and teachers, host an annual conference, visit students at high schools, and facilitate a weekly philosophy club at a local high school. While the goal of the project is to increase access to philosophy for high school students so they can experience the benefits of philosophical engagement, the project has a significant impact on the college students as well. Most of these students join the project because of a commitment to and belief in the value of philosophy. Through the project, they encounter structural and cultural barriers to their work, and through these encounters, they often develop a critical consciousness. Paolo Freire emphasizes that the goal of the educator or facilitator is to engage in dialogue with the participants, who are members of an oppressed class, such that the oppressed are given a space to identify their own problems and create their own solutions. But because the university students have been a part of the same neoliberal educational system as the high school students with whom they work, they have been subject to many of the same disciplinary mechanisms. Engaging in communities of philosophical inquiry, or following Freire's problem-posing method, they too become conscious of the social and political structures that impact their lived experience. By interviewing former university participants of the Philosophy Outreach Project, Vitale examines how the project impacts the development of their critical consciousness.

Keywords: Philosophy for Children, pre-college philosophy, high school philosophy, neoliberal education, education reform

***

One of the key principles of pre-college philosophy is increasing access to philosophy education for those in elementary and secondary programs. Aware of the value of philosophy, advocates of pre-college philosophy do not believe philosophy education should be available only to those at institutions of higher education, nor do they believe philosophy should be treated solely as a professional pursuit.

The question of increasing access, however, requires us to question why access is currently limited. One reason is because of a failure to recognize the benefits of philosophy on a social level, which is part of an overall assault on the humanities over the past couple decades. Another reason is the rise of neoliberal school management practices, which create situations in which teachers must overemphasize "teaching to the test," leaving less time for open-ended philosophical engagement. Additionally, socio-economic disparities across school districts, intensified by neoliberal economic policies, limit access to enrichment programs for many students in the country. All of these reasons stem from what I call a productivist logic. Sometimes called instrumental rationality, this logic values practices that increase productivity and profits and devalues practices that fail to do so.[1] It converts all practices to economic ones and prioritizes market exchange over all other human interactions.

In what follows, I suggest that to engage in pre-college philosophy in neoliberalism can be a radical practice, one that promotes public philosophy and public investment in education overall and challenges the large-scale neoliberal assault on public goods and the productivist logic undergirding it. To do so, I discuss the barriers to pre-college philosophy listed above and the Philosophy Outreach Project I founded in 2015.

Barriers to Philosophy for Children

The Assault on the Humanities

A key barrier to the creation of pre-college philosophy programs is the failure to recognize the benefits of philosophy on an institutional and social level, coupled with an overall assault on the humanities. According to the productivist logic, a process is only as good as its products, and the faster it can produce those products, the better. Efficiency is of paramount importance. The practice of philosophy, however, demands reflection, listening to others, and engagement with texts, all activities that take a great deal of time. It demands the development of certain sensitivities and dispositions, whose cultivation also takes time. The space to do philosophy is crowded out when every moment

---

[1] Horkheimer and Adorno, *Dialectic of Enlightenment.*

must be accounted for and when every activity is subjected to a cost/benefit analysis.

However, the university historically has been a space somewhat sheltered from the influence of economic trends, and philosophy has been a core discipline in liberal arts education since the birth of the modern university system. While the greater Western culture was becoming increasingly market-driven, the university still provided a space for the cultivation of ideas not necessarily tied to the production of goods – ideas about philosophy, art, and literature. But academia has simply been slower to change than other institutions, not immune to change. Today, while many schools still require philosophy classes as part of their general education curricula, the number of academic positions in philosophy is decreasing, and many programs are shuttering.

The shift away from the humanities is evidenced by university funding. Since 2009, for example, there have been significant cuts to spending on university humanities programs, even though enrollment declines in humanities programs began in the 1970s and leveled off in the 1990s.[2] The political rhetoric has recently emphasized the value of STEM degrees and the funding has followed. Schools like the University of Wisconsin at Stevens Point, Purdue University Fort Wayne, Claremont Graduate University, Liberty University, and University of Louisiana at Lafayette have closed entire humanities departments. Several others have responded by merging departments. Former governor Rick Scott of Florida even floated a proposal to reduce tuition for majors in high demand on the job market, ignoring data that humanities majors do very well in mid-career.[3]

Neoliberalism and the Corporatization of Education

In the age of neoliberalism, defined by David Harvey as "a theory of political economic practices that proposes that human well-being can best be advanced by liberating individual entrepreneurial freedoms and skills within an institutional framework characterized by strong private property rights, free markets, and free trade, wherein the role of the state is to protect this institutional framework, productivist logic has permeated more aspects of our lives."[4] In this section, I consider neoliberal school management practices in particular and the barrier they pose to the creation of pre-college philosophy programs.

---

[2] Halevi, and Bar-Ilan, "Trends in Arts and Humanities Funding."
[3] Alvarez, "To Steer Students Toward Jobs, Florida May Cut Tuition for Select Majors.";
Dorfman, "Humanities Degrees Provide Great Return on Investment."
[4] Harvey, *A Brief History of Neoliberalism*, 2.

Neoliberalism has hurt students through weakening teachers' unions, establishing "school choice" programs, and promoting school management practices, including the rise of standardized testing and assessment culture, which have further increased inequality in schools and impeded the access to enrichment opportunities, such as pre-college philosophy programs.

A key component of school choice programs are vouchers, which are used to send students to private and parochial schools. As of 2017, fourteen states and the District of Columbia have voucher programs.[5] All of these programs have eligibility requirements, ranging from admitting only students with disabilities or individual education plans to students from low-income families, to students in specific geographic areas, and many require students to have attended public school in the past.[6] However, while they were originally intended to support low-income families, vouchers increase inequality by sometimes providing additional support to families with economic means and by supporting private schools with discriminatory agendas. For example, when the voucher program was introduced in Indiana, it was sold as an option for parents who wanted to get their children out of failing schools. Today, however, many of the students who attend private schools with vouchers have never stepped foot into a public school. Vouchers are thus supporting families who were already paying for and affording private tuition. In fact, 30% of vouchers go to families making $90,000 and above for a family of four.[7]

While vouchers allow students to attend private schools, other types of school choice legislation allow students to attend public schools in districts where they do not live. In states with such programs, parents choose what schools their children attend and in what districts. The state funding, then, follows the student. Schools are left without knowing how many students they might have in the fall, and the final count that is tied to state funding often occurs in mid-September, over a month after classes begin. This means that schools are likely to under-hire teachers and staff and then be forced to look for new faculty mid-year, if they end up having more students enroll than expected. School choice decimates urban schools and furthers inequality because those who can exercise choice are those whose parents have the time and resources to drive them to another school district.

Finally, charter schools receive public funds but are managed privately. Most do not have to follow the same rules as public schools do, and many operate as

---

[5] "State Education Reforms (SER)."
[6] "School Voucher Laws."
[7] Wang, "Indiana Still Has the Nation's Largest Voucher Program."

for-profit institutions. Charter schools have grown in number and size in the U.S. In the 2000-01 school year, 2% of public schools were charter schools, while in the 2015-16 school year, 7% were. In fall 2000, 1% of public-school students attended charter schools, and in fall 2015, 6% attended charter schools.[8]

Charter schools have also been shown to contribute to inequality, specifically greater racial segregation. They have been called by UCLA's Civil Rights Project a "civil rights failure" due to their higher rates of segregation.[9] In addition, charter schools are exempt from many of the laws regulating public schools, such that they can expel students more easily, hire uncredentialled teachers, and ignore bargaining rights of teachers. There is also significant corporate interest behind the charter school movement, which indicates how it benefits neoliberal players rather than the students enrolled.[10]

One key problem with the school choice movement is that its neoliberal market model demands a mentality of winners and losers. It presumes there are and will be failing schools, and in the market model, parents, motivated as rational actors, would take their children out of these schools. Following the market model, those failing schools would need to compete to get students to return or they would necessarily shutter. Rather than improving all public schools, this model leaves significant populations of children underserved – those inevitably left in the "failing" public schools, the schools that suffer because of the mass exodus of students and of tax dollars.

In addition, the model leaves those in the classroom, in both public and charter schools, receiving an education that is almost singularly focused on standardized assessments, making these schools unwelcome places for philosophy for children or pre-college philosophy programs. Schools that meet the assessment requirements and are able to stay open. Schools are often rated by how well students do on these measures, and teachers' jobs can be tied to the performance metrics.[11] The very space to do philosophy has been crowded out in an age where every moment is accounted for and every moment has been commandeered to prepare for relentless assessments. According to the

---

[8] "Fast Facts: Charter Schools."

[9] Orfield, "Foreword."

[10] Prothero, "Charter Sector to Get $1 Billion From Walton Family Foundation - Education Week."

[11] Even the future of the schools can be tied to the students' performance on these tests. In Indiana, for instance, the state passed HB1321, which changed school reviews to a portfolio measure, akin to stock portfolios. If the school "underperforms," it becomes a charter (Morello, "Plan For IPS, Charter Collaboration Draws Backlash From Teachers Union.").

Council of the Great City Schools, students take about 112 tests between pre-K and their senior year of high school.[12] During the course of one school year, a student spends about 25 hours taking tests, roughly four or five whole school days.[13] There is little to no time left in the course of the day to engage in open-ended discussion, to allow students to employ their critical thinking skills, let alone to develop a committed and sustained community of philosophical inquiry.

Economic Disparities

School districts have also been hurt economically due to other neoliberal practices, including a measure that began in the 1970s -- the debt-funding of U.S. cities. As Ann Larson explains, "The debt financing of U.S. cities and towns, a neoliberal economic model that long precedes the current recession, has inflicted deep and growing suffering on communities across the country."[14] Cities began to receive significantly less federal funding, and Republican legislatures also slashed taxes. Without adequate tax revenue and federal funding, municipalities needed to raise funds in a different way. They turned to Wall Street, offering the municipal bond.

Municipal bonds were used to pay for city projects that taxes had previously funded. They are quite attractive for investors, as they are tax-exempt and highly reliable. Cities do not default on these loans. Since the Great Recession of 2008, U.S. cities have been forced to operate in the mode of austerity in order to repay their Wall Street investors. Unable to fund basic projects, municipalities respond through personnel cuts, cancelling projects, modifying health care benefits of city employees, cutting human services, cutting funds to public safety, etc.[15] In some cities, the services formerly provided by the city are now provided by volunteer citizen organizations.

Public education is a key victim in this process. With decreased revenue from the state, municipalities must rely on revenue from the property taxes alone to fund school programs, which has been increasingly untenable in low-income areas. As state funding disappears from districts, enrichment programs are now supposed to rely on philanthropy and volunteerism. In fact, one of the key ideologies of neoliberalism is that of volunteerism. Working parents, overburdened teachers, and compassionate community members are expected to put in the hours to do the work of previously paid staff. Citizens are expected to provide for their

---

[12] Hart et al., "Student Testing in America's Great City Schools," 83.
[13] Hart et al., 83.
[14] Larson, "Cities in the Red."
[15] Lubin, "Frightening Charts Show Record Low Revenue, Worst-Ever Austerity Measures For US Cities."

communities the services previously provided by the state. This is at the same time, however, as they are receiving lower wages, working more, and still paying taxes. It is not as if the state and the federal government are not investing in anything, however. Rather, the government invests in things other than public education, and those who remain committed to public education are asked to put the time, money, and energy in to keep the venture afloat.

Philosophy for Children

The Philosophy for Children (P4C) movement developed during the same period as neoliberalism took hold in the U.S., though not as a neoliberal alternative to public school education. The main principle of pre-college philosophy is that children are capable of engaging in philosophical dialogue and reflection and that such reflection and dialogue are beneficial for children for a host of reasons. In addition, pre-college philosophy advocates seek to provide more opportunities for K-12 students to engage with philosophy.

Pre-college philosophy, however, does not appear at its face to be a radical venture. It looks like many other enrichment opportunities, even sharing many things in common with them. Engagement with philosophy in high school has many instrumental benefits that accord with a neoliberal educational model, including improved academic performance and career readiness. Students who engage in philosophy programs demonstrate improved reasoning, discussion, and argumentation skills, all skills that will help them at the collegiate level.[16] Those who end up studying philosophy in college receive higher scores across the board on grad school entrance exams.[17]

However, pre-college philosophy is unlike neoliberal enrichment programs and is indeed a radical project for several reasons. First, it challenges the very structure of the traditional K-12 classroom and anticipates the current emphasis on learner-centered pedagogy. In "Does Philosophy for Children Belong in School at All?", Jana Mohr Lone considers whether philosophy for children belongs in traditional schools because of their historically hierarchical and coercive elements.[18] Even though the traditional classroom may not seem on its face conducive to philosophy for children, Lone argues that P4C should remain in the schools in order to reach more students and advocate for change in the school system.

The analysis Lone and others in P4C offer of the traditional educational model echoes the analysis offered by Althusser in "Ideology and Ideological

---

[16] Trickey and Topping, "Philosophy for Children: A Systematic Review."

[17] "Value of Philosophy - Charts and Graphs."

[18] Lone, "Does Philosophy for Children Belong in School at All?"

State Apparatuses." Here, Althusser argues that the reproduction of the working class occurs not only by means of wages which procure the means of subsistence, but also through the reproduction of certain ideas that allow the ruling class to rule with less brute force. Such reproduction occurs largely through education. Althusser explains that "the school...teaches 'know-how,' but in forms which ensure *subjection to the ruling ideology* or the mastery of its 'practice.'"[19] It also teaches "rules of good behavior." While the church was the dominant ideological apparatus under feudalism, Althusser explains that the school has become the dominant ideological apparatus under capitalism because everyone is required to attend school. The school passes itself off as neutral, but it works to support the capitalist economy, preparing students for their respective roles in the economy and then "ejecting" them into the workforce at the appropriate level of preparation.

Second, and relatedly, philosophy for children provides a space for students to be critical and engaged. One of the methods used in the P4C setting is the "Community of Philosophical Inquiry." The teacher or club leader acts as a facilitator rather than one who delivers content, and students are encouraged to take time to reflect on a prompt and form their own questions, thus shaping the direction of the subsequent discussion.[20] This method challenges the content-driven assessment culture in the current education system, where teachers must focus on preparing students for large-scale assessments.

Finally, philosophy for children is radically democratic insofar as it holds that young people are capable of accessing the truth and exercising reason just as adults can. Jacques Rancière, one of the key thinkers of radical democracy, argues that equality is not something we achieve but is in fact the very presupposition behind our communication.[21] When we communicate, we must presume the other can understand us, and we thus presume their equality with us. These others can be children, and those who practice pre-college philosophy begin with the assumption that young people are rational and possess the full capacity to engage in philosophical dialogue.

The Philosophy Outreach Project (POP)

While Philosophy for Children is a radical venture, to establish a pre-college philosophy program, one must work within the confines of neoliberalism and in a culture guided by a productivist logic. In addition, if establishing a program

---

[19] Althusser, "Ideology and Ideological State Apparatus," 7.
[20] Lone and Burroughs, *Philosophy in Education: Questioning and Dialogue in Schools*, 53–65.
[21] Rancière, *Disagreement*; Lone and Burroughs, *Philosophy in Education: Questioning and Dialogue in Schools*.

under the aegis of a university, one likely faces additional barriers. However, I believe that the university still offers some of the most promising avenues to starting pre-college philosophy programs, even though some of those avenues may not be immune to neoliberal logic. In this section, I discuss these phenomena while addressing the pre-college philosophy program I founded at a midsize public university in the Midwest.

Background and Initial Outreach

Not only are there structural and ideological barriers to beginning high school philosophy programs in the K-12 system, but there are also barriers at the university level. An increasing percentage of faculty are non-tenure track or adjunct and are not compensated for service work, which disincentivizes such faculty members from starting outreach programs. In addition, tenure requirements often dissuade tenure-track faculty from engaging in such projects before promotion to the associate level. Most universities give more weight to scholarly publications in tenure decisions, which means pre-tenure faculty members should spend more time on their research than on service endeavors. While publications may result from service endeavors, the time invested in the project is rarely commensurate with the reward. After receiving tenure, one has established an identity as a faculty member, and it is more difficult to reinvent one's self as a community-engaged scholar. Finally, colleges and universities are cash-strapped as well, and faculty may find it difficult to find the resources to begin a program readily available.

I began the Philosophy Outreach Project in an extra-curricular capacity. I was in my second year of a tenure-track position, and I was not as worried about tenure as I likely should have been. I was the advisor to my institution's philosophy club and a mentor to a high school student in the community, and I derived a great deal of satisfaction from these activities. Because of my work as a mentor, I became interested in what opportunities were afforded to my mentee at the local high school. I decided to investigate the field of pre-college philosophy in Indiana.

In December 2015, I contacted roughly 250 public and private high schools across the state.[22] I asked whether the schools had philosophy clubs and received responses from over half the schools. Of those who replied, only seven had philosophy clubs. Another eight indicated they had philosophy classes in

---

[22] I repeated the survey in November 2017, and in this survey, I asked whether the school had a philosophy club or class, indicating that the class might come in the form of Theories of Knowledge or Critical Thinking. I learned that 11 schools had courses and six had clubs. Two clubs had stopped meeting, and three schools who had not indicated they had classes during the first survey responded positively when I asked this question.

their curricula, even though I had not asked that question. Of those without clubs and classes, some expressed an interest in starting a club and many more expressed an interest in some sort of partnership. In the project's first phase, I brought a group of my institution's philosophy majors and philosophy club members to visit several schools with existing clubs, in part to learn about existing pre-college programs and to offer engagement opportunities for my own students. Between December 2015 and April 2017, we made ten site visits to six different high schools.

The college students involved with the first phase of the outreach project noticed that three of the five schools we visited were in affluent school districts in the Indianapolis suburbs and another was a high-performing school in the Indianapolis district. The exception was a rural school in a small city with a poverty rate of 15.4%, which is below the state average (18.5%) but above the national average (12.7%), and well above the average in the three affluent districts (3.6%).[23] They drew a parallel between access to enrichment opportunities and socio-economic status. They also inquired about starting a philosophy club in the high school in our own city, Muncie, Indiana. Muncie has a 28.1% poverty rate, well above the national rate and significantly above the rate of the communities we had initially visited.[24]

It was relatively easy to start the club at the high school, since I found a social studies teacher willing to host it in his classroom during the afterschool period for club meetings. The club began in February 2017. Quickly, the university students were very impressed with the level of curiosity and intellectual engagement displayed by the high school students at the club and on the site visits. My students were eager to continue and develop the outreach program. In addition to starting the club at our local high school, they expressed a desire to visit schools without existing clubs to provide students with an initial encounter with philosophy. Until that point, however, I was performing the labor for the project outside my teaching load, ostensibly as part of the service portion of my appointment. The department compensated me for gas mileage, and I purchased the snacks for our visits. At that point, now in the spring of my third year on the tenure track, I realized that I could no longer perform such a project in this fashion. I needed more institutional support, especially if I wanted to reach more high school students. The "Philosophy for High School" course grew out of this recognition.

---

[23] "Monticello, Indiana (IN) Poverty Rate Data"; "Carmel, Indiana (IN) Poverty Rate Data"; "Fishers, Indiana (IN) Poverty Rate Data."
[24] "Muncie, Indiana (IN) Poverty Rate Data."

My university provides grants to support classes engaged in community-based projects, which they call immersive-learning classes. The university prioritizes projects in which "the proposed scope of work solves a problem or fills the needs of a community partner."[25] Part of the goal of this grant program is to help students gain project-based experience, similar to what they would experience on a job. In this way, the immersive-learning project accords with neoliberal demands. In addition, the grant program has other neoliberal demands – "deliverables" or "products" – and echoes corporate language of "risk-taking" and "real-world engagement." But the university is more committed to what pedagogical experts call high-impact experiences, and there is great room under the umbrella of the grant program for projects that challenge various economic models.[26] The grant program involves a public engagement element as well, which makes it perfect for a pre-college philosophy program.

I have earned these internal grants to offer the class in spring 2018, spring 2019, and spring 2021. In part because of these grants and the work the project was able to accomplish through them, I was well-positioned to receive external grants from PLATO (the Philosophy Learning and Teaching Organization), the American Philosophical Association, and Indiana Campus Compact. These grants allowed me to offer the course in spring 2020 and to fund the efforts in the summers and falls when the class was not in session.

In the Philosophy for High School course, the community partners are the high school faculty and students with whom we engage, and, instead of corporate deliverables, what my students provide are resources for teachers and students, site visits, and a day-long engagement. These products serve a very real need, one ignored by our current educational model and its creation of false needs.

The class also involves risk-taking on the part of the teachers and students, but not the kind of risk-taking typically associated with neoliberal, productivist logic. Rather, it is the type of risk that involves vulnerability. For the student who is accustomed to a clear syllabus with deadlines, to receive a syllabus with expectations such as "host a conference," "work well with your classmates," and "step up to take on new tasks," without any deadlines, the process seems risky from the start. For the teacher who is used to managing all the parts of her class and her projects, stepping back to let students take the lead involves a certain degree of risk and vulnerability.

---

[25] "Provost Grant Application."
[26] Kuh, *High-Impact Educational Practices: What They Are, Who Has Access to Them, and Why They Matter.*

In every iteration of the course, my university students have risen to the challenge. They read the literature on pre-college philosophy and P4C, and, in a sense, became experts. The class itself becomes a community of philosophical inquiry, in which the prompt is "How can we encourage philosophical engagement at the high school level in Indiana?" We spend the course of each semester engaging that question.

Components of the Philosophy for High School Class

A. Site Visits and Muncie Central Philosophy Club

A key element of the course is maintaining and improving the outreach portion that began in 2015. My students and I together visit approximately five schools per academic year. During these visits, the university students lead discussions. The discussions begin with a brief presentation of material, followed by structured activities and unstructured but guided discussions. The high school students are very active as they address topics such as censorship, Nietzsche, Marxism and capitalism, and various topics in ethics. Additionally, the college students field questions about their own experiences with philosophy and college in general.

B. Resources

POP students also create resources for high school students and teachers. In the first year of the program, the students in the course created an extensive guide for high school students interested in philosophy. Through their engagement with students on site visits and at Muncie Central, the Outreach Team decided what would be most helpful to include in the packet. They included information on how to start a philosophy club, how to find philosophical material, and how to read philosophy, as well as information for those interested in studying philosophy at the college level, including how to find philosophy departments, the benefits of studying philosophy at college, and information on what it is like to study philosophy at college. The packet has been published on PLATO's website (https://www.plato-philosophy.org/downloadable-resources/). In subsequent years, the university students have improved and expanded the resource.

Students in the course have also created white pages on pre-college philosophy for high school faculty, as well as detailed lesson plans on various philosophical topics. For high school students, they have created interactive online starter packs, which introduce high school students to a philosophical topic through the use of humor and memes and by curating other material on the internet, including podcasts, videos, and articles. The starter packs and teacher resources, as well as the packet, can be found on the project's website, which is also managed by students in the course (https://philosophyoutreachproject.azure websites.net/).

To disseminate resources, reach more students and faculty, and encourage engagement, students in the course manage several social media accounts. Grant funding has allowed the project to pay someone to manage the accounts when the class is not in session.

C. Conference for Pre-College Philosophical Engagement

Perhaps the signature event of the Philosophy Outreach Project is the Conference for pre-college Philosophical Engagement (CPPE), a one-day interactive conference for high school students held at the end of the spring semester. The conference is free to attendees, and any high school student in the state of Indiana is welcome to attend. In the first year, 64 students from five high schools attended. In the second year, 88 students from 9 high schools attended.

Barriers to hosting conference include lack of funding, scheduling around standardized tests and other events at the participating high schools, and securing speakers. In terms of funding, the most significant cost for our conference is catering. To encourage participation from high school students regardless of income level, I have sought to make the conference free and to provide a meal to every attendee. The funding has come from internal grants, external grants, as well as a partnership with the university's honors college. I invited the dean of the honors college to attend the first two conferences, and he recognized the event as an opportunity to recruit students who might be good candidates for the university's honors program. He therefore agreed to partner with the project for the third conference, which was unfortunately cancelled due to Covid-19. Strategic partnerships with other members of one's university and even departments at neighboring universities can help mitigate expenses and also expand the program's reach.

While the conference was free to attend in the first and second years, and meals were provided, inequalities in district funding still affected attendance. Those who attended in the first two years were primarily students from school districts with below-average poverty rates. I discovered that I had not considered transportation costs for high schools when I considered barriers to attendance. Attending the conference, despite the lack of registration fees and the provision of meals, was still prohibitive for students in many districts. Because of this, in the third year, we used grant funds to offer travel stipends. But because the conference was cancelled due to the pandemic, no travel stipends were awarded.

Above, I discussed the constraints secondary teachers face due to neoliberal school management practices, such as standardized tests. The mandate that teachers "teach to the tests" also affects the success of our site visits and conference. Some principals with whom I communicated said there was no way students could miss a day of class in the spring semester. In other cases, even if the administrators and teachers were open to attending the conference, it was difficult to find a date that did not overlap with at least one school's spring break or testing day. I have found that it is essential to find ways to communicate the value of philosophy to high school administrators, and I have since incorporated a "principal pitch" as an assignment in the course.

Finally, a strong conference needs engaging speakers and facilitators. Through the grant, the project has been able to offer a small stipend and cover the travel expenses for a local academic to offer a keynote address. The students in the university course were very selective when considering a keynote speaker. They looked at potential speakers' bodies of work and presentation styles, and, because of what is known as the pipeline problem in philosophy, they also considered identity issues.[27] They made it a priority to invite speakers from underrepresented groups in philosophy, as they believed that it would be important for a high school student's first experience in philosophy to be one that challenged traditional notions of who a philosopher can be.

To facilitate the breakout sessions, they petitioned faculty members at the university, and students in the class also facilitated sessions. After faculty members submitted their session descriptions, the university students designed sessions that would complement those. Sessions have included "The Privilege Line-up," "Drawing Your Identity," "Gender & Race & Class…Wait, Is That Right?," "Treehuggers 101," "Feeling of the Creeps," "Nietzsche's Guide to Greatness," "Wake Me Up Before You Gogh Gogh," "What Came First, God or Matter? A View from Africa," "Three Yeets for Consciousness," and "How to Start a Philosophy Club," among others. Past conference agendas and session descriptions can be found on the project website.

University students used feedback from attendees at the first conference to improve the second conference. In the first year, the "Speed Philosophy" breakout session was so popular that they made it into an event for all attendees to follow the keynote address during the second year. During speed philosophy, a group of five to six high school students sit at a table with a university student facilitator. They are given a question and five minutes to discuss it. After the time is up, they are presented with another question. As five minutes is never enough to address one of the questions in a satisfying manner,

---

[27] Calhoun, "The Undergraduate Pipeline Problem."

students become energized for the future discussions throughout the day. The keynote session then followed "Speed Philosophy," and then students attended one breakout session before lunch. Because of the popularity of the breakout sessions in the first year, the university students reorganized the day to allow students to attend four breakout sessions rather than three.

The university students organized the day through a careful registration process. First, they received a list of attendees along with their dietary restrictions from the high school teachers, and then they provided the high school students with a form to rank their selections for sessions. During each time slot, several sessions were offered. Because of room size and to maintain an appropriate number of participants for engagement, the university student coordinators used the high school students' preferences to create an individualized agenda for each student. They were able to ensure that everyone participated in either their top or second choice during each breakout session.

Conclusion: Sustainability and Looking toward the Future

The effort to create and sustain a pre-college philosophy program is significant. Several factors coalesce to make it difficult, including an inhospitable educational system. But like Lone, who believes that Philosophy for Children still belongs in the schools in order to expose more students to it and to hopefully serve a voice for change in the school system, we believe in the importance of working with students in the public school system.[28] The learning experience, for both high school students and university students, makes it worth the effort. High school students who engage in philosophy are provided a space to articulate and develop their critiques of their own institutions and imagine possibilities for a better world. One of the things the neoliberal logic does is reduce all thinking to the market model, but philosophy broadens the horizon of possibility and allows students the space to reconstrue their worldviews. They are able to question the reigning ideology that tells them that something is only valuable insofar as it is quantifiable or produces exchange value, and they are able to rekindle their own innate capacity for wonder and questioning. Incorporating university students in the project allows them to see that philosophy is not something that exists solely within the halls of their university. Rather, it is an approach to the world and a practice.

Ultimately, to allow more people to begin such programs, what is needed is policy change. Only movement at the state and federal levels will allow the structural change necessary for more students to be exposed to important programming. In the interim, however, we can pursue constructive efforts that

---

[28] Lone, "Does Philosophy for Children Belong in School at All?," 156.

allow high school students to interact with college students in very productive ways. There are "win-wins" available, even in neoliberalism. I was able to set up a program within institutional parameters, for instance, such that the participating students receive credit, I teach the course as part of my teaching load, and high school students are afforded a new opportunity.

There still are pitfalls. The course only runs in the spring, and the club at the local high school runs throughout the academic year. The university students who run the club in the fall still do so in the spirit of volunteership. One way to change this in the future would be to offer the club advising to one or two students as an independent study. Another problem is that it is unlikely that we will receive the same grants annually *ad infinitum*, so we will likely have to search for other funding sources, and this is part of the difficulties of doing public philosophy in the age of austerity, when we rely on donors and philanthropists for the survival of ostensibly public goods.

Nonetheless, if universities remain the sites most committed to humanistic pursuits and least affected by productivist logic, then they remain important sites from which to promote public engagement. In an article in *The Chronicle Review*, Gary Gutting argues that the very existence of research institutions in the United States indicates our commitment to promoting an intellectual culture, even when many factors mitigate against that.[29] It is therefore the responsibility of the people afforded the opportunity to work in these spaces somewhat protected from economic pressures to struggle against the impact of productivism in the greater public, and one way to do this is through promoting pre-college philosophy

Bibliography

Althusser, Louis. "Ideology and Ideological State Apparatus (Notes Towards an Investigation)." In *Lenin and Philosophy and Other Essays*, translated by Ben Brewster. New York: Monthly Review Press, 2001.

Alvarez, Lizette. "To Steer Students Toward Jobs, Florida May Cut Tuition for Select Majors." *The New York Times*. December 10, 2012, New York edition, sec. Education.

Calhoun, Cheshire. "The Undergraduate Pipeline Problem." *Hypatia* 24, no. 2 (2009): 216–23.

City-Data.com. "Carmel, Indiana (IN) Poverty Rate Data," 2016. http://www.city-data.com/poverty/poverty-Carmel-Indiana.html.

City-Data.com. "Fishers, Indiana (IN) Poverty Rate Data," 2016. http://www.city-data.com/poverty/poverty-Fishers-Indiana.html.

---

[29] Gutting, "Why College Is Not a Commodity."

City-Data.com. "Muncie, Indiana (IN) Poverty Rate Data," 2016. http://www.city-data.com/poverty/poverty-Muncie-Indiana.html.

City-Data.com. "Monticello, Indiana (IN) Poverty Rate Data," 2016. http://www.city-data.com/poverty/poverty-Monticello-Indiana.html.

Daily Nous. "Value of Philosophy - Charts and Graphs." Accessed November 19, 2018. http://dailynous.com/value-of-philosophy/charts-and-graphs.

Dorfman, Jeffrey. "Surprise: Humanities Degrees Provide Great Return On Investment." *Forbes*, November 20, 2014. https://www.forbes.com/sites/jeffreydorfman/2014/11/20/surprise-humanities-degrees-provide-great-return-on-investment/#73ca9732031b.

Gutting, Gary. "Why College Is Not a Commodity." *The Chronicle Review*, September 25, 2015.

Halevi, Gali, Elsevier Barl-Ilan., and Judit Bar-Ilan. "Trends in Arts and Humanities Funding 2004-2012." *Research Trends*, no. 32 (March 2013). https://www.researchtrends.com/issue-32-march-2013/trends-in-arts-humanities-funding-2004-2012/.

Hart, Ray, Michael Casserly, Renata Uzzell, Moses Palacios, Amanda Corcoran., and Liz Spurgeon. "Student Testing in America's Great City Schools: An Inventory and Preliminary Analysis." Washington, DC: Council of the Great City Schools, October 2015. https://www.cgcs.org/cms/lib/DC00001581/Centricity/Domain/87/Testing%20Report.pdf.

Harvey, David. *A Brief History of Neoliberalism*. Oxford: Oxford University Press, 2007.

Horkheimer, Max., and Theodor W. Adorno. *Dialectic of Enlightenment: Philosophical Fragments*. Stanford, CA: Stanford University Press, 2002.

Humanities Indicators. "Bachleors Degrees in the Humanities," May 2017. http://www.humanitiesIndicators.org/content/indicatorDoc.aspx?i=34.

Immersive Learning. "Provost Grant Application." Accessed November 19, 2018. https://www.bsu.edu/about/administrativeoffices/immersive-learning/for-faculty/grant-opportunities.

Kuh, George D. *High-Impact Educational Practices: What They Are, Who Has Access to Them, and Why They Matter*. Association of American Colleges and Universities, 2008. https://secure.aacu.org/imis/ItemDetail?iProductCode=E-HIGHIMP&Category=.

Larson, Ann. "Cities in the Red: Austerity Hits America." *Dissent Magazine*, November 16, 2012. https://www.dissentmagazine.org/online_articles/cities-in-the-red-austerity-hits-america.

Lone, Jana Mohr. "Does Philosophy for Children Belong in School at All?" *Analytical Teaching* 21, no. 2 (June 2000): 151–56.

Lone, Jana Mohr., and Michael D. Burroughs. *Philosophy in Education: Questioning and Dialogue in Schools*. Lanham: Rowman and Littlefield, 2016.

Lubin, Gus. "Frightening Charts Show Record Low Revenue, Worst-Ever Austerity Measures For US Cities." *Business Insider*, October 6, 2010. https://www.businessinsider.com/record-low-revenue-record-austerity-measures-for-us-cities-2010-10#now-meet-some-of-the-worst-cities-12.

Morello, Rachel. "Plan For IPS, Charter Collaboration Draws Backlash From Teachers Union." *StateImpact Indiana* (blog), January 24, 2014. https://indianapublicmedia.

org/stateimpact/2014/01/24/plan-ips-charter-collaboration-draws-backlash-teachers-union/.

National Center for Education Statistics. "Fast Facts: Charter Schools." Accessed January 2, 2019. https://nces.ed.gov/fastfacts/display.asp?id=30.

National Center for Education Statistics. "State Education Reforms (SER)." Accessed January 2, 2019. https://nces.ed.gov/programs/statereform/tab4_7.asp.

National Conference of State Legislatures. "School Voucher Laws: State-by-State Comparison." Accessed January 2, 2019. http://www.ncsl.org/research/education/voucher-law-comparison.aspx.

Orfield, Gary. "Foreword." In *Choice Without Equity: Charter School Segregation and the Need for Civil Rights Standards*, by Erica Frankenberg, Genevieve Siegel-Hawley, and Jia Wang. UCLA: The Civil Rights Project / Proyecto Derechos Civiles, 2012. https://escholarship.org/uc/item/4r07q8kg.

Prothero, Arianna. "Charter Sector to Get $1 Billion From Walton Family Foundation - Education Week." *Education Week*, January 13, 2016. https://www.edweek.org/ew/articles/2016/01/13/charter-sector-to-get-1-billion-from.html.

Rancière, Jacques. *Disagreement: Politics And Philosophy*. Translated by Julie Rose. 1st ed. University of Minnesota Press, 2004.

Trickey, S., and K.J. Topping. "Philosophy for Children: A Systematic Review." *Research Papers in Education* 19, no. 3 (2004): 365=80.

Wang, Stephanie. "Indiana Still Has the Nation's Largest Voucher Program. But Growth Is Slowing Down." *Chalkbeat* (blog), March 1, 2018. https://chalkbeat.org/posts/in/2018/03/01/indiana-still-has-the-nations-largest-voucher-program-but-growth-is-slowing-down/.

Chapter 7

Bringing Philosophy into Philadelphia Classrooms

Dustin Webster

University of Pennsylvania

Stephen Esser

University of Pennsylvania

Karen Detlefsen

University of Pennsylvania

Abstract

The Penn Project for Philosophy for the Young (P4Y) at the University of Pennsylvania was founded in 2014 by Professor Karen Detlefsen, a faculty member in the philosophy department. From a once-a-week philosophy club with 12 high school students to a multi-pronged program, Penn's Project for Philosophy for the Young aims to bring philosophy into the pre-college, public school classroom, both through self-standing philosophy classes and clubs, and through the integration of philosophy into existing school subjects. The Project is also committed to the development of pedagogical and other skills in college and graduate students, and we are in the process of laying foundations for a robust research program in pre-college philosophy. In this essay, we outline the philosophy behind Penn's P4Y project, detailing the range of our initiatives, and offering some reflections on our successes and failures. Before turning to these aspects of the project, however, we turn to the roots of our work.

Keywords: community partnerships, curriculum development, ethics bowl, philosophy club, public philosophy, teacher collaboration

***

Launching the Project

The project's first initiative was a philosophy club in association with the college readiness and success organization Philadelphia Futures,[1] which offers programming and support to local high school students through to the completion of college. Detlefsen and Robert Willison, a graduate student from Penn, traveled to the Philadelphia Futures program space, and ran various philosophy activities and discussions. This programming was very well received by everyone involved and garnered the initial interest to expand the opportunities around engaging young people in philosophy.

In an effort to involve more of the university community and students, the Philadelphia Futures partnership transformed in spring 2015 into an Academically Based Community Service Course in the University of Pennsylvania Philosophy Department. These courses, often referred to as ABCS courses, involve a mix of traditional college classroom work, and involvement of Penn undergraduate students in the local community. ABCS courses are supported financially and programmatically by the Netter Center for Community Partnerships.[2] In this particular course, undergraduate students learned about the philosophy of education in a college seminar during the week and were trained in the necessary skills to teach philosophy to high school students. The high school students met on Saturday mornings on Penn's campus to take a course, taught by the Penn undergraduates, on the philosophy of education. Bringing high school students to campus allowed them to get a sense of college life, which was especially welcomed by the pre-college students as they would be the first members of their families to attend college. In addition to teaching the high school students content in philosophy of education, the Penn undergraduates then supported the high school students in the drafting of papers. Then, for the culmination of the course, everyone came together on the university campus for an academic conference in which the high school students presented their work. Audience members included: the students' friends, families, mentors and other supporters; members of the philosophy department; and members of the wider Penn community, including Deans. Central to the success of this first year of Penn's P4Y initiative were the close relationships built between undergraduate and high school students; long lunches after Saturday morning classes built a camaraderie and sense of community amongst the students that contributed

---

[1] https://philadelphiafutures.org/

[2] http://www.nettercenter.upenn.edu/ The Netter Center was founded at Penn in 1992 and focuses on civic and community engagement of the University with the surrounding neighborhoods in West Philadelphia, but also beyond into other areas of the city.

to the high schoolers' extraordinary academic achievements throughout the year.

This course solidified the commitment to developing these efforts into a larger project. From these initial activities, the Penn Project for Philosophy for the Young (Penn P4Y) has grown each year. It is now a robust program with multiple initiatives and directions involving pre-college philosophy including direct engagement with local K-12 schools, teacher collaborations, student development and courses at the university, and the beginnings of a research program. Currently, Dr. Detlefsen serves as the director of the project, and Dr. Stephen Esser serves as Associate Director. The project is further staffed by a number of graduate and undergraduate students. It is also undergirded by a philosophy that underscores the importance of philosophical thinking in the lives of young people.

The Philosophy Behind Our Mission and Programming

Philosophy for Children (P4C) is a long-standing phenomenon, and Penn's P4Y project is in the general spirit of such P4C projects found across the world. At the same time, Penn's P4Y initiatives have largely targeted Philadelphia's public school population. As such, we are driven by a range of values especially relevant to local conditions. So, the driving philosophies behind the Penn P4Y project are as follows: (a) philosophical thinking – e.g., wondering about the nature of goodness, what one values, social justice, how to live well, how to determine the right course of action – shows up very early in children, and children greatly enjoy thinking about philosophical questions; (b) helping the young to cultivate philosophical thinking sharpens a range of skills that are helpful across all school subjects; (c) helping the young to cultivate philosophical thinking can directly address content in a range of subjects from K-12, and can deepen understanding in those subjects; and (d) bringing philosophy into underserved schools can help address the issue of equal access to educational goods.

Part of the success and growth of the projects in which we have engaged, as evidenced by our experiences over the past six years and detailed below, is that pre-college students are enthusiastically eager to think about, discuss and write about philosophical topics. At least in part, this eagerness comes from the fact that these young people are already grappling with the kinds of problems that drive philosophical inquiry as is evident by the questions they themselves generate in our discussions. These pre-college students are interested in thinking about such topics partly because it is satisfying to wrestle with hard questions one is curious about, a point we are all familiar with. But the problems that are absorbing these young people also connect directly with their lived experience and with the problems they face. Grappling with these questions can help them to formulate their own values and to decide what choices they ought to make when faced with important decisions. It is not just the content that is of value in teaching philosophy. Philosophy cultivates valuable intellectual skills and habits of mind, for it requires both clarity and creativity of thought. Three crucial skills at the heart of philosophical inquiry are: the need to be clear in understanding the precise nature of the question at hand, the uncovering of various tacit assumptions one might hold that may constrain one's understanding of possible solutions to the problem as clarified, and the creative canvassing of a wide range of possible solutions to the problem at hand. Uncovering one's tacit assumptions in particular can be a difficult task – both as an exercise in clear thinking and as an exercise in recognizing that closely-held beliefs may be reasonably doubted. But the difficulty of this task contributes to another intellectual virtue as well – the ability to tolerate, and even embrace, intellectual ambiguity. We want to equip our students to defend with confidence their own conclusions, but also to recognize the merits of the opinions of others, in matters where certainty cannot reasonably be achieved.

These values have been at the foundation of our projects since that first philosophy club at the Philadelphia Future's conference room, where we sat with those 12 talented high school philosophers a little over six years ago. In what follows, we outline the projects we have added to our program since our inception.

Current Penn P4Y Initiatives

A. Self-Standing Philosophy Clubs and Classes

A major component of the Penn P4Y has been and continues to be direct engagement with local K-12 public school students. These initiatives involve students or staff from the university directly running programming with students. Because of this in-person interaction, they tend to be the most exciting types of activities the program runs, and also the programming that gets the most attention. The challenges of running a program like the Penn P4Y will be explored later, but an inherent limitation to in-person programming is the numbers of students and staff required to reach just a tiny fraction of the Philadelphia School District's (PSD's) 200,000-plus students spread among more than 300 schools. While there has yet to be a major staffing shortage for our programming thus far, we are quickly approaching the point where we will have more demand than we can fulfill, which is where other types of initiative such as teacher collaborations become important. We will turn to such collaborations in the next section, devoting the current section to self-standing philosophy projects.

The direct engagement with philosophy, which is at the core of much of our programming, is extremely rewarding for both Penn students and staff on the one hand, and the public school students on the other hand. As such, it will always have a place in Penn's P4Y project. One of the longest-running of these initiatives is a variety of philosophy classes and clubs at the Benjamin B. Comegys School in West Philadelphia. This program started in 2016 when Detlefsen and a group of graduate students in Penn's philosophy department began to work with a class of about 30 eighth-grade social studies students to discuss questions related to social justice. We created philosophy lessons related to the topics they were studying in social studies, and we taught these lessons once per week, breaking the class into smaller groups of about 5 students and a mentor. We had originally tried to teach the whole group at once, but we quickly discovered that the students were exceptionally keen to contribute to oral discussion. And so, by breaking into smaller groups, students got a better chance to talk about the philosophical concepts.

Following this successful launch at Comegys, we have continued to offer a variety of lunchtime, after school, and early morning philosophy clubs, now called the Think and Talk Club. Over the years, we have interacted with students from fourth through eighth grade, and we have covered a wide range of topics, including ownership, friendship, how to distribute scarce resources, the metaphysics of time, what makes a game a game, the difference between children and adults, and much more.

In addition to the ABCS course model discussed above -- bringing high school students to campus for philosophy class culminating in a conference -- we piloted a second model with a group of fifth-grade students at Comegys in Fall 2018. This course built a 13-week philosophy curriculum around interests expressed by the fifth graders. Drawing upon the pedagogical expertise of Charlette Walker -- a fifth-grade teacher at a local school (Tilden Middle School) -- a group of twelve Penn undergraduates developed a course covering topics such as "The Good Life," "How Do We Know Unicorns Don't Exist?" "Definitions," "Classification," "Colorism," and more.

Other examples of after school clubs that we have run over the years include a Middle School Film and Philosophy Club at Penn Alexander School, a High School Philosophy Club at Carver Engineering and Science High School, and continued partnership through 2017 with Philadelphia Futures, which spawned a second ABCS course on the class culminating in a conference model.

Another more recent initiative which adds a slightly more academic focus to something like a philosophy club is our partnership with a program called

Mighty Writers.[3] Mighty Writers offers free workshops and activities for K-12 students in and around Philadelphia with the goal of supporting the development of writing skills. Our partnership with Mighty Writers has so far been very successful, and is a good example of how philosophy programming can be flexible, and can adapt to fit in a variety of after-school settings. The initial partnership began as a two-week workshop which met for one hour each day as part of the Mighty Writers summer programming for students ages 8-11. This program was then run again in the Fall of 2020 in a slightly new format, meeting once each week for eight weeks. Stephanie Wesson, the Penn P4Y staff person and graduate student in philosophy who created the programming, has worked to merge the Mighty Writers mission of improving writing skills, with our mission of getting kids involved in philosophical thinking.

The topics for these initial two iterations of the Mighty Writers workshop were the philosophy of technology and the philosophy of nature. Each day of the program focused on a philosophical concept or skill, coupled with a writing skill. For example, to work on the philosophical thinking skill of perspective-taking, and the skill of writing descriptively, the students were asked to write descriptions from various perspectives and taking on the identities of various natural entities. Another activity asked students to write a story from the perspective of something which has been taken out of nature, or placed back into nature. One student wrote of a dog, who when he returned to the woods, realized he was a wolf. These activities also developed concepts in metaphysics, such as what makes something what it is. Another activity used poetry writing to help students develop the use of metaphor, and to see how a metaphor can sometimes explain abstract concepts like emotions more clearly than a description. The technology unit explored similar concepts. One particularly successful lesson involved the students writing a dialogue between a person and an artificial intelligence entity, such as an Amazon Echo device. The students were then asked to reflect on which is more like a human, Amazon's Alexa, or a dog.

Much of pre-college philosophy is very heavily focused on oral dialogue. There are significant virtues to this approach, especially in a public school district with large classes (often well over 30 students) where oral participation allowing extensive contributions by each student is very difficult. This virtue notwithstanding, one of the major benefits of the Mighty Writers programming is that it offers young students a chance to engage in the practice of philosophical writing, which is far less common in the pre-college population. Philosophy based in oral dialogue, while a very important part of the practice, can also privilege certain types of students, such as those with greater

---

[3] https://mightywriters.org/.

confidence speaking to a group, and be more difficult for students like those who need more time to think over ideas. Philosophy through writing can give students who might have more trouble with dialogue a chance to shine. Additionally, it should be noted that this workshop began in the summer of 2020 during the Covid-19 pandemic and shutdowns. Because of this, it took place remotely via video conferencing meetings. The facilitator found the focus on independent writing to be slightly more compatible with the virtual format than a traditional dialogue model. Mighty Writers seems very happy with the philosophy workshops so far, and we hope to continue and expand this partnership. Indeed, within a week of the final writing of this essay, Penn's P4Y workshop was selected as one of the Mighty Writers' workshops to be offered at The Southwest Leadership Academy in West Philadelphia in the early spring of 2021. This workshop will be 6 weeks long, and will run as part of the school day. It will include approximately 50 sixth-grade students, taught by a team of two staff from Penn P4Y along with two classroom teachers and two additional teaching assistants from Mighty Writers. The topic of this workshop will be the 'Philosophy of the Future.'

Another program, in place since 2018, has a somewhat more formal instruction format: this is a series of 8-week courses on the "The Philosophy and Ethics of Science" offered at the Science Leadership Academy (SLA), a high school in the Philadelphia School District. SLA offers ninth-grade students a choice of "mini-course" electives in non-traditional subjects, and our course was developed as one of the options. Like the Mighty Writers initiative described above, the SLA Philosophy and Ethics of Science course was initially developed and piloted by a staff member of P4Y, in this case, Nicholas Friedman, building on their specific interests.

SLA has a science and technology focus, and our course is designed to complement this using scientific themes as a launching point for engagement with philosophy. Our objectives are fourfold: to introduce the students to philosophical topics; to cultivate their reasoning and critical thinking skills; to have them gain experience engaging with challenging ethical issues; and to deepen their understanding of science by reflecting on its complexities. We also hope to motivate the students to further explore these ideas in their other coursework and in their everyday lives as consumers of scientific information. The sessions are organized by topic, with added modules on reasoning and argumentation and one or two classes devoted to ethics case studies. The class activities feature small group work, debates, and role-playing (a tabletop exercise and a mock trial). The emphasis is on independent thinking, constructive dialogue, and respect for other viewpoints.

We have focused on the following themes and key questions. "The Demarcation Problem" - How do we distinguish science from non-science and pseudo-science? "The Nature of Scientific Evidence" - What counts as evidence? What makes some evidence preferred over others? "Scientific Reasoning" - What kind of reasoning supports scientific claims? What are facts vs. opinions? Do scientists prove claims? "Science and Moral Questions" - Can science answer moral or ethical questions (or contribute to their answer)? "Values and Objectivity" - How do values influence the sciences? Should we aspire to a value-free ideal? "Ethics Case Studies" - What ethical problems arise in research? What moral principles guide application of scientific discoveries? In reflecting on this initiative, we felt that these 9th-grade students were able to critically examine their intuitions and assumptions regarding these topics and science in general. Many of the students have clearly enjoyed getting the opportunity to discuss and debate deep questions.

At the end of each course, we have surveyed the students, and the responses have been positive on format and content, with criticisms focused on a desire for even more interactive (and "fun" or "exciting" elements). Challenges include the variation in the background knowledge of students, and keeping everyone on pace to complete activities. We intend to continue developing and improving this course while looking for other applications for this or similar curricula.

Because the University of Pennsylvania has in place the ABCS course format, these courses have been a great way to both run and staff this kind of direct programming in schools, as well as to involve Penn's undergraduate students. For these reasons, ABCS courses have been a big part of Penn P4Y programming. In addition to the Philadelphia Futures partnership built around paper writing and conference presentation courses (offered twice) and the fifth-grade curriculum development and implementation course (offered once) described earlier, we have used the ABCS course opportunity to help launch the Philadelphia Regional Ethics Bowl -- an initiative described below.

While Detlefsen offered the initial ABCS courses in the philosophy department, recently, we have moved to have graduate students develop and teach their own ABCS courses, an opportunity which we hope graduate students will continue to pursue in future years. In the spring of 2020, Michael Vazquez, a doctoral student in the philosophy department, was one of two inaugural Provost's Graduate Academic Engagement Fellows at the Netter Center, and in this capacity, Vazquez developed and implemented an ABCS course entitled "Public Philosophy." The course partnered with Mastery Charter School, Shoemaker Campus to bring Penn undergraduate students into an economics and civics class to lead the high school students in philosophical lessons on a variety of topics related to their regular curriculum. The goal of the course was to explore 'public philosophy' by bringing philosophy outside of the academy, and it sought to do this in two ways. First, the undergraduates were directly involved with public philosophy by bringing philosophy into a high school classroom. The course meetings consisted of developing lesson plans to use with the high school students, and also engaging in a meta-analysis of what public philosophy is, the purposes it might serve, and why it might be important to engage in it. Second, the culminating project for the undergraduate students was writing a philosophical op-ed on a current topic of their choosing that ostensibly could be published as a piece of public philosophy itself.

The partnership with the school - and specifically the teacher with whom we worked, Griffin Pepper - was very important in the success of this program. Pepper assisted the undergraduate students in working from the standard 12th grade economics curriculum, and the undergraduates built lesson plans to highlight and augment the philosophical themes in the class topics. Lessons included explorations of issues and concepts like fairness and equality, environmental justice, duties to the poor, corporate responsibility, the role of education, and more. Additionally, because of the investment of this particular teacher, he instituted this partnership in all four of the groups of seniors he taught, reaching more than 100 students each week. This wide reach along with the subject matter of the lessons led to an underlying focus on the democratic purposes of education, and the class even garnered the attention of the University president, Amy Gutmann, who visited the class. Unfortunately, the plans of the course were forced to change abruptly due to the move to online and remote learning caused by the Covid-19 pandemic. This included the cancellation of the culminating event with the high school students which was planned to take place on Penn's campus. But, the success of this program, the support from the university and high school, and the fact that a full semester of lessons synced to the standard high school economics curriculum was developed and tested by the students will surely lead to this program being replicated in the future, either as another ABCS course or otherwise.

A relatively new project for Penn P4Y which brings together many of the types of initiatives in which we are engaged has been our involvement with establishing a new regional competition for the National High School Ethics Bowl,[4] an achievement realized through the vision and work of Dustin Webster. The National High School Ethics Bowl is an annual event sponsored by the Parr Center for Ethics at the University of North Carolina, Chapel Hill. In the event, teams of students use a set of case studies to discuss ethical dilemmas. The event is similar to debate, but markedly different in that the conversations are meant to be collaborative as opposed to adversarial. Teams are meant to work together to gain a better understanding of the ethical dimensions of each case. They are scored on how thoughtful they are in various parts of these

---

[4] https://nhseb.unc.edu/.

discussions. There are regional competitions throughout the United States, which send winners to the national competition which takes place at UNC.

In 2019-2020, Penn P4Y founded a new regional competition, the Philadelphia Regional High School Ethics Bowl, to be hosted at Penn. In this first year, we supported and helped to develop a foundation of High School teams through the use of another ABCS course, as mentioned above. In this course, we trained undergraduate students to be Ethics Bowl coaches, and once each week the students traveled to five local high schools where they helped to develop and coach teams. In addition to these student coaches, we also had a number of graduate students who helped to coach the teams alongside the undergraduates, and continued that coaching after the ABCS course ended. While the ABCS course will not take place every year, we are committed to the ongoing support of Ethics Bowl teams. Participation in an event like the Ethics Bowl can be more difficult for under-resourced schools because of the demands for time which it places on both the teachers and students. A big part of our development of this project is to continue to provide undergraduate and graduate students who help those teams, should their teachers request such coaching.

Additionally, we are in the early stages of a few other initiatives related to supporting Ethics Bowl participation. These include creating an Ethics Bowl coaching manual, as well as offering training in the early fall for teachers who wish to coach, both on the basics of coaching an Ethics Bowl team, and, since many teachers might view their lack of knowledge of philosophy as a barrier to participation, a workshop in basic ethical theory.

In many ways, the Ethics Bowl can be an anchor of expanded philosophy programming for high schools. The Philadelphia Ethics Bowl culminates in the competition which takes place in late winter, but Ethics Bowl clubs can and have continued at schools through the spring led by the same graduate students. These clubs have continued working with the case studies and in ethics, or have also shifted to explore other topics in philosophy. Additionally, teachers who coach teams have sometimes continued to develop or initiate philosophy classes at their schools.

To expand the Ethics Bowl beyond just the teams' individual meetings and the single competition day, we sponsor other events and programming before and after the bowl on Penn's campus. For example, leading up to the 2020 bowl, we offered several weekend workshops at Penn for any teams or students who wanted to gain some extra preparation and coaching. The high school students worked with Penn students, and we are exploring the possibilities of hosting practice ethic bowl rounds to help teams prepare. We plan to hold similar types of weekend workshops to continue involvement after the bowl takes place.

One final thing to note about the Ethics Bowl is that it is an extremely popular and well-received event. We have received support - financial and otherwise - from across the university including from the Graduate School of Education, Penn Law School, the School of Arts and Sciences, and several other centers and units on campus. On competition day, faculty and staff from across the university volunteer to function as judges. The Ethics Bowl event has been valuable to Penn P4Y not only because it is enjoyed by everyone who participates, but also because it helps to build strong connections between area high schools and the university.

B. Philosophy Integrated into Existing School Curricula

The Ethics Bowl is one way in which K-12 teachers have been engaged by Penn P4Y. In addition, we have also cultivated a valuable relationship with the Teachers Institute of Philadelphia (TIP).[5] This is the primary avenue by which we collaborate with teachers to integrate philosophy into existing school curricula. TIP is a chapter associated with the Yale National Initiative, which aims to strengthen teaching in public schools.

Both the Yale initiative and TIP are rooted in the belief that teachers have professional expertise in education, professors at local universities have expertise in their subject areas, and that by bringing together these two sets of expertise, public school students stand to reap significant benefits by improved teaching and content in the classroom. Each year in the spring, TIP offers five or six seminars, each serving 12 public school teachers, and each involving a different specialization. In spring 2018, Detlefsen was invited to offer a seminar in philosophy, focusing on science and society. The Fellows -- TIP term for PSD educators participating in the seminars -- collectively covered all K-12 grades except fifth grade, and a wide range of subjects including literature, social studies, sciences, mathematics, computer technology and more. Together with the Fellows, Detlefsen designed a philosophy curriculum covering philosophy of science, including bioethics, and a range of issues in social-political philosophy. The Fellows each produced a curriculum unit of about 20 pages, addressing the philosophy covered in the seminar, and developing a number of lesson plans that engaged with the philosophy. The subsequent year, the Fellows piloted their curriculum with their classes.

The model of TIP Seminars (and of the Yale National Initiative more generally) holds a great deal of promise for bringing philosophy to school-age students in

---

[5] https://theteachersinstitute.org/ The Teachers Institute of Philadelphia offers teachers the opportunity to enroll in semester-long courses taught by university professors on a variety of topics at no cost to the teachers.

a way that is developmentally appropriate, and in a way that directly compliments their existing school subjects. Moreover, because teachers teach large numbers of students, year after year, and because the curriculum units developed by the PSD educators are publicly available on TIP's website for any teacher anywhere to implement with their students, the TIP model holds a great deal of promise for bringing philosophy to large numbers of school-age students.

After her initial TIP seminar, described above, Detlefsen collaborated in 2018-19 with a high school literature teacher from that seminar, Jessica Waber, to design an experimental version of the TIP seminar. Focusing on a specific group of teachers -- high school teachers of literature -- Waber and Detlefsen recruited a handful of other teachers to try out a new model. Starting with about a dozen books that the teachers regularly taught their students, the group together designed a philosophy curriculum to directly address philosophical problems at the heart of those novels. Covering topics such as evil, race and racism, social construction, love, parents and children, and more, and connecting these topics with texts such as *Hamlet, Frankenstein, The Hate U Give, I Know Why the Caged Bird Sings,* and *The Things They Carried,* the teachers designed a number of lessons to connect their class material with philosophy. In the academic year 2019-2020, Stephen Esser and Detlefsen collaborated with a retired elementary school teacher, Terry Anne Wildman, to offer another variant on the TIP seminar. This time working with teachers of third through fifth-grade students, the team built 48 lesson plans and accompanying philosophical material around a commonly-used elementary school curriculum based in the ReadyGEN reading program.[6]

Detlefsen and P4Y more generally will continue partnering with TIP -- for example, in spring 2021 on the topic of Democracy and Expertise, collaborating with a group of history, literature, and science teachers -- to pursue this second major prong of our project, namely integrating philosophy into existing school curricula.

Student Development and Research within Penn

A. Penn Student Development

Penn Students have been enthusiastic and thoughtful participants across all of our activities, and graduate students in particular have provided new ideas for engaging pre-college students which have led some important new initiatives.

---

[6] "ReadyGEN" is a literacy curriculum developed by the Savvas learning company which is one of the curricula used by the Philadelphia School District.

In doing so, they have been developing valuable new pedagogical and communication skills to complement their academic training. In recognition of this student development dimension of our P4Y work, along with that of other public outreach efforts at Penn, our Philosophy Department has established a Graduate Certificate in Public Philosophy in order to create a formal path for our students to develop their capabilities as they engage members of the community.

This new Certificate Program reflects our belief that philosophical tools and knowledge can contribute to improving civic dialogue about contentious issues. To make this happen, we think that those with academic training must cultivate the knowledge and skills needed to effectively engage with the public. Ultimately, it requires *doing* public philosophy: interacting with diverse sets of people in non-academic settings to explore issues and critique the reasoning methods used to evaluate them. In particular, we think it is especially worthwhile for academics to reach out to members of their communities who might have fewer opportunities to participate in this kind of dialogue.

The Certificate Program incorporates coursework, research, and community engagement. It is open to any student already enrolled in a graduate program at the University of Pennsylvania. These students should gain professional benefits from participating. We have observed that postings for new academic positions increasingly feature components of public outreach or community engagement. The research, training, and practical experience gained from completing the program will demonstrate that our students have a level of proficiency in building relationships between the academy and the public. We have already seen our alumni contribute to new public philosophy efforts after leaving Penn, and we look forward to much more of this in the future.

B. Research

There is no shortage of anecdotal accounts of the positive effects that engaging in philosophy can bring to pre-college students, teachers and schools, and it is important to demonstrate these outcomes through empirical research. There is a small but growing body of work in this area to which we hope to make a contribution. At the time of writing this chapter, we are in the early stages of thinking through what such a research project would look like. We plan to build from the research framework used by Keith Topping and Steven Trickey to conduct a large-scale and high-quality study.[7] The Topping and Trickey study

---

[7] This study is described in detail in a number of papers by the authors, and is nicely summarized in Topping, Keith J., Steven Trickey, and Paul Cleghorn. *A Teacher's Guide to Philosophy for Children*. Routledge, 2019.

included 105 experimental students who engaged in one hour of philosophy each week, and 72 students matched with them in a control group. It also included follow-up testing 16 months after the intervention. Their evaluative tools included standardized tests to measure both cognitive ability as well as self-esteem, questionnaires completed by children to measure social development, and the analysis of video recordings of classroom sessions. The authors found significant gains for students engaging in P4C over the control group in cognitive abilities (verbal, non-verbal, quantitative), and in how students reported seeing themselves as learners (self-as-learner esteem score). Additionally, through analyzing videos and transcripts, they found students in the experimental group had increased participation, gave more elaborate answers, and demonstrated increased reasoning through their justification for those answers.

For our project, we hope to follow a cohort of students from kindergarten through third grade who engage in a philosophy program each year. The curriculum we will develop will be closely based on an adaptation of Matthew Lipman's method created by Paul Cleghorn, entitled 'Thinking Through Philosophy.'[8] It also works from elements of a program for young children created by Sarah Stanley.[9] With the help of a kindergarten teacher or teachers from the Philadelphia School District we will test and hone this curriculum. We will then work closely with the Penn Graduate School of Education (GSE) to develop and implement the study. Our hope is that this initial foray into research, as well as the partnership with GSE, will lay the groundwork for regular and continued collaboration in research around pre-college philosophy. As Penn P4Y grows, we plan to support both teachers and graduate students who wish to undertake such work.

Future Plans and Directions

Aligned with this intention to eventually be able to offer robust support for research, the broad goal for the Penn P4Y moving forward is to develop into a center focused on this work. The program has already expanded to a scale that goes beyond a project that can be run by faculty and others with full-time commitments to regular jobs and studies, and it would benefit from one or more part-time staff to take over general operations. We realize that the key to

---

[8] Paul Cleghorn, and Stephanie Baudet. *Thinking Through Philosophy: Book 1*. Educational Printing Services Limited, 2004; Matthew Lipman, along with Ann Margaret Sharp are widely considered to be the founders of the contemporary philosophy for children movement. See Matthew Lipman. *Thinking in Education*. Cambridge University Press, 1991.

[9] Sara Stanley. "A Skills Based Approach to P4C—Philosophy: Fairy Tales and the Foundation Stage." *Gifted Education International* 22, no. 2-3 (2007): 172-181.

truly scaling our programming, and getting philosophy into more classrooms is through collaboration with K-12 teachers and curriculum development. There is a great deal of value in faculty, project staff, and graduate students entering schools and engaging young students directly, and maintaining such opportunities through our relationships will remain an important part of our work. However, the bigger picture must necessarily be more easily scalable, and this involves helping teachers themselves use philosophical tools, and integrate philosophy into their classrooms. In the near future and beyond, we will place a strong emphasis on providing teachers the opportunities and support they need toward this end.

What Works and What Doesn't

Finally, we would like to add a small handful of lessons which we have learned over the past six years of growth and program development. This is far from an exhaustive list, but offers a few of the major takeaways and themes from our experience.

By far one of the most significant factors in the success of any initiative is buy-in from the teachers, administrators, or staff of the school or program where the philosophy curriculum is being implemented. This is important whether or not the philosophy program is being run by Penn P4Y staff, or the teachers themselves. When others see the value in engaging their students in philosophy, it makes all aspects of implementing a program more successful. For example, our P4Y staff of mostly philosophy graduate and undergraduate students have varying degrees of experience working with and teaching K-12 students. Classroom management and organization is often new to them, and can be a challenge. When the classroom teacher is ready and willing to step in to assist, and is interested in being involved, it can help support the P4Y staff in a way that more quickly enables them to develop their own skills working with the younger students. Invested teachers can keep aspects of philosophical practice, formally or informally, as part of the normal classroom routine, further enforcing the skills which we hope to develop in the students.

Alternatively, when teachers are not on the same page as our staff and program, many unforeseen challenges can arise. For example, our staff might arrive to find far more, or far fewer students than they were expecting, forcing last-minute changes to the plans for the day. Teachers might also be expecting, or in need of, something different from what our staff is planning on providing. At one of our sites, staff arrived to implement an after-school club, but found that most of the students were engaged in their homework, and the teachers asked them to provide homework help instead of running the philosophy programming. Of course, such support is important and helpful to teachers, but it is not what we are aiming to provide. Another example is from a school where our staff was engaged in preparing a team for the Ethics Bowl. The same small group of high school students making up the team who had been meeting for some time was planning on working through a case on which they had already put in a great deal of effort. The teacher, however, had an influx of students into her room, as she was covering the class of a colleague during the period. These students needed something to do, and without consulting our staff, she offered extra credit to anyone who wanted to join the Ethics Bowl discussion. Unsurprisingly, we were met with a wave of new students, which on one hand we were happy to have, but which also made the original plan for the day impossible. and took away from the progress that the team was hoping to make in that period.

Teacher involvement can help with consistency as well. As with the examples above, depending on the type of programming, consistency of students who participate can be very important. Teachers are in the primary position to control this aspect of our programming. Consistency in staffing is also important, and can be a challenge if programs are staffed by graduate and undergraduate students, as their schedules and availability are often subject to frequent change. An invested teacher can help smooth out such transitions and staffing changes, and provide continuity even if our staffing has to be adjusted.

Lastly, as we are learning as our program grows, organization and standardization of the materials and programming we develop and offer to schools is becoming increasingly important. Much of our curricula has been developed in a piecemeal fashion by a number of different students and staff over the years. As such, we found ourselves with a wealth of material that was not so easy for new participants to access or implement. At the time of writing this chapter, we are engaged in a large-scale effort to comb through all of these various lessons, standardize their format, and organize them into easy-to-use units.

Conclusion

From its inception a little over six years ago, the Penn Project for Philosophy for the Young has grown rapidly into a multipronged effort covering self-standing philosophy classes and clubs within K-12 public schools, afterschool programs, philosophy merged with existing school subjects, Penn student development, and research. Rooted in beliefs about young folks' ability to engage in philosophy in age-appropriate ways, and in their love of thinking deeply about hard questions that matter to them, and also rooted in a commitment to bringing excellent humanistic education to students in Philadelphia's Public School District, Penn's P4Y strives to continue its growth to reach more students across the city in coming years.

Bibliography

Cleghorn, Paul., and Stephanie Baudet. *Thinking Through Philosophy: Book 1.* Educational Printing Services Limited, 2004.

Lipman, Matthew. *Thinking in Education.* Cambridge: Cambridge University Press, 1991.

Stanley, Sara. "A Skills Based Approach to P4C—Philosophy: Fairy Tales and the Foundation Stage." *Gifted Education International* 22, no. 2-3 (2007): 172-181.

Topping, Keith J., Steven Trickey, and Paul Cleghorn. *A Teacher's Guide to Philosophy for Children.* New York: Routledge, 2019.

Chapter 8

Once A Philosopher-In-Hiding: Teaching Philosophy in Spanish in the USA

Joseph Aloysius Murphy

Dwight-Englewood School, NJ

Abstract

This chapter describes how students can read and discuss philosophical concepts in a new language. The author shares his experience teaching a full-year course in the History of Philosophy in Spanish in an independent school in New Jersey. In this class, students never speak or read a word in English. The class focus is on engagement and inquiry-based discussion. The author guides his students to learn to think audaciously as they gradually acquire academic language. A growing understanding of logic helps students to scaffold their emerging ideas and reasoning. Students learn how to critique classic philosophical texts and take on multiple perspectives as they discuss and write essays about some of the most influential ideas in the world. In the process, philosophically and linguistically fluent students grow the ability to create and defend their own arguments. "The History of Philosophy in Spanish" course also prepares students to compete in both the American Philosophy Open (APO) and ultimately the International Philosophy Olympiad (IPO) essay contests. Both opportunities require that students write their essay in a language other than their national language. The chapter fully describes the qualifications and requirements of both the APO and IPO.

Keywords: American Philosophy Open, Critical Thinking, Ethics, Euthyphro, International Philosophy Olympiad, Knowledge, Language, Opinion, Philosophy, Spanish

***

What time is it? That's an easy enough question. Just look at any clock available to you right now. Okay, done. Even in Spanish, that's an easy enough question: *¿Qué hora es?* But if I were to ask you *"¿qué es el tiempo?,"* as Fernando Savater does in his history of philosophy book for Spanish high school students, then everything changes. "What is time?" is not an easy question for native speakers of English. When I ask my native English speakers the same question in Spanish, the double struggle begins. It includes a lot of silence, false starts and a plethora of mistakes. I love it.

As my students walk into our honors History of Philosophy in Spanish course, they leave their English behind. They walk into a new realm where they study *la historia de la filosofía*. They are high school juniors and seniors who have been studying Spanish since middle school and probably for a few years before that. The course is an Honors, level 6, sometimes post Advanced Placement course. It is a Spanish language class, but it is also a philosophy course. Besides the Spanish language requirement, there is another prerequisite for this class at Dwight-Englewood School (D-E), the required Ethical Thinking 1 course, which is an introductory course in moral philosophy.

Before I describe more about what happens in my History of Philosophy in Spanish course, I want to give you some personal background to see how this opportunity came about at my school. Twenty-five years ago, I started teaching Spanish at D-E. Five years later, I became Language Department Chair in 2000. In 2005, after a series of events at my school, I was able to use my degree in Philosophy to help create a small Ethics and Philosophy Department. The *Historia de la Filosofía* course has grown out of my particular background, but my experience is just an example of what is possible in American high schools. English, History, Mathematics and Science teachers, as well as other philosophers-in-hiding in all kinds of American schools around the country, could develop an analogous philosophy course from within their academic departments. If you look, you will see that there is someone in your school who majored or minored in philosophy in college. I'm sure they would love to help develop and teach a philosophy course at your school. Students will learn to do some serious critical reasoning, logic and philosophical thinking. These are skills they will be able to use across the academic spectrum to their benefit in every discipline.

Now imagine that you are one of my students. You cross the threshold of our classroom—or come on-screen via Zoom in this COVID time of a worldwide pandemic, which is a major interruption in our normal lives—and you are transported to Spain. No one here speaks any English at all. I am rather extreme as a Spanish teacher. No one may even ask for a translation of any word or concept. Hand signals, drawings, pantomime, elaborate descriptions and enough circumlocution to make anyone dizzy are all tools at one's disposal to make a point and understand a concept, but not translation. Your text is the *Historia de la Filosofía sin temor ni temblor* (*History of Philosophy Without Fear or Trembling*) by the Spanish philosopher, Fernando Savater[1]. It is an authentic text written for high school students in Spain. It's a 300-page book. The course is divided into two semesters; Ancient and Modern Philosophy. Students read the first half of the text in Semester 1 and the second half in semester 2. Along the way in the first semester, students also read Plato's *Apología de Sócrates*[2] (*Apology*) or *Eutifrón* [3](*Euthyphro*) in Spanish, of course. In the second semester, students read René Descartes' entire *Discurso del método* (*Discourse on Method*), which, by the way, was one of the first books of philosophy ever written in a vulgar language. Descartes wrote it in French. Most if not all of his other books were written in Latin, but in this class we read it in Spanish translation.

At first, my students stumble. Most of them are used to being able to fall back on English in some way. Most of them have used bilingual dictionaries, have asked in English for particular words in Spanish, perhaps have even looked up concepts on a website in English, then have spoken about it or written about it in faltering Spanish. Not here. Students may certainly use dictionaries, but only monolingual Spanish ones. They may certainly ask for an explanation of particular words and concepts, but only in Spanish. They may only express their thoughts in Spanish, both in their speaking and in their writing. Efficiency is not the point. The goal in this class is to learn to think directly in Spanish. Of course, students make a lot of mistakes in grammar and syntax, in vocabulary, and even in style. Sometimes they consciously or unconsciously translate from English thinking. They express a thought in Spanish that is a phrase or a word that obviously, is English dressed up in literal Spanish words or elementary Spanish syntax. Often, they use English syntax using Spanish words. This is normal for students learning a second language. It is all fine as long as they continue to *struggle* with the language and with the philosophical concepts. This is learning at a deep level. It is also acquiring perspective that will pervade their social lives as well as their thinking.

The struggle is all good if the teacher is understanding and maieutic. My own struggles learning Spanish in Spain and my personal reflections about it, as well as later advanced study in language help me to be understanding of my students' struggles acquiring a new language. My background in philosophy has also been a struggle for me. I wrestle with concepts, ideas, points of view and logic. But I have a good example to follow. My first real philosophical inspiration was Socrates. He was strong, quick-witted and profoundly

---

[1] Savater, Fernando. *Historia de la filosofía sin temor ni temblor*. Madrid, Spain: Espasa Calpe. S. A., 2009. This book was written by Professor Savater for high school students in Spain.

[2] Platón. *Apoligía de Sócrates. Obras completes de Platón.*

[3] Platón. *Eutifrón o de la santidad. Obras completes de Platón.*

insightful. He was irrepressible with supposed experts, the Sophists, while at the same time, he would behave like a conceptual midwife with his disciples who would struggle with his questions. I join in the struggle of my students as they wrestle with concepts. I try to think with them. I listen very carefully to them while they attempt to express a new thought in a language that is not their own. I might offer a word or add direction to their thinking by interpolating into their speech what I think they are trying to say in Spanish. I know the material, the languages, and I know the students. I know where they're coming from and where I think they're going. Sometimes we meander through a wilderness of concepts to arrive at what we hope will be, to echo Descartes, a clear and distinct idea. We usually arrive at a place of some epistemic satisfaction. Sometimes there is an epiphany when a student understands a brand-new concept in his, her, or their life that they understand first in a second language.

Socrates Lives in My Classroom

Socrates asked my students the following question in Spanish: *"¿Lo santo es amado por los dioses porque es santo, o es santo porque es amado por ellos?"*[4] ("Is the holy loved by the gods because it is holy, or is it holy because it is loved by them?" – My translation from the Spanish.)

This question causes the same consternation for an adolescent in Spanish as it does in English or in any other language. I put this question to my students in Spanish the same way I would in an English language philosophy course. Are you good because God says you're good or are you good because you are good? If God does exist, does He, She or They actually do any ethical thinking? Perhaps what God or the gods say is good is proclaimed by the godhead/s by divine fiat. If that's so, then couldn't anything be good, even the bad? What? Wait, if the bad were proclaimed to be good by the divine being/s, which would it be and how would we mere mortals know it? Or does that which many people call the Creator go through some kind of ethical thinking of His, Her or Their own? Or perhaps God just knows what is good and bad not by some Divine Command Theory, but by recognizing the good for what it is. But if this is true, doesn't that mean that God had nothing to do with the decision? Who made the original judgment?

Yes, this whole conversation is held in Spanish. It is all very confusing, even in English for a native speaker. But as I work through it with my students, there is a tremendous satisfaction when the problem is understood and the students

---

[4] Platón. *Eutifrón o de la santidad. Obras completes de Platón.* Translated by Patricio de Azcárate. Madrid, Spain 1871-72: Proyecto Filosofía en español ©2005 www.filosofia.org. http://www.filosofia.org/cla/pla/azc01009.htm.

start to form their own ideas about such heady topics in Spanish! Could it be that there's another option? Maybe God has nothing to do with it other than recognizing the good for what it is in the moment. Maybe God leaves the whole question up to us! Then what? And what's the plan? Or my atheistic students look at this question in another way that is entirely different from the Divine Command Theory. Enter secular ethics using reason to decide what is good and bad and to make ethical decisions. There is a lot to all of this and doing it in a language that is not the native language of the student is extra exciting.

Of course, the original question is asked in Plato's words, which he ascribed to his teacher, Socrates. Plato wrote this question in his dialogue, *Euthyphro*, which my students read in the Spanish from Ancient Greek as, "*Eutifrón o de la santidad*". My students in the "History of Philosophy in Spanish," mostly high school seniors, read Plato's *Euthyphro* in Spanish. They are not native speakers of Spanish. Occasionally heritage or native speakers take my "History of Philosophy in Spanish" course, but for the most part, they are students who have been studying Spanish since they were in elementary school. Sometimes they will have already taken our Advanced Placement Language or Literature course in Spanish before they take my History of Philosophy course. There have been some students who have taken this course instead of either of the AP courses in Spanish. They struggle a little bit more with the language, but I help them with it in my role as a language teacher. The "philosophy bug," as some of the parents of my students call it, carries them through.

There's a model of disruption here. Euthyphro was an important theologian in the time of Socrates. Whom better to ask than an authority on the subject? The subject of the holy or pious or good is a subject that any self-respecting theologian should know about. So, of course, Socrates would ask Euthyphro the questions concerning this subject. Socrates is our best model of a critical thinker.

An Ethics Requirement

Although I came to my school as a Spanish teacher, I was a philosopher-in-hiding. I noticed that the administration and the teachers at D-E all talked about critical thinking. I was very excited to hear this. It seemed to me that there must be some philosophical thinking and at least elementary logic being taught throughout the curriculum. There was also an ethics program at the school, but as I found out, the program was little more than a senior essay requirement.

For their essay requirement, seniors would meet with one of the English teachers who was also the summer school principal. One of his titles was also, "Ethics Coordinator." He would meet with the seniors in the fall. He'd meet with groups of 15 students or so to prepare them to write the essay. This preparation was nothing more than the presentation of ethics vocabulary; consequentialism, character, deontology, values and virtue among other words used in moral philosophy. With this one session done, the students were told to write an essay on an ethics topic of their choice. Most of the essays were two or three pages long. They would be handed in to the coordinator of the ethics program who would ask for volunteers from among the faculty to be readers and evaluators. Most of them had no training in philosophy or ethics besides, perhaps, a philosophy course that they may have taken in college. I would always volunteer. My reading of the senior essays was an education. Most of the essays were a free expression of popular opinion with no argument. They were mere opinions written on topics like abortion, the death penalty, or plagiarism. Sometimes a few students would write about euthanasia, war, the inquisition or a critique of authoritarianism. Each teacher would read five or six or more essays, give them a pass—most of the students who graduate from my school are good writers by the time they are seniors—and return them to the coordinator marked as a requirement fulfilled. Almost none of the poor students whose essays I would read would ever receive a 'requirement fulfilled' before meeting with me for a tutorial on ethics in which I would ask them to justify the point of view they'd expressed in their essays. I would ask them why they would think that something is right or wrong, good or bad, then I would help them to construct a clear argument and to look for counterarguments. After that short session, I'd send them off to rewrite their essays. Sometimes their second essay would meet the requirement.

After having this experience for a couple of years and meeting with the coordinator of the ethics program, I started to develop ideas for an ethics program that I thought we could implement at the school that would approach teaching the students some elementary ethical thinking before they were sent off to write their essays. For several years my proposals went nowhere. After five years at the school, I was invited to become Chair of the Language Department. My proposals were getting more elaborate even to the point that I asked for space in the curriculum to create a minor ethics class. As Chair, I now had more say in the curriculum of the school. So I proposed an Introduction to Philosophy as well as my regular updated ethics proposals. My fellow chairs told me that high school students were too young and not yet mature enough to study philosophy. One Chair told me that philosophy was a college subject, that it was inappropriate for high school students who would only be frustrated by it. Besides, we don't have room for it in our schedule, they said. Other Chairs and the Principal acquiesced. I was the only member of the Curriculum Committee composed of all Department Chairs and principals of the three divisions of the school, who had a degree in Philosophy. I was bewildered by what my fellow leaders of the school said, especially because I had taught Philosophy For Children (P4C) and had worked directly with Matthew Lipman, the creator of the P4C method of teaching philosophy to children in the 1970's. I had taught philosophy to fifth graders while I worked with Dr. Lipman. It was an outstanding experience, but my arguments and experience to create an ethics class at my school went nowhere. Once I sent one of my ethics proposals to Peter Singer, Professor of Bioethics at Princeton University, to have a look at it. Professor Singer very graciously read my proposal and gave me some suggestions for improvement, complemented me for it and wished me luck. It and all my other proposals were rejected until 2005.

In late summer, 2005 the Ethics Coordinator left the school to take a position as Vice Principal in a New York school. The Principal of the Upper School called an emergency meeting. We needed to fill the position of Ethics Coordinator. I submitted another proposal. This time the Principal asked me to lead a discussion with the Chairs using my new proposal as the exclusive agenda item. This time my proposal was more audacious than the ones I had submitted in previous years. The next day the Head of the School asked me to teach the ethics program I had proposed. I suggested that an ethics class be a required minor course for sophomores. I would teach all the sections. There are five sections per semester. I said I would give up the Language Chair to do it if we would create an Ethics Chair position with all the rights and requirements of the other academic Chairs and the one I was leaving to take it. He agreed and my office as Language Chair became the office of the new Ethics Chair. That was 2005. In 2021 there are eight philosophy and ethics courses taught at my school including the History of Philosophy in Spanish, which is a course shared by both the Language Department and the Philosophy and Ethics Department. We have found a way to include philosophy and ethics courses in our curriculum, which now includes the original ethics requirement and seven other courses as major and minor electives for juniors and seniors. The current Head of School and the Upper School Principal fully support the work of the Philosophy and Ethics Department. Currently, we not only successfully teach ethics and philosophy at my school, but frequently some of our graduates go on to college to major in philosophy. They learn that it is possible to major in philosophy in college because they discovered it in high school.

Critical Thinking

Critical thinking and rational analysis in various disciplines have figured prominently in D-E's literature and in the syllabi of the classes. It is taught to one degree or another in my school and in most American high schools. I have been informally surveying my Ethical Thinking 1 students over the years by asking my students if their teachers have told them that critical thinking would be an important part of their classes. They have told me that most of their teachers say that critical thinking is important in their classes. I follow up my initial question by asking the students if their teachers have explicitly explained to them what critical thinking is. Many of the students say no. Students seem to have come away with the idea that critical thinking is just deep reading and careful listening to the teacher to make sure they understand what the teacher is saying. I'm sure that teachers explain it much more clearly than that, but students seem to equate critical thinking with good understanding. Certainly, school administrators say that critical thinking is central to a good education. They're right. Schools across the country include critical thinking as one of their school values, but little time is spent teaching it explicitly. Critical thinking can be traced back to Plato and Socrates. With the systematic use of inquiry, for which Socrates is best known as the origin of this skill. In my Ethical Thinking 1 class, I use a book by Lewis Vaughn; *Beginning Ethics: an introduction to moral philosophy*. Critical thinking and an introduction to logic are central to this book and to ethics as I teach it. Vaughn's description of critical thinking or critical reasoning is important to quote here.

"As a division of philosophy, ethics does its work primarily through critical reasoning. Critical reasoning is the careful, systematic evaluation of statements, or claims—a process used in all fields of study, not just in ethics. Mainly this process includes both the evaluation of logical arguments and the careful analysis of concepts."[5]

Critical thinking or critical reasoning is one step toward teaching philosophy already appreciated in school curricula, but the link to broader philosophical analysis doesn't seem clear in schools. Certainly, the inclusion of the concept of diversity in the curriculum as well as the conscious inclusion of diverse people in the student body, faculty and staff of a school, and the perspectives that come with deepening awareness of racism and sexism are serious moral issues. The questions that arise in anti-racist work and anti-sexist social life are complex issues that are now widely discussed in many schools. The social and emotional learning that is becoming more common in schools is necessary to this work, but it is not sufficient. These issues raise deeply philosophical questions. Indeed, they are moral issues of the first order that need philosophical analysis and ethical decision-making strategies. But, generally, including a philosophy and / or ethics course in a school's curriculum to help teach a broader and more coordinated understanding of how a philosophical perspective can help, is not appreciated. These issues scream out for the kind

---

[5] Vaughn, Lewis. *Beginning Ethics: an introduction to moral philosophy*. New York and London: W. W. Norton and Company, Inc., 2015, 16.

of clarification that philosophical and ethical analysis and reflection can provide in schools.

Character education is a perspective that some Independent Schools appreciate and provide mostly in the context of professional development for the faculty. An example of this is the training that is provided by "The Center for Spiritual and Ethical Education.,"[6] but ongoing classes in ethics or moral philosophy are not usually provided for the students. Indeed, these concerns are at the core of who we are as human beings and how we treat each other as moral agents. These questions both create and challenge the meaning that we create for ourselves in our personal, social, moral, cultural, educational and philosophical lives. I see all of this as a paradoxical presence of philosophy in American high schools[7] because educators are calling for the skills that philosophy provides while at the same time, administrators are saying that the study of philosophy as an academic subject is impractical and cannot be accommodated in our school curricula. In fact, serious courses in philosophy and ethics would greatly benefit our students right now. The skills that philosophy and ethics provide are exactly what our students need in a moment in their adolescence in which students see social problems as real. They are asking authentic questions of themselves, their parents, teachers and the leaders of our society. It is also a moment in which they are coming to understand that they themselves are becoming capable of confronting these problems and helping to resolve them for themselves and for the broader society. Indeed, they are not only capable of doing this work, they must do it for themselves now and in their immediate future. Educators consistently tell these young people, they are the future leaders of society. It is time that they learn the skills they need to make good ethical decisions and to build these leadership capacities. It is time for them to take the moral responsibility of their own lives and help make society a more coherently moral community.

I see a paradoxical situation in our schools. We are yearning for philosophical analysis that clarifies our thinking, helps us distinguish good arguments from bad, and adds perspective and skills to help us live more meaningful lives, but we reject philosophy as a subject of direct study in most of our pre-college schools. We yearn for truth in our schools, but when we look to the broader society we see some leaders of our country make a mockery of truth when some of them offer what have been called "alternative facts." This is unclear thinking

---

[6] "The Center for Spiritual and Ethical Education" www.csee.org.

[7] In 2015 I published an article in a journal of philosophy in Spain "*Diálogo Filosófico*" (written only in Spanish) in which I elaborated on what I called "*La paradójica presencia creciente de la filosofía en los institutos en Estados Unidos*" (The paradoxical increasing presence of philosophy in high schools in the United States). It will soon be available online.

or intentional deception. Either way, our students need to be able to see through it and distinguish it from clear thinking and sincere, good rational arguments. Reason is what holds us together when we share ideas, strategies, plans and policies. This is why we value critical thinking and this is what philosophy in our schools can provide.

We urge our children not to tell a lie, not to plagiarize, to search for truth in history, to learn the scientific method, to study the characters in literature searching in part for positive and negative examples of living a good life. We look askance at the kind of behavior that has brought a President of the USA to a second impeachment citing his violent rhetoric, his persuasive exhortations to storm the capitol of the US government, his fallacious arguments and the general confusion that his outlandish behavior and example has had on voters and even on elected government officials. Then we avoid talking about it directly in schools and we don't provide our students with a philosophical study of logic, fallacies and the kind perspective of argumentation that could help clarify our serious discussions and general conversation. We want the kind of solutions that moral thinking can provide, yet we don't make time for moral philosophy in our schools. We decry philosophy as impractical, yet we don't make time for philosophy per se in our curricula or give much time to it in our extracurricular schedules. We say we want to teach practical skills to our students to help them live lives that will assure them of a strong financial future to make sure that they are happy people, but happiness is prior to financial success not a product of it. The developing consciousness of meaning in our personal and social lives can only be enhanced by making an explicit commitment to the philosophical basis of the issues that concern us.

Furthermore, it seems to me that every academic discipline is rooted in philosophical thinking. A person's self-concept, understanding of the world and human behavior are all molded by it. It is a sense of wonder and philosophical investigation that structures our consciousness, shapes our world and helps to give rise to culture. Actual Pre-college Philosophy and Ethics classes can help students realize this and help them develop their early ruminations into clear and explicit thinking about life and their place in it. The Ethical Thinking 1 course, which I teach as an initial course for students at D-E, is designed to teach ethical and moral decision-making by helping students develop the conceptual and rational skills of philosophical thinking built on a sense of empathy and compassion for others that students can use as they try to live a consciously good life.

The methodology of all of my classes is primarily Socratic and inquiry-based. I believe that epistemological humility is an important value for students and teachers. At the same time, it seems to me that taking good pre-college philosophy and ethics courses can inspire students to give full reign to their imaginations and sense of inquiry to pursue and develop knowledge to the clearest and fullest extent possible. In the context of critical thinking and moral philosophy, what I mean by knowledge here is the skill to be able to distinguish honesty, sincerity, and truth from dishonesty, deception, and misrepresentation.

I'm Not Interested in Your Opinions

In this section, I'll give the reader a window into my Ethical Thinking I class. Most of the fifteen-year-old students in this class are naïve relativists. They believe that they have a right to their 'opinions.' They believe that if they believe something, then it's true. They believe the same about others, too. In this sense, they are being tolerant of others' opinions, but they seem to be confusing aesthetic or prudential norms with moral or more broadly rational norms. Many of my students think that they are being open and understanding of the 'opinions' of each other and I know that they have good intentions, but they don't have a right to their own 'opinions' in the way that they might have a right to genuine knowledge. Students learn that mere opinions are empty when they are offered without the structured decision-making process needed to take a systematic stance.

"I'm Mr. Murphy," I tell students on the first day of class. "Please take out a piece of paper and a pen or pencil. Write your name and today's date at the top of the page." Other than issuing these requests, I'm playing my cards close to the vest. "I'm going to give you ten topics. Please write your 'opinion' of each topic. Don't ask any questions. Don't ask for clarification, spelling or meaning. Just write your 'opinion,' nothing else." "How much should we write?" one of them inevitably asks. I tell them that they will have time to write their 'opinion' of each topic until I announce the next one. Then I tell them not to ask any more questions. "Topic one...."

I proceed to walk around the Ethics Classroom, a room especially designed by D-E for philosophical inquiry. The classroom has a built-in bookcase over which hangs a copy of Raphael's *School of Athens*. Around the periphery of the room are easy chairs and sofas. The center of the room is an open space with a long-running Persian-style rug that is well worn, lying diagonally from near the room entrance to the opposite corner. There is no assigned place for a teacher to sit that is any different from where the students sit nor is there a teacher's desk. The very structure of the room has been created to foster our daily exercise of "Philosophy in the Round," as I call it. "Philosophy in the round" is a place where all ideas can emerge and be shared equally, judged by the merit of the arguments put forth, their reasonable structures and the speaker's thoughtfulness. It is in this setting that my eager new students begin to scribble or type a response to the topics I dictate to them.

Topic 1: Euthanasia. ("Yes, I'll spell it for you. And, no, it's not youth in
    Asia....")
Topic 2: DACA.
Topic 3: Honor Killing.
Topic 4: Abortion
Topic 5: Waterboarding
Topic 6: Pre-marital sex
Topic 7: Cheating...

I usually give them ten topics. Then I collect the papers with a very serious affect. (This year during the pandemic I've had the students who were virtual in my hybrid class take a picture of their page and send it to me. I look at theirs on my iPad and treat it like paper.) I walk around the room reading all the opinions. The students are always silent and serious. They don't know what I'm going to do. When I'm finished with the reading, I look around the room dramatically, then I proceed to rip up all the papers, throw them up into the air and let the pieces fall like snow as I say, "that's what I think of your opinions!" There is stark silence in the room, which I don't let last very long. Some students grimace or widen their eyes, others meet the gaze of confused classmates. I proceed to tell them that some of what they wrote is very interesting and good. "Some of you wrote that you didn't know what X meant or that you have no opinion. Those are perfect answers. If you don't know something, say so! If you have no opinion or no idea, don't invent one." On the other hand, there are always students who say that waterboarding sounds like a fun sport that they'd like to try this coming summer. Oh, boy. Some of the students start to laugh out loud. I explain that I understand the confusion. "Waterboarding" could sound like "Surfboarding," but after I explain what waterboarding is, the laughter stops and students usually understand why it might be quite dangerous to invent an opinion.

Now I read the definition of opinion from The American Heritage Dictionary, which I have framed on the wall. "**o-pin-ion** ... *n.* 1. A belief or conclusion held with confidence, but ***not substantiated by positive knowledge or proof.***" (My bold and italics.) I explain this and tell a story about how many mere opinions are formed and expressed. It's sort of parrot-like, I tell them. You hear an opinion of someone else and later find yourself saying what you heard and calling it your own opinion.

At this point, I tell them why I was so dramatic. I want them to remember what an opinion is. "I am not interested in your opinions," I tell them. "I am interested in your questions, your arguments, and your sincere speculation. In this class, I hope we will learn how to recognize good and bad arguments and learn how to prepare good arguments using our most sincere and best reasoning and logic to do so. We're here to learn some of the conceptual tools you will need to make the best ethical decisions you can. So I'm not interested in mere opinions, but I am terribly interested in your serious thinking." As I introduce students to the difference between having mere opinions and learning how to construct solid arguments, I hope to help them to develop the conceptual tools they need to make the best decisions they can using sincere language and arguments.

As the class proceeds, we begin to observe that in popular conversation, one often hears that there are no answers in ethics or in philosophy in general. Students will say that everyone has a right to whatever opinion they have because in a democracy, "we can say whatever we want to say." They believe that each individual is free to say whatever they please without critical thinking since there really are no answers and no standard of comparison. As we sort out what an opinion means, we begin to discover that an "opinion" is like an object over which an individual can claim ownership. As students closely examine this view, however, they learn that it is a form of "subjective relativism," the idea that everyone is right just because they say so. As we wonder together what this might mean in a society, students conclude that subjective relativism is a convenient way for people to avoid the hard thinking that is involved in making good decisions because, in fact, there are reasonable standards that we can use to examine and understand our thinking and decisions.

Some philosophers who facilitate inquiry-based forms of conversation typical in a Philosophy for Children (P4C) approach to teaching Philosophy may give students the impression that they can say whatever they like with no critique. It is my intention, however, to inspire students to give full reign to their imaginations and sense of inquiry to pursue and develop knowledge to the fullest extent that is possible, but notice that I said "knowledge," not "opinion." I think that the Socratic method used in a pre-college classroom doesn't just leave things hanging in the air with no resolution. Pre-college philosophy teachers inspire and elicit thoughts from students for consideration, but a good teacher will pursue a student's thoughts socratically to the point of epistemological satisfaction even if it is temporary, with gentle and critical follow-up questions that will help a student to be reflective, self-critical and insightful. Even the *aporia* with which many of Plato's dialogues ended was not really the end of the discussion. *Aporia* is a kind of impasse at the end of a Platonic dialog which does not actually answer the question posed in the dialog. Similarly, a student may pursue their line of inquiry to the extent that it is possible and might later pick up their thinking to further develop it, but such thinking is governed by reasonable standards, logical arguments and a systematic approach to the topic. In the end, the "knowledge" one gains at the end of a rigorous thought journey is their best approximation of "knowledge," given what one knows at that moment. Such "knowledge" is subject to scrutiny and modification as new perspectives and information are learned and indeed, the conclusions one reaches can and often are modified. Such knowledge is a far cry from simply spouting opinions without any method or transparency. "Opinions" assume that each person's thought is infallible, that there is no way that way we can push back because an "opinion" is an island unto itself. Students begin to realize that "knowledge" is our best and most transparent human attempt at understanding our increasingly complex world and that the very history of philosophy is simply a continuation of the conversation that is pursued with reasonable standards.

The foundation of my philosophy courses is inquiry-based in the Socratic sense that leads to logical or rational arguments. Mere opinion might be an adequate start to an argument, but it can never be a good place to end up. Students learn that "Expert opinion" is not the same as "mere opinion." A good example of "expert opinion" can be the opinions of Dr. Anthony Fauci, the American immunologist and head of the U.S. National Institute of Allergy and Infectious Diseases. Dr. Fauci gives recommendations about our behavior vis-à-vis the COVID-19 pandemic. His opinions are expert opinions and they are based in knowledge and experience. They are based on good science and a sincere, honest attempt to tell the truth. Mr. Donald Trump, former President of the United States, has also given recommendations about what to do in the face of this pandemic. His opinions are mere opinions. They lack scientific knowledge. They are at best arrogant ignorance. At worst, they express a disregard for truth. They are dishonest, political manipulation. This is opinion at its worst.

As students grow and learn about how to use ethical decision-making tools and logical arguments, they begin to notice that the world is full of the kinds of philosophical topics we consider in class. The extraordinary relevance of their studies becomes clear as they notice fallacies in political debates, class arguments and their own thinking. Frequently, families comment on lively dinner conversations that might take off after a parent or sibling talks about a topic in the news or that came up in a class at school. Every single aspect of life is seen anew when students have the philosophical lens to examine, inquire and see-through arguments with a kind of laser-like scrutiny that they have never had before. Though it might seem harsh to so dramatically disregard students' opinions at the onset of our studies, the experience remains a visceral reminder of the importance of backing up one's thoughts, structuring thinking and relying on tools that we learn in our "Philosophy in the Round" discussions.

The APO and the IPO

Some schools do include philosophy and ethics in their curricula. The American Philosophy Open (APO)—a national high school philosophy essay writing contest, which I direct—has compiled a list of schools where philosophy is explicitly taught. They are not easy to find across the nation, but they are growing. Literature is sent to more than 200 schools for the APO every year. Some of the schools identified that do teach pre-college philosophy do so as a course in English, History, or Science departments. Existential literature in English classes, Kantian ethics and utilitarianism in History classes, Bioethics in Science departments are some examples. Sometimes there are standalone philosophy courses organized by these academic departments taught by teachers who have a background or strong interest in philosophy. My own example of a Spanish teacher who was a philosopher-in-hiding is one that might reveal a source of teachers already teaching other subjects in schools who can teach philosophy in schools. Sometimes schools organize Philosophy Clubs. There is also an Ethics Bowl movement across the nation, which has more than 30 regional Ethics Bowl competitions and a national championship competition that is centered at the University of North Carolina at Chapel Hill.[8]

The American Philosophy Open[9] is a pre-college philosophy writing contest across the USA that is the US national branch of the International Philosophy Olympiad (IPO).[10] There are more than 50 national contests that compete every year in the IPO. This is a unique contest in that the essays that students write may not be written in the student's native or national language. IPO essays may only be written in one of the following languages; English, German, French or Spanish. US high school students may not write in English. The APO's essay contest is a qualifying round to compete in the IPO and therefore the language requirements are the same. The top two national winners from all competing countries are eligible to compete in the IPO.

The students in my History of Philosophy in Spanish course may prepare for this competition. Any student who studies philosophy in high school or is a member of a club or is on an Ethics Bowl team and speaks or studies one of the three non-English languages may compete. The key mission of the APO and the IPO is to contribute to the development of critical, inquisitive, creative, and international thinking. One of the main reasons for which the students may not write in their own language is to exercise perspective at a very deep level.

---

[8] If you don't know about the Ethics Bowl, take a look at the National High School Ethics Bowl website: https://nhseb.unc.edu/.

[9] Here is the blog in which much of the annual information about the APO is published: http://pre-collegephilosophy.blogspot.com and the APO email address: PhilosophyAPO@gmail.com.

[10] Here is the website of the International Philosophy Olympiad: http://www.philosophy-olympiad.org/.

The qualifications for participation in the APO as written in the APO brochure every year are as follows.

- Be U.S. citizens and current U.S. high school students
- Participate in a high school philosophy class, club, or core subject with a philosophical bent or concentration
- Be proficient in writing in French, German, or Spanish

The IPO annual contest is almost 30 years old. It is held in a different host country every year. In 2020 the host country was scheduled to be Lisbon, Portugal, but it was cancelled because of the COVID-19 pandemic. There was an e-IPO celebrated instead. In 2021 Portugal was again going to host the IPO, but again it has been cancelled because of the pandemic. There will be an e-IPO organized by the Slovenian member country for all national teams. The benefits of participation for the students are many. I will quote from the APO 2020 brochure to explain the benefits.

"The two victorious 2020 APO contestants win the opportunity to travel to Lisbon, Portugal to share a once-in-a-lifetime experience networking face-to-face with other high school students from around the world. Winners of the IPO competition receive international recognition by UNESCO, the Federation of International Philosophy Societies (FISP), and other international philosophy organizations—honors that will make you, your parents, your friends, your school and your community proud."

The opportunity of high school students from around the world to meet other high school students who share an interest in philosophy is the beginning of a personal relationship that can last for a lifetime and can enhance the understanding of people all over the world.

Conclusion

American educators value philosophical thinking, but call it by other names; critical thinking, ethics, values, inquiry, Socratic Method, character, diversity, perspective, even the word philosophy, when it is not attached to the actual discipline itself. A course in Philosophy *per se*, however, is misunderstood and undervalued perhaps even feared unnecessarily. For several years I taught English as a Second Language (ESL) in Spain. When my friends in the US would ask me what I was doing in Spain, I would tell them that I was an ESL teacher. Inevitably they would tell me that they could teach my classes since they already speak English. When I was arguing to incorporate a freestanding ethics course into the curriculum, teachers would tell me that it wasn't needed since all teachers and administrators teach their students right from wrong. Everyone knows something about personal history. That doesn't mean they can teach history. Everybody knows something about chemistry if they can make a pot of coffee, that doesn't qualify them to teach science. All native speakers of English can speak English. That doesn't make them explicitly aware of the structure of language and methods to teach it. Just because many if not most teachers try to be good people, that doesn't prepare them to be able to teach ethics. No, a dedicated course in ethics is necessary. The right kind of philosophy course in the high school curriculum could help to create better critical thinkers. A course in ethical thinking could be used to explain the importance of rational thinking as an important critical thinking and intellectual skill set. Social and Emotional Learning is necessary to understand much of the social and emotional makeup of our society and our individual identities today, but it is not sufficient for our students to understand how to use ethical and philosophical skills to make good ethical decisions and create good strategies to help disrupt the problems of systemic racism of our society, for example.

Finally, I would suggest that if administrators would like to create a philosophy course in their schools, the first thing they could do would be to look around the school for any philosophers-in-hiding in other disciplines on staff. If graduate students in philosophy would like to teach philosophy they might look into getting certified in another subject to teach in a high school. Perhaps you could help to create a philosophy course you could teach as well. This is also an avenue for current teachers of other subjects who have a background in philosophy. You could come out of hiding and teach philosophy in your schools. It has been done before.

Bibliography

Aloysius Murphy, J. "*La paradójica presencia creciente de la filosofía en los institutos en Estados Unidos,*" *Diálogo Filosófico* no. 93 (September/December 2015): 417-432. https://www.dialogofilosofico.com/index.php/dialogo/article/view/91/98.

Descartes, René. *Discurso del método.* Translated by D. Manuel García Morente. Madrid, Spain: Colección Austral-Espasa Calpe, 2010.

Platón. *Apoligía de Sócrates. Obras completes de Platón.* Translated by Patricio de Azcárate. Madrid, Spain 1871-72: Proyecto Filosofía en español ©2005 www.filosofia.org. http://www.filosofia.org/cla/pla/azc01049.htm.

Platón. *Eutifrón o de la santidad. Obras completes de Platón.* Translated by Patricio de Azcárate. Madrid, Spain 1871-72: Proyecto Filosofía en español ©2005 www.filosofia.org. http://www.filosofia.org/cla/pla/azc01009.htm.

Savater, Fernando. *Historia de la filosofía sin temor ni temblor.* Madrid, Spain: Espasa Calpe. S. A., 2009.

Vaughn, Lewis. *Beginning Ethics: an introduction to moral philosophy.* New York and London: W. W. Norton and Company, Inc., 2015.

Contributors

Danielle Colburn

Danielle Colburn is a PhD student at the University of Iowa. Her areas of interest are the intersection between philosophy of mind, philosophy of psychology/neuroscience, and philosophy of education. Her current research focuses on the nature of "self" with an eye towards the unique, and often overlooked, experiences of those with mental illness. Danielle has been a Iowa Lyceum program director since Fall 2019.

Dr. Karen Detlefsen

Karen Detlefsen is a Professor of Philosophy and Education at the University of Pennsylvania. She has research interests in early modern philosophy, including women in the history of philosophy. She is the Founding Director of Penn's Project for Philosophy for the Young.

Marisa Diaz-Waian

Marisa is a public philosopher and "generalist" by nature, training, and practice. After completing her M.A. in Philosophy from San Diego State University, she moved to Montana to live off-grid as a resident-steward of Merlin Nature Preserve and founded Merlin CCC – a philosophy non-profit that offers opportunities for people of all stripes and ages to have fun with and do philosophy together. In addition to directing her non-profit, Marisa also serves on the Board and the Executive and Education Committees for The Philosophy Learning and Teaching Organization, is a member of the Mellon Philosophy as a Way of Life Network, and a regular speaker for Humanities Montana. Her work focuses on philosophy in community and frequently involves an interdisciplinary, environmental, and intergenerational bent.

Dr. Stephen Esser

Stephen Esser, PhD is Associate Director of Penn's Project for Philosophy of the Young at the University of Pennsylvania. His research specialization is philosophy of science with a focus on the role played by causation in scientific explanations.

Cassie Finley

Cassie Finley is a PhD student at the University of Iowa. Her research interests include Aristotle, ethics of algorithms, and philosophy of education, with a particular focus on the intersection of virtue ethics and moral responsibility in algorithm ethics. She is a program organizer for the Iowa Lyceum.

Joe Glover

Joe Glover is a philosophy PhD student at the University of Iowa. His primary philosophical interests are in philosophy of language (esp. modal language), history of analytic philosophy (esp. Wittgenstein and Carnap), and ancient philosophy. He is a co-organizer for The Iowa Lyceum.

Dr. Erik Kenyon

Erik Kenyon is author of *Augustine and the Dialogue* (Cambridge, 2018) and co-author of *Ethics for the Very Young* (Rowman and Littlefield, 2019). From 2012 to 2020, he taught courses in Philosophy, Classics and Humanities at Rollins College in Winter Park, FL. Since 2020, he has served as a Latin and Humanities teacher at Friends Academy in Dartmouth, MA, where he is helping develop an integrated middle-school Humanities curriculum.

Christian Kronsted

Christian Kronsted is a Ph.D. candidate at The University of Memphis who specializes in embodied cognition, aesthetics, and the philosophy of dance. He currently is the fourth graduate student director of the Philosophical Horizons outreach program at UofM. He is also a former professional breakdancer and has previously worked on integrating dance and philosophy with kids.

Stephen Kekoa Miller

Stephen Kekoa Miller has taught Philosophy and Religious Studies at Oakwood Friends School and Marist College in Poughkeepsie, New York for 19 years. Stephen is the Treasurer, member of the Executive Committee of PLATO (Philosophy Learning and Teaching Organization) and chairs the Advocacy Committee. Stephen has served on the Teachers Advisory Council of the National Humanities Center and currently serves on the Ethics Board of the Town of Poughkeepsie and has begun serving as the Chair of the Committee on Precollege Philosophy for the American Philosophical Association. Stephen speaks and publishes in the areas of pre-college philosophy, philosophy of emotions, ethics education, moral imagination and virtue ethics.

Joseph Aloysius Murphy

Joe Murphy has been teaching at Dwight-Englewood School in NJ since 1995. He began at Dwight-Englewood as a Spanish teacher, then was Chair of the Language Department from 2000 to 2005. During that time, he wrote curricula for philosophy and ethics courses, which he proposed to the school. Currently, Joe is Chair of the Philosophy and Ethics Department, which was established in 2006. In May of 2011, Joe became the USA Delegation leader of the International Philosophy Olympiad to Vienna, Austria. Since then, he has created the American Philosophy Open and has led the US Delegation to the IPO to Norway, Denmark, Estonia, Lithuania, Italy and other countries. Before coming to Dwight-Englewood, he taught Professional Translation at New York University, was president of the New York Circle of Translators, was Chair of the Professional Advocacy Committee of the American Translators Association and co-owned and directed an N.J. language school and translation company for over a decade. Joe has his degree in Philosophy from Montclair State University, where he worked with Matthew Lipman in the early days of the Institute for the Advancement of Philosophy for Children. He also has a degree in Hispanic Studies from the *Universidad de Salamanca* in Spain. He is currently a member of APA's Committee on Pre-College Instruction in Philosophy.

Dr. Sarah E. Vitale

Sarah Vitale is Assistant Professor of Philosophy at Ball State University in Muncie, Indiana. She teaches classes on critical theory, existentialism, and social institutions. Her research focuses on Marx and post-Marxism, especially on the notions of production, labor, and human nature, as well as contemporary feminist theory. She is co-editor of the *Radical Philosophy Review*, the journal of the Radical Philosophy Association, as well as co-editor of *The Weariness of Democracy* (Palgrave Macmillan 2019), and her recent publications include "Beyond *Homo Laborans*: Marx's Dialectical Account of Human Essence" (*Social Theory and Practice* 46, no. 3) and "Post-Marxist Political Ontology and the Foreclosure of Radical Newness" (*Philosophy Today* 64, no. 3). She is also the founder and director of the Ball State Philosophy Outreach Project, a pre-college philosophy program.

Dustin Webster

Dustin Webster is a doctoral student at the University of Pennsylvania Graduate School of Education and a former elementary school teacher. In addition to philosophy for children, his research interests include conceptions of virtue and character, and their relation to education policy and practice.

Dr. Jonathan Wurtz

Jonathan Wurtz graduated from The University of Memphis with a PhD in Philosophy and specializes in Social and Political Philosophy and 20th Century French Continental Philosophy. Their primary research interest is twofold. On the one hand, they are interested in highlighting how philosophers deploy the concept of the deficient child to support their normative claims about ethics and justice. On the other, they are also interested in the current attempts by philosophers to rethink the concept of childhood. During their time at The University of Memphis they volunteered with Philosophical Horizons for seven years and became the third graduate student director in 2017.

Index